Population and Social Policy in France

Also available from Pinter:

Voices of France, edited by Sheila Perry and Máire Cross

POPULATION AND SOCIAL POLICY IN FRANCE

edited by Máire Cross and Sheila Perry

PINTER

London and Washington

PINTER
A Cassell imprint
Wellington House, 125 Strand, London WC2R 0BB, England
PO Box 605, Herndon, VA 20172, USA

First published in 1997

British Library Cataloguing-in-Publication Data
A catalogue record for this book is available from the British Library.

ISBN 1-85567-393-2

Library of Congress Cataloging-in-Publication Data
Population and social policy in France/edited by Máire Cross and Sheila Perry.
    p. cm.
   Includes bibliographical references and index.
   ISBN 1-85567-393-2 (hc : alk. paper)
   1. France—Population policy. 2. France—Population. 3. France—Social policy. I. Cross, Máire. II. Perry, Sheila, 1952–   .
   HB3593.P64 1997
   363.9'1'0944—dc20   96–45999
                                                           CIP

Typeset by York House Typographic Ltd, London
Printed and bound in Great Britain by Biddles Ltd, Guildford and King's Lynn

Contents

Notes on contributors

Christine Bard lectures in contemporary history at the University of Angers. She has written widely on French feminism in the first half of the twentieth century, notably in *Les Filles de Marianne* (Fayard, 1995) and *Les Garçonnes* (Flammarion, 1997), and is currently completing a textbook (co-authored with Gabrielle Houbre) entitled *Les Femmes dans la société française* for the Collection 'U' (Armand Colin, 1997).

Máire Cross is Senior Lecturer in French at the University of Sheffield where she teaches aspects of contemporary French politics at post-graduate and undergraduate level. She has co-authored two books on French feminism, contributes items regularly to the journals *Modern and Contemporary France, European History Quarterly* and *French Studies* and is a member of the Editorial Board of *Modern and Contemporary France.*

Michel Dreyfus is a historian and research fellow at the CNRS. He specializes in the workers' movement, trade unionism and welfare, and has published several works, most recently *Histoire de la CGT. Cent ans de syndicalisme en France, 1895–1995* (Complexe, 1995) and, together with Claude Pennetier and Nathalie Viet-Depaule, *La Part des militants* (De L'Atelier, 1996).

Margaret Gibbon is a Lecturer in the School of Applied Language and Intercultural Studies, Dublin City University. Since she completed her thesis on *Gender and Class Consciousness* (University of Reading, 1987), she has continued to develop her research interests in feminist theory, ethnic minorities and race. She is currently writing a book on language and patriarchy.

Françoise Gollain is Lecturer in French at La Sainte Union College in Southampton. She specialized in philosophy and sociology at Caen University and is completing her PhD in Orléans on the critical evaluation of work ethics and practices in the field of French political ecology.

Eleonore Kofman is Professor of Human Geography at Nottingham Trent University. She has published books and articles on gender, political geography and national identity in France, including *France* (Paul Chapman, 1989), and is co-editor with Gillian Youngs of *Globalization: Theory and Practice* (Pinter, 1996).

Hervé Le Bras is a leading researcher in population studies in France. A graduate of the Ecole Polytechnique, where he qualified in mathematics and demography, he has since led his own research group in demographic history for the EHESS/CNRS. A Research Director at INED, Paris, and Associate Professor at the University of Geneva, he is the author of *Marianne et les lapins: l'obsession démographique* (Hachette, 1992), *Le Sol et le sang* (De L'Aube, 1993), *Les Limites de la planète: mythes de la nature et de la population* (Flammarion, 1994), *Les Trois France* (Odile Jacob, 1995) and *Le Peuplement de l'Europe* (La Documentation Française, 1996).

Neil MacMaster is a Lecturer in Contempory European Studies at the University of East Anglia. His research is on migration and racism, and recent works include *Spanish Fighters. An Oral History of Civil War and Exile* (Macmillan, 1990) and *Colonial Migrants and Racism. Algerians in France 1900–1962* (Macmillan, 1997).

Catherine Morel is a Lecturer in French and European Business at Sheffield Hallam University Business School. Her current research encompasses the analysis of the socio-political French business environment, specifically the interrelationships between business and arts.

Geneviève Parkes lectures in language, marketing and contemporary French civilization at the University of Portsmouth. She has published extensively on aspects of the market economy in France and is currently completing her thesis on British family policy.

Sheila Perry is Principal Lecturer in French and the Modern Languages Departmental Research Coordinator at the University of Northumbria at Newcastle, where she teaches French language and politics at under-graduate and postgraduate level. She specializes in the study of politics and the media in France and has published articles and conference papers on French television and political communication. She is currently researching the development of political programmes on French television since the 1960s.

Jacques Reland is Senior Lecturer in French Studies at London Guild-hall University, where he teaches courses on French social, economic and European policies. Since 1988 he has been a consultant on France for Oxford Analytica and more recently for the BBC. He has recently completed a chapter entitled 'The impact of European integration on French monetary policy' for a book edited by Anand Menon and James Forbes, as part of a series (Oxford University Centre for European Policy Studies, 1997).

Yvette Rocheron is a Lecturer in French Studies at the University of Leicester. She has held teaching posts in secondary and higher educa-tion in France and Britain and researched questions related to health and ethnicity in both countries. She has published articles on social aspects of the ethnic minority question in France and French television and culture.

Rob Turner is Senior Lecturer at the University of Northumbria at Newcastle, where he teaches and researches French politics with a special interest in the presidency and the higher education system. He has forged many links with sister institutions in France, giving him a practical insight into the French university system and its problems.

Jan Windebank is a Senior Lecturer in the Department of French, University of Sheffield. She is the author of *The Informal Economy in France* (Avebury, 1991), co-editor (with Dr Renate Gunther) of two volumes of essays on the subject of violence and conflict in modern France, and has written extensively on the gender division of domestic labour, cross-national comparative methodology as applied to women's employment, social policy and child care and paid informal work in the European Union.

TRANSLATORS

Máire Cross: see above.
Christopher de Luchi (University of Portsmouth)
Anabel Taylor (University of Westminster)

Preface

This volume arose out of the proceedings of the annual conference of the Association for the Study of Modern and Contemporary France held at the University of Northumbria at Newcastle in September 1995 on the theme of 'France, Population and Peoples'.[1] The editors would like to thank the Committee of the Association for the advice and assistance it provided in the organization of the conference, and members of the Modern Languages Department, University of Northumbria, for administrative, technical and clerical support. Special thanks also go to the Department of French, University of Sheffield, for financial backing and to the official sponsors, the French Embassy, North East Water, Tyne and Wear PTE and Newcastle Airport, for their generous donations.

Máire Cross
Sheila Perry
June 1997

1. See also M. Cross and S. Perry, *Voices of France*. London: Pinter (1997).

List of abbreviations

ADRI Agence pour le développement des relations interculturelles
AGED allocation pour garde d'enfant à domicile
ASFNE allocations spéciales du fonds national pour l'emploi à mi-temps
ASMCF Association for the Study of Modern and Contemporary France
ASSEDIC Association pour l'emploi dans l'industrie et le commerce
BNP Banque nationale de Paris
BTS Brevet de technicien supérieure
CAF Caisses d'allocations familiales
CAM Caisse d'assurance maladie
CCAS Caisse centrale d'activités sociales
CCNE Comité consultatif national d'éthique pour les sciences de la vie et de la santé
CCSS Commission des comptes de la sécurité sociale
CECOS Centre d'étude et de conservation des oeufs et du sperme humains
CFDT Confédération française et démocratique du travail
CFTC Confédération française des travailleurs chrétiens
CGC Confédération générale des cadres
CGT Confédération générale du travail
CGT–FO Confédération générale du travail – Force ouvrière
CGTU Confédération générale du travail unitaire
CIP Contrat d'insertion professionnelle des jeunes
CNAF Caisses nationales d'allocations familiales
CNAM Caisses nationales d'assurance maladie
CNAV Caisses nationales d'assurance vieillesse
CNRS Centre national de la recherche scientifique

CSG cotisation sociale généralisée
DARES Direction de l'animation de la recherche, des études et des statistiques
DEA Diplôme d'études approfondies
DESS Diplôme d'études supérieures spécialisées
DEUG Diplôme d'études universitaires générales
DEUST Diplôme d'études universitaires des sciences et de la technologie
DPM Direction de la population et des migrations
DUT Diplôme universitaire de technologie
EDF Electricité de France
EU European Union
FAS Fonds d'action sociale
FEN Fédération de l'éducation nationale
FLN Front de libération nationale (Algeria)
FN Front National
FNE Fonds national pour l'emploi
FO Force Ouvrière (see CGT–FO)
FPSC Family Policy Studies Centre
FSU Fédération syndicale unitaire
FSV Fonds de solidarité vieillesse
GDF Gaz de France
GP general practitioner
GREC Groupement de recherche d'échange et de communication
GRIT Groupe de réflexion inter et transdisciplinaire
HCSP Haut Comité de la santé publique
HMSO Her Majesty's Stationery Office
INED Institut national d'études démographiques
INSEE Institut national de la statistique et des études économiques
INSERM Institut national de santé et de recherche médicale
IUP Institut universitaire professionalisé
IUT Institut universitaire de technologie
IVF in vitro fertilization (French term FIVETE)
JOC Jeunesse ouvrière chrétienne
JOCF Jeunesse ouvrière chrétienne féminine
MIAGE Maîtrise de méthodes informatiques appliquées à la gestion
MNA Mouvement national algérien
MST Maîtrise de sciences et techniques
MST maladie sexuellement transmissible
OCDE Organisation de coopération et de développement économique

OECD Organization for Economic Co-operation and Development
PCF Parti communiste français (French Communist Party)
PIB produit intérieur brut
PMA procréation médicalement assistée
PS Parti socialiste
PTT Administration des postes et télécommunications et de la télédiffusion
PRP préretraites progressives
RATP Régie autonome des transports parisiens
RDS remboursement de la dette sociale
RMI revenu minimum d'insertion
RPR Rassemblement pour la république
SAINA Service des affaires indigènes nord-africaines
SMIC Salaire minimum interprofessionel de croissance
SNCF Société nationale des chemins de fer français
SOFRES Société française d'enquêtes pour sondage
STS Section de techniciens supérieurs
SUD Solidaires unitaires démocratiques
UDF Union pour la démocracie française
UFSF Union française pour le suffrage des femmes
UNEDIC Union nationale pour l'emploi dans l'industrie et le commerce
UNESCO United Nations Educational, Scientific and Cultural Organization

Introduction

MÁIRE CROSS

Population and social policy are two important themes of study of any society. The purpose of this book is to explore the familiar, using less-familiar methods, in order to increase our understanding of how the French people view themselves and are viewed in their daily lives. For the purpose of organization the work is divided in two, although many of the themes overlap.

Population growth and its related issues have long been on the political agenda in France in a way which distinguishes her from her European neighbours and particularly from Britain. This book explores the latest developments in population studies and policies which spring from them. It begins with the question: does France still have a population policy? Geneviève Parkes shows how a desire for demographic growth has been allied to the idea of the well-being of the nation in the French approach to population. While this policy may be shifting slightly, the degree of collaboration between researchers and the state apparatus is as strong as ever and crucial in the political consensus ·on the necessity of encouraging births. The extent of this dominant pro-natalist ideology emerges in Chapters 2 and 3. Since the end of the nineteenth century, demographic scientists and feminists have succumbed to this way of thinking. However, the political adjustment to the soaring costs of the state in terms of medical spending, retirement costs, unemployment and training, discussed in Chapters 9, 11, 12 and 13, have caused a rethink in some quarters. Also in question is the requirement of economic alignment with other European countries where steady falls in birth-rates do not provoke such anxiety.

Hervé Le Bras, demographic researcher, outspoken critic of the high-level pro-natalist policy-makers, demonstrates the political consensus on the matter, elaborates the mythical constructions of the dominant ideology and reveals the flaws in the dubious proposals of those who claim to see potential national disaster in an ageing population and a declining birth-rate. Natalist doctrine can be as morally dangerous as eugenics was in the hands of the Nazis: it encourages xenophobia and conservatism in its moral and political functions. Chapter 3 is a further demonstration of the strength of the dominant ideology of pro-natalism, this time affecting the successes and failures of the moderate feminist groups during the inter-war period when they sought to dissociate themselves from the opinion that emancipated women were part of the demographic peril that threatened the nation's future. In order to combat the influences of the anti-feminist movement, Christine Bard argues that feminists developed a concept of modern femininity which lay half-way between the traditional role of motherhood and the desire to enjoy new freedoms of education and work. While moderate feminists eagerly took part in the moral crusade of placing the family as the indispensable core of society, they considered that the state should intervene with regulations to ensure better conditions for motherhood. The government response was a policy of repression in 1920 which severely penalized abortion and neo-Malthusian propaganda. State family allowances did finally come in 1932, a pioneering step among European countries. None the less reformist feminists were disillusioned by then. Their unsuccessful demands for maternity welfare were part of a campaign for suffrage but they were attacked from all sides by those who wished to see women restored to their traditional domestic role. This attack on the right to work is still the essential part of the debate on female employment today, discussed in Chapter 5.

State intervention and the lack of it is the subject of Chapter 4. Margaret Gibbon reveals how technological advances in reproduction were achieved in the late 1980s and early 1990s and momentous decisions were made by doctors without any government regulation. She presents a critique of the IVF techniques developed in France, a leader in the field, and the moral, legal and political questions this expensive technique fails to address. It reinforces the control of a largely male obstetrical and gynaecological élite which has suddenly discovered media interest. The dangers of eugenics loom once more.

The association of fertility rates, family policy and employment are placed in a different contemporary setting by Jan Windebank in Chapter 5, where she examines the strategy women adopt to chart a course of survival between motherhood and employment. Contrary to the wishes of the government for women to have a third child, statistics show that this propaganda policy did not succeed, as current employment rates for women after the birth of a third child drop dramatically. Demand for women in the workforce has been traditionally high, family policy provision has increased the role of the state in the question of childcare provision but, even so, the ideal of the mother at home still prevails and there is very little flexibility for women at work. Until men contribute to domestic arrangements in a radically different way, there will be little alteration to the imbalance of opportunities on the labour market.

Shifts in cultural values are needed in another domain, according to Eleonore Kofman in Chapter 6. Family reunification and labour migration cannot be distinguished easily in official statistics but in the rare assessments of women immigrants either it is wrongly assumed that they only come for family reasons or else they are simply invisible in immigration studies. As a new subject of interest to researchers and policy-makers alike, women immigrants still remain in a precarious position, however. They are now seen as a vehicle for governments' measures for integration of difficult groups of second-generation immigrants in deprived suburbs without necessarily being considered as players and actors in French society with their own economic aspirations.

The one-sided story of French integration policies and universalism is revisited in Chapter 7 where Neil MacMaster discusses the matter of racial intermarriage against a background of the colonial history of Algeria. Sexual relations between colonizer and colonized were a potent form of racial tension. This chapter portrays the evolution of the issue from the early colonial concern for loss of authority to the end of the earlier intermarriage trends with the shift to family reunification in emigration and the Algerian War. Colonial values persist, however, in the flawed interpretations by eminent sociologists of the changes in marriage patterns between nationalities. Yvette Rocheron's Chapter 8 analyses the contradiction between those wishful thinkers who see the increase of mixed marriages as a positive sign of integration in the republican tradition, with the foreigner accepting the 'universalist' values of France (which has one of the highest rates of intermarriage among Western countries), and the politicians who vilify mixed marriages as a threat to French traditions. With the official end of immigration and the increase in unemployment, there are new social trends in France which affect mixed marriages.

These same trends have provoked a controversy, discussed in Chapter 9, which now dominates debates on active population trends, that is the distribution of a certain form of wealth, namely labour, between the working population and the retired (as well as between the working and the unemployed, discussed in Chapter 11). In spite of forecasts of a shrinking and older working population there is considerable reluctance on the part of employers to keep on older staff. In the past, the usual methods of supplementing numbers in the French working population have been to import labour to increase productivity or to increase the numbers of women and older people in employment. By means of a case-study, Catherine Morel shows how regrettable it is that the last method is the least-popular solution to a potential labour shortage.

Chapter 10 presents the different traditions of militancy for workers' rights in one of France's oldest and largest trade unions, the CGT. Social questions were part of the mutualist tradition which goes back to early nineteenth-century practices of self-help organizations. The other strong syndicalist tradition of strike action began to take an interest in the advantages of social benefits with the development of the social security system established after 1945. The nationalization programmes strengthened the position of the unions, which by then were keen to be involved in running the welfare administration. Michel Dreyfus assesses the reasons for the decline of membership of the CGT and sees a desire on the part of other unions to unite to combat a common problem, apathy and employee powerlessness when faced with imposed changes of working practices. In Chapter 11 Françoise Gollain proposes an analysis of French ecologists' solutions to the uneven distribution of labour which unions have been unwilling or unable to address.

Just how to educate future generations of workers is the subject of the penultimate chapter, in which Rob Turner shows how successive governments have oscillated between radical proposals and conservative approaches in an effort to cope with huge pressures of numbers in higher education and dwindling resources when faced with powerful lobbying by the interested parties.

Diminishing state resources faced with population changes have provoked massive strike reactions in the past in France, as Michel Dreyfus shows in Chapters 10 and 14. The most recent demonstration of militancy and mass discontent of the population which erupted in December 1995 features in each of the last three chapters. Crucial for an understanding of the reasons behind the strike was the plan of the newly appointed Juppé government to solve the deficit crisis of the social security system. Jacques Reland explains how this was to affect the health service, which plays a crucial role in medical care and as an employer. History was in the making as these chapters were being written; students were out on strike for weeks and the government's handling of a massive display of solidarity during the December strikes is the subject of study in Chapter 14 by Michel Dreyfus, who followed the events closely. The mass solidarity of millions of strikers pushed the union leaders into united opposition. The movement involved public-sector employees, who had the tacit support of private-sector workers, since it was considered a defence of social rights that concern the whole population in one way or another. Whether this defence of the *Sécu*, the familiar term for the French social security system, means that France will still have a social policy for its population in a similar form in years to come can only be a matter of speculation.

In each chapter there is a discussion of at least one aspect of the pressures of demographic changes, long-term population trends, ideological debates, political short-term expediencies and sociologists' analyses from French sources which give an intimate view of trends which have their own French specificity and at the same time provide a universal appeal to readers from many disciplines who will be able to draw their own conclusions.

Part One

Births, Marriages and Migration

1.

Does France still have a population policy?

GENEVIÈVE PARKES

TRANSLATED BY CHRISTOPHER DE LUCHI

Similar causes do not necessarily produce the same effects. Several member countries of the European Union have taken the first steps towards common agriculture and defence policies. In other fields, such as justice and the right to work, there are signs of progress in the medium term. European demographic policy, on the other hand, has not been defined since 1984, at which time the first outlines could have been drawn had there been a common desire to achieve this.[1] This is where the trouble lies. Although all countries in the EU are facing similar demographic trends, that is, a slowing down of growth due to a drop in the birth-rate, what some see as an alarming situation is for others a matter of indifference or even relief. The 'same' words do not correspond to the 'same' realities. France and Britain illustrate perfectly this mutual lack of understanding, although certain traditions may be starting to disappear.

The French approach to demography

In studies of population, the priorities of sociologists, demographers and official bodies, such as associations interested in the family, differ considerably between France and Britain. Whereas in France the concern is with what might happen, such as the demographic future of the country and preventive medicine, in Britain it is the well-being of children already born, rather than those who might or might not be born, which is of utmost importance. Certain social phenomena, such as the impoverishment of one-parent families or the protection of children at risk, are the subject of numerous analyses and general reports and books in Britain. The branch of sociology called 'poverty studies' is particularly developed within 'family policy'. *Politique familiale* and 'family policy' have of course some points in common, and increasingly so, as will be seen later, but they cover different realities.[2]

'Family policy' suggests a rather grim reality: poverty, social problems, violence towards children, the generation conflict. As for *politique familiale*, this is identified in the French mind with many forms of family aid, state intervention, more proactive than reactive and with encouragement to increase the birth-rate; the term is thus often synonymous with *politique démographique*, or in English, 'population policy'. The word 'demography' itself is less frequently used and is semantically more restricted than its French equivalent; in fact, *démographie*, in everyday use, has three meanings: demographic science, the dynamics of population growth and population itself. In France, the adjective *démographique* is part of the non-specialist public's store of passive knowledge, whereas in Britain, in the same circumstances, the term 'demographic' needs to be explained.[3] Juxtaposed with the word 'problem', it is automatically associated in the British mind with the risk of overpopulation of the world; French people questioned out of context would tend to interpret it either as the drop in the birth-rate in France and other Western European countries, or as the difference between the demographic surplus in the Third World and the French or European deficit.[4]

Compared with that of the British, the French perspective tends to be centred on the national rather than on the world situation. For some, the world population explosion is partly compensated for by the slowing down of population growth in Europe and at home, a fine example of international good citizenship: for others, the two problems, although connected, are to be considered independently; it would be as appropriate to increase the birth-rate in our countries as to restrict it in the Third World. The examination of two broadly comparable journals devoted to demography underlines this divergence of preoccupation: *Population* is published in France under the aegis of INED (Institut national d'études démographiques), whereas *Population Studies* is produced by the Population Investigation Committee, founded in 1936. In the British journal, most articles deal with general demographic theories such as division into socio-economic groups, the working population or demographic questions concerning either the whole world or countries outside Europe (including the former USSR) and 18.6 per cent of published articles deal with national or European questions. In the French journal *Population*, there is a majority of articles on general theory or analyses relating to various countries of the world (outside Europe), but the proportion dealing with national and European matters is higher, at 32.2 per cent.[5] Furthermore, in both publications, a look at the list of contributors is revealing: when the subject matter happens to concern the various birth-rates in European countries, demographers with a French cultural background are often those who report with relief the slightest upturn, or with concern yet another drop (Pressat, 1980; Monnier, 1981; Calot and Blayo, 1982; Prioux, 1990). Thus we begin to see how a difference of approach can correspond to a different intervention policy.

Pro-natalism as a 'nationalized' concept

One of the aspects which perhaps most characterizes French demography is the degree of collaboration and interaction between researchers and the state apparatus. Although in the 1930s the same fear of depopulation and degeneration of the race affected both France and Britain, in the latter country corrective measures were initiated by what we might today call ideological movements or pressure groups.[6] The British Population Society, formed in 1928, the national branch of the International Union for the Scientific Study of Demographic Problems, had no brief to make political recommendations. There was no convergence until 1943, when the government announced the setting up of the Royal Commission on Population, whose investigators were recruited from among experts such as David Victor Glass.[7] The report of the Commission, however, was not published until 1949, by which time Beveridge had already set up the structures of the Welfare State which, although favourable to an increased birth-rate for Britain, did not include all the measures recommended by the Commission (Royal Commission on Population, 1949). Researchers in Britain are less empowered to put their recommendations into practice.

In France, on the other hand, Sauvy, statistician, economist and demographer at the Fondation Carrel, which was not unlike the Positive Eugenics Committee of the same period, was also technical adviser to the Finance Minister, where he enjoyed considerable powers. The Fondation Carrel was itself attached to the Secrétariat d'état à la famille et à la santé. It was Sauvy who in 1939 introduced the *Code de la famille*, and when INED was founded in 1945 on the ashes of the Fondation, it was Sauvy who accepted its directorship, which he held until 1962, and who chose his collaborators. One of these was Adolphe Landry, one of the 'great' demographers of the same period, who was both a writer and a minister. These relations between research and implementation worked to the satisfaction of all parties concerned: there was a consensus on the need to encourage births. It is undeniable that the freedom of action enjoyed by the principal researchers of the period such as Sauvy helped to cement this bond, which has lasted until today.[8] The initials of numerous organizations publishing data or demographic analyses in France bear the N of 'National' (INED, INSEE, CNRS, CNAF, INSERM). The subsidies that the state pays to run them support a mutual interest.

Without this consensus, would France have experienced such militancy? France was the first country to discover and implement contraception, at the beginning of the nineteenth century, without having to read Malthus or the neo-Malthusian works which had a notable impact in Britain.[9] The risk of depopulation appeared real enough to bring about a clear reaction: in 1896, the Alliance nationale pour l'accroissement de la population française (National Alliance for French Population Growth) was created. Pro-natalist propaganda by the Alliance was then assisted by the parallel development of moral campaigning, such as anti-alcoholism, a drive for public hygiene and proper baby care. This had the effect of rallying women to the cause (see Chapter 3). Thus Associations familiales (associations run on the principle of today's Consumers' Associations, but based on family units) spread through the *départements*, with Clémenceau's blessing. From then on, pro-natalism and *démographie* became close allies indeed.

Thus it is no longer in the number of births itself that an explanation can be found as to the difference in attitude between France and Britain, since, until 1989, both countries have shared similar birth-rates: 13.6 per thousand and slightly higher in Britain since 1990.[10] France has acquired a model of ideology which is self-perpetuating and involves the state, the opinion leaders and the public at large.

Pro-natalism, theory and practice

France has known no real ideological break as to the merits of pro-natalism since the inter-war period; from Vichy to the trend of one-parent families, through the baby boom and the feminist movement, this national characteristic has survived. The French have had, however, ample time to compare their population statistics with those of other countries, and perhaps, in so doing, to evaluate the low impact of government measures responding to the evolution of demographic trends. For many French people, the idea of abolishing family allowances is as absurd as suggesting the end of free schooling. The *quotient familial* (tax relief in respect of dependants) is an obvious form of taxation: large families have greater expenses than families with one child, that goes without saying, and anyway the prospect of having to spend one's old age in relative poverty is worrying. Are the French thus a nation of 'passive' pro-natalists?

There are areas in which things are perfectly clear: for the Right, there is a birth deficit and the authorities have a duty to facilitate the arrival of children who are wanted. This message, from Edouard Balladur, the then Prime Minister, could have come from any other previous right-wing Prime Minister:

> En premier lieu, le rayonnement de la France dans le monde dépend pour une large part de la vitalité de sa démographie. L'évolution pré-occupante constatée ces dernières années imposait que des dispositions fussent prises par les pouvoirs publics pour faire en sorte que le choix des familles ne se heurte pas à des obstacles matériels et financiers trop dissuasifs.[11]
>
> (Lettre des Caisses d'Allocations Familiales, 1994, V)

As for the Front National, it follows the tradition of demographic nationalism as a means of defence against the threat from abroad.[12] Women of the far Right, belonging for example to the Cercle national des femmes d'Europe or the Front national de la jeunesse, still call for French motherhood to be used as a weapon; some of these also call themselves feminists.[13]

Certain other movements with a religious motivation explicitly include pro-natalism in their declaration of principles, together with the fight against abortion; see, for example, the Union pour la vie, a federation which unites organizations like the Confédération nationale des associations familiales catholiques, Choisir la vie, and Renaissance catholique.[14]

To those groups which include pro-natalism in their programme of action are added other groups of 'practitioners'. Respect for life can be seen as belonging to the code of ethics of the medical profession. The extreme medicalization of pregnancy and childbirth (Stewart-Richardson, 1995), the reluctance of French doctors to suggest sterilization (female or male) as a contraceptive measure, the lack of commitment on the part of the medical profession when there was a question of legalizing abortion or dispensing birth control services which were none the less authorized in France,[15] would seem to indicate a desire to help all wanted children to be born (Ferrand, 1982). In the field of medically assisted conception, science itself seems to be serving the 'demographic effort': IVF is more readily available in France than in Britain, being both subsidized and particularly well developed (see Chapter 4).[16] Of course, the medical profession does not legislate, but it can standardize certain practices: for example, childbirth today is frequently declared by doctors to be *pathologique* (with complications), which allows the mother to benefit from extended maternity leave. A tacit commitment on the part of the medical profession? Some doctors are outspoken pro-natalists:

> D'après notre expérience, ce chiffre [de deux] ne suffit pas. Il nous semble que sur l'image de la famille heureuse, on doit compter de trois à six enfants.[17]
>
> (Debré, 1974: 404)

It is also perfectly natural to find the same demographic concerns amongst demographers themselves, whether members of the INED, of the Haut Conseil de la population et de la famille or of centres for research in social sciences. Nor should we be surprised by researchers who publish in specialist or fairly widely distributed journals such as *Cahiers Français, Problèmes Economiques, Recherche Sociale* and *Futuribles*. The peculiarity of the French in this field is the wide diversity: national daily newspapers, weekly news magazines, television programmes, women's magazines, the popular press. Although journals devoted to sociology, economics, politics and even literature publish articles on demography, the fact that some can also be found in the general press emphasizes the public interest in them. Between popular newspapers and academic journals, usually only the tone changes: it is still a question of missing babies. Pro-natalism is thus a national attitude in France.

Demographic worries mobilize the Right, demographers, journalists and also, it would seem, the medical profession. They are, however, equally felt on the Left: François Mitterrand widened the definition of *politique familiale* during his two terms of presidency, but kept pro-natalism, even though he briefly thought that it was not necessarily compatible with a Socialist definition of equal opportunities for women. Georgina Dufoix, Pierre Bérégovoy and Jacques Delors (all one-time Socialist ministers) have also swollen the ranks.[18] As for the Communist Georges Marchais, he thought that 'si le désir, la volonté des femmes et des couples étaient satisfaits, la tendance à la dénatalité serait renversée' (Girard and Roussel, 1980: 1010).[19]

The history of family allowances since the end of the war shows that the family, a traditional value, has been the subject of constant legislation up until today. There has been no inertia as in Britain. The aggressive pro-natalism of the period from 1946 to 1967 gradually gave way to a more sophisticated system, less based on the concept of the full-time mother, more 'politically correct' and introducing the means test. The fourteen Mitterrand years did not completely break with the incentive approach, alternating the promotion of reproduction with measures for social justice (Steck, 1994).

The 'new', watered-down nationalized French pro-natalism is affected by current concern over the financing of pensions (see Chapter 12), and by women's freedom of choice, whether they stay at home, with subsidies taking over and partially compensating mothers for their loss of income, or whether they go out to work (in French, there is no term laden with accusatory connotations such as 'working mothers' even if opinion in favour of working mothers is far from unanimous in the polls), and they have the choice between different forms of childcare. It is also affected by employment policy and the general trend towards the 'rolling back of the state'.

For all this, the legacy of the demographic nationalism of the inter-war period has not totally disappeared. A few vestiges remain, such as are found in the magazine *Bonheur*, distributed by the Caisse nationale des allocations familiales to all families, in the Front National's call for *préférence nationale* (priority being given to French nationals for access to subsidized accommodation, jobs, children's places in popular schools and so on over existing criteria such as need or merit), as well as the unshakeable pessimism of numerous experts. There remains above all a part of French culture that encourages reproduction and which may or may not recognize itself in the alarmist pronouncements of statisticians forecasting demographic decline.

Rémi Lenoir has analysed (Lenoir, 1985) the decline of *familialisme* (the promotion of family values) in France. The erstwhile associations for the promotion of large families have now disappeared and we have new definitions for the family. The cult of the family in France is no longer what it was. Since the publication of *Fécondité* by Emile Zola, whose heroes find their fulfilment in their large family, literature and the cinema have often featured the idea of family life as the source of happiness, albeit in a somewhat more restrained way. The popular iconographic representation of the blessed union has itself also changed. One no longer finds on sale wedding cards to send to the happy couple in which, apart from the gold rings, hearts and white lace, were to be found wishes for a happy life together, thanks to a family of four or five children, drawn in order of descending size. French baby boomers will recall wedding celebrations enlivened by crackers popping at the banquet, showering the table with pink and blue ribbons attached to plastic micro-babies in their prams. Other 'fun' cards were, until the end of the 1970s, sent to young parents or those who 'should have been' after so many months of marriage, suggesting foolproof fertility methods, such as visits to kitchen gardens, harvesting cabbages and roses, or capturing carrier storks in flight. Tales in which the love story ends well do not finish as in English with 'and they lived happily ever after' but with 'ils vécurent heureux et eurent beaucoup d'enfants' (they lived happily and had many children). Love songs today certainly no longer speak of marriage and 'deux bébés roses faisant la ronde gentiment' (two pink babies happily bouncing along) two years later (Louguy and Larue, 1950), but when in 1985 advertising agencies in France were seeking a non-controversial theme to sell their hoarding space during the quieter summer period, it was indeed pink babies who greeted passers-by with appropriate texts like 'Ai-je l'air d'une mesure gouvernementale?' (Do I look like a government measure?), 'Il n'y a pas que le sexe dans la vie' (Sex isn't the only thing in life) or 'Il paraît que je suis un phénomène socio-culturel' (So I'm a socio-cultural phenomenon!), subtitle: 'La France a besoin d'enfants' (France needs children). This spontaneous expression of commitment goes well beyond official policies.[20] Similarly, although shopkeepers no longer offer a 5 per cent discount 'aux économiquement faibles et aux familles nombreuses' (to low-wage earners and large families), French supermarkets often have a checkout reserved for 'mothers to be', who should be exempt from queuing.[21] The SNCF has seats reserved for pregnant women and persons accompanied by young children, and continues to offer discounts to large families. Motherhood is still a currency which can buy housing benefit, the right to compete for some national professional examinations (*concours*), or a little tranquillity for one's old age: *assurance-vieillesse des parents au foyer* (old-age insurance for parents in the home) (Steck, 1994).

From council-run crèches and playgroups to family unit taxation, from subsidized *colonies de vacances* (holiday camps) to the parsimony that characterizes the provision of free abortions compared with other EU countries (Festy, 1993), from the discreet availability of contraception to family consumerism (Ragot, 1984), so many things in France still function according to the principle of co-operation between state and pro-natalism. But is this going to change?

Why pro-natalism is now obsolescent

Despite the survival of tradition, currently aided by the lowest ever birth-rate figures, by the scientific and media cover of these figures (Bichot, 1992; Calot, 1994; Lamy-Festy, 1994) and by the arrival of a president clearly favourable to 'demographic support' for France,[22] French pro-natalism seems to be threatened on three fronts: Europe, the new role of the state concerning intervention and a sudden questioning at grass-roots level.

The Commission and the Council of the European Community declared in 1989 the necessity of promoting a family policy in member countries, but the difference in principles and objectives constitutes a considerable obstacle. Furthermore, perception of the legitimacy of state intervention in domains (in this case the family) seen as public in certain countries and private in others varies considerably. The position of women, as understood from one country to another, in particular concerning the juxtaposition of work and family responsibilities, constitutes another factor. 'Intergenerational solidarity', for that is what is in question in France in 1995, does not necessarily find an answering echo elsewhere. European harmonization, unlikely in the short term,[23] will have to be based on compromise. France represents only one current among the countries of the EU. It has allies in Belgium, Luxembourg, Sweden (and would have had more if the central European countries such as Hungary, who had manifested their desire to join the Union, had been integrated), but other countries such as Spain, Greece and Portugal have no 'family policy', and Britain does not want global commitment, especially one that favours an increased birth-rate. On the other hand, in 1990, France ratified the UN convention on children's rights, thus widening further the definition of *politique familiale* towards 'family policy' (this has been called *pédo-centrage*, or sliding towards a policy of support for the child) (Raymond, 1994). Thus the definition of *politique familiale* is adaptable.

The rolling back of the state, faced with a dramatic increase in potential demand – medical spending, retirement costs, unemployment and training, education – has left gaps in the social cover, and priorities have to be defined. In the area of family benefits, the proportion of allowances that are means tested compared with mandatory allowances has increased appreciably. With all *transferts sociaux* (various benefits) added together, it has risen from 14 per cent of the total in 1970 to 50 per cent in 1993.[24] This indicates a move towards, but not an adoption of, a social policy. The 'mission' has been redefined at the same time that public expenditure had to be curbed. Less state involvement also signals the return of a number of private initiatives, such as *crèches parentales* (not unlike private playgroups in Britain) (coll. *Nouvel Observateur*, 1992; Berthet and Prat, 1992), to fill the gap.

The *revenu minimum d'insertion* (equivalent to Income Support), and the *aide personnalisée au logement* (Rent Rebate) are both managed by the Caisses d'allocations familiales (Family Allowances Bureaux), which emphasizes a new orientation in family policy towards protection from destitution.[25] (Naturally, not all recipients of RMI have dependent families.) On the other hand, the strengthening of action connected with family employment, like the AGED (*allocation pour garde d'enfant à domicile* – allowance given for looking after a child at home), has a double effect: *politique familiale* in the traditional sense[26] plus helping people to obtain paid employment. The payment of the *allocation parentale d'éducation* (state subsidies for the parent leaving paid employment to look after children at home) from the second child in 1994, instead of from the third child, also has this double aim: to ease the arrival of the second child, and provide temporary jobs corresponding to the compulsory leave taken by one of the parents. Family policy blends with employment policy.

The steady fall in the birth-rate (1.65 children per woman in 1993) was indeed the reason behind the measures proposed by Colette Codaccioni, ex-Minister for Intergenerational Solidarity during Alain Juppé's first government. The key proposal was to be the *allocation parentale de libre choix* (self-elected parental allowance), amounting to 50 per cent of the official minimum wage, and granted from the first child, seen by some as a desperate but costly way to stop the decline, with no more special bonuses for the third child, since the previous encouragement had not been responded to. The Codaccioni plan undeniably and explicitly had an incentive basis, as explained in the introduction of the long document: 'Si le phénomène se poursuit linéairement, notre pays arrivera à un indice de 1,5 maximum en 1994' (If this trend continues, our country will reach the figure of 1.5 maximum in 1994). Other measures included in the plan were to use the family as a unit for the purpose of local taxes and housing (on the existing model of the *quotient familial*) and to create a Comité d'évaluation de la politique familiale (Committee for the Evaluation of Family Policy) in order to increase or withdraw state effort according to the demographic results obtained (i.e. number of babies produced). This plan, not yet implemented to date (March 1996), is an ambitious, all-embracing child blueprint covering childcare, allowances, simplification of benefit procedures, a simple penalty-free alternative between home and career for the parent, housing and taxation. The Codaccioni programme is pro-natalist, since every child is welcome, yet at the same time it seeks, by the neutral attitude of the authorities with regard to working women, to ensure equal treatment between families. It is also difficult to put into practice: with a negative balance since 1994, the CNAF could not meet the increased expense. It is therefore unlikely that all the reforms suggested will see the light of day. In an economic climate which tends to encourage economies, the Codaccioni plan looks extravagant.

However, French pro-natalism is not threatened by economic factors alone. The publication in 1991 of *Marianne et les lapins* by Hervé Le Bras and the storm that this book created (both before and after its publica-tion) constitute an historic demographic event. The title itself was sufficient to cause a chill: to mock in four words a pro-natalist ideology which seemed harmless enough (using the connotation of lubricious rabbits), and also in the same breath its attachment to sentiments perceived as honourable (France = Marianne), smacked of black humour. But it could not just be wished away: it was no pamphlet which had surreptitiously escaped moral censorship, written by a British pen and translated into French, but the thesis of an expert historian demographer, not only French but a member of INED, and of the Haut Conseil de la population et de la famille, those institutions the pro-fessed faith of which is precisely a commitment to population. As this was an isolated voice amid well-tuned and harmonious sounds, it had to be loud. This was the case: accusation, defence, prosecution, witnesses, libel, suddenly the good people of France are made to feel xenophobic and reactionary when they simply thought they liked children. *Mari-anne et les lapins* is an encouragement to take stock of what had been taken for granted. Furthermore, to accuse the INED of being a mouth-piece for the Front National was sufficiently serious for the matter to be referred to the President of the Republic. Hervé Le Bras was removed from the upper echelons of the INED hierarchy (the list appears regularly in *Population*). In July 1990, he disappeared from the list of technical advisers, and in January 1992, a new head of the department of Methods and Forecasts, named 'N' took his place. The harmony was broken. Among the experts, the quarrel over fertility calculations served to prove or to refute the theory of non-replacement of genera-tions (for which the figure of 2.1 children per woman had been calculated).[27] There was henceforth more than one thesis: one can now question the innocence or the respectability of pro-natalism, and one can also question the calculations on which the statistics are based. In

Marianne (141), Hervé Le Bras mentions the three wise men committee commissioned by the Minister of Research to draw up a report on this *question démographique.* Their laconic findings were in fact neither published nor debated, but public reaction arrived later. The INED, as a scholarly institution, could not but authorize the ensuing debate. Since 1992, Gérard Calot (understood to be a 'traditionalist' demographer) is no longer director of the INED – a sensitive post.

Links have been shown to exist between demographers and political power in France. As for the media, they too, like *Paris-Match,* quoted as the chronicler of the initial confrontations of H. Le Bras and the pronatalists, can get hold of the facts.

Conclusion

Although French pro-natalism has a century of tradition behind it, despite a net population increase, and has survived the winds and tides of equality for women, fourteen years of Socialism, and the new trends in society – new family structures, the cult of individualism – it is doubtful whether it will survive under its consensual form. Destined to be modified, faced with the practices and attitudes that prevail in other EU countries, to be widened to include the concept of social policy, whilst accepting the progressive disengagement of the state, it is henceforth also questioned as national second nature. A hardening of positions is observed, such as the Codaccioni plan which, in its catastrophe-evoking tone and in-built threat of punitive measures, reminds us of France's darkest (demographic) hours.

Notes

1. Bérégovoy, then Minister for Social Affairs, proposed to define 'une politique commune de redressement démographique' (a common population recovery policy). See *Le Matin,* 30 November 1983: 2–3.
2. The Family Policy Studies Centre is an independent research centre, founded in 1983. Its publications comprise mainly articles on children, the aged and family income, but not on population issues. In France, the Caisse nationale des allocations familiales, the official function of which is the management of family benefits, has its own research department. The CNAF publications deal with topics similar to the FPSC's, but state help for families is very prominently represented.
3. The author verified this whilst conducting open interviews in 1993 and 1994 on non-means-tested family benefits in Britain.
4. A group of 64 undergraduates at the University of Portsmouth were asked to write about 'current demographic problems' (shortly after the World Conference on Population that had just taken place in Cairo). The ten French students in the

group clearly interpreted the 'problem' as being one of European depopulation compared to world trends – unlike their British counterparts.

5. The author's calculations, rounded up to the nearest tenth of a percentage point, were based on a comparison of the 736 articles published in *Population Studies* and 855 articles in *Population* between 1969 and 1993. Naturally, certain articles cover more than one aspect and had to be allocated to the category that fitted them best, which may introduce a margin of error. One should also note that both journals publish special thematic issues, and that there has been a slight shift in recent years towards world demography in *Population*.

6. Such as the Fabian Society, or the Positive Eugenics Committee, created in 1934.

7. See London School of Economics (1993) *Population Investigation Committee Annual Report 1992*.

8. Alfred Sauvy's autobiography *La Vie en plus, souvenirs* (1981) mentions this well-documented collaboration. See also Girard, 1986; Lévy, 1990; Bisseret-Moreau, 1990; Kraeger, 1992.

9. There was in fact a neo-Malthusian movement in France. Paul Robin had to send his 'appeal' from London, in 1879, having met with considerable opposition on French territory. This movement started later and waned earlier than its British equivalent and had a relatively small impact.

10. Eurostat, 1989: 122; Eurostat, 1990: 123; Eurostat, 1992: 136; Eurostat, 1994: 132.

11. In the first place, the influence of France in the world depends largely on the vitality of its population. The worrying trends observed these last few years necessitated measures being taken by the authorities to ensure that family decisions should not run into material and financial obstacles that are too dissuasive.

12. See in particular the fifth (*préférence nationale*) and sixth items in the twelve areas of commitment found in the Jean-Marie Le Pen's Front National manifesto sent to all voters in the 1995 presidential elections: 'le revenu parental à 6000 francs par mois, l'augmentation des allocations familiales, une protection sociale personnelle pour chaque mère de famille' (an income of 6000 francs per month for parents, increased family allowance, personal social cover for all mothers).

13. Such as Trève de Dieu, Association pour l'objection de conscience à l'avortement, Union féminine pour le respect et l'aide à la maternité (God's Truce, an anti-abortion association). See Venner, 1993, who in a most interesting piece of research on women and the far Right, illustrates the link between motherhood, a certain perception of civic duty and a different brand of feminism. This at least in part reminds us of the early French feminists mentioned by Christine Bard in Chapter 3.

14. Each year in Paris, these many associations march together, singing hymns (*Marche pour la vie*). Leaflets are distributed with a message that clearly links anti-abortion ideology and pro-natalism: 'Pour le respect de la vie sous toutes ses formes, contre l'avortement et l'euthanasie, pour une politique familiale en France et en Europe' (We must have respect for life in all its forms, ban abortion and euthanasia, and support a population policy for France and Europe). The author wishes to thank Michel Valadier, of Renaissance catholique (interview, 22 August 1995).

15. The Pill has been available in France since 1967, but there is a reluctance to disseminate information about contraception (Fournier, 1980).

16. Treatment for infertility is sometimes associated with treatment of French demographic problems (Leridon, 1982).

17. 'According to our experience, this figure [two] is too low. It seems to us that for a happy family, you need between three and six children.' Or 'In our modern industrialised society, everything is constantly conspiring to reduce the size of the family, the birth rate gets lower and lower' (Odent, 1987).

18. 'Il faut résolument faire des enfants' (We must definitely have more children), said Dufoix, then State Secretary for the Family (Durand, 1983: 46–7).

19. If the wishes and the will of women and couples were satisfied, the downward trend in the birth-rate would be reversed.

20. Certain organizations like the Banque nationale de Paris (BNP), the old PTT, the Ministry of National Education, the CAF and the SNCF have paid voluntary childcare allowances to their employees (Office social et culturel rennais, unsigned, 1980: 7–8).

21. It could be argued that similar preferential treatment is practised in Britain, where mothers now have trolleys capable of seating two young children, or equipped with a baby basket, and special wider car spaces by the entrance of supermarkets. The author would suggest that the motive is to please young mothers in order that they do not take their custom elsewhere rather than to celebrate motherhood. Also, if British mothers had a real choice and were helped by a national *politique familiale*, they would leave their babies in available crèches and their small children in *écoles maternelles* (nursery schools) or *haltes-garderies* (crèches) in order to enjoy stress-free shopping.

22. 'Ses atouts sont nombreux, sa démographie, malgré ses faiblesses actuelles, sa recherche scientifique' ([France's] assets are many: her population, in spite of its current weakness, her scientific research): Chirac, as a presidential candidate, 1995.

23. The CNRS together with the CAF launched in 1992 a European-wide research programme: a comparison of European Family Policies. The first report was published in 1994.

24. 47.9 per cent according to Steck (1994: 112) and between 50 per cent and 55 per cent according to Rossillon (1993).

25. Since 1993, for example, low wage earners no longer contribute to the 'family' section of national insurance.

26. The AGED can give parents up to 3800 francs per month in tax relief (in 1995); therefore, like the *quotient familial*, it favours taxpayers. It must be seen as a pronatalist measure rather than a social one.

27. With women marrying later and opting for motherhood later in life, should we calculate the total number of children they will have by the end of their reproductive years (*descendance finale*), rather than calculating the global number of children produced in a year?

References

Berthet, G. and Prat, H. (1992) Les crèches parentales, *Silence*, **149**, 16–17.

Bichot, J. (1992) *La Politique familiale, jeunesse, investissement, avenir.* Paris: Cujas.

Bisseret-Moreau, N. (1990) De la décadence de la race au vieillissement de la population, *Les Temps Modernes,* **45,** 529–30.

Calot, C. and Blayo, C. (1982) The recent course of fertility in Western Europe, *Population Studies,* **36**(3), 349–72.

Calot, G. (1994) Droit fiscal, état matrimonial et nombre d'enfants, *Population,* **6,** 1473–99.

Chauvière, M. (1992) L'expert et les propagandistes, *Population,* **6,** 1441–52.

Chirac, J. (1995) Presidential Election Manifesto.

Codaccioni, C. (1993) *Politique familiale, Rapport Codaccioni.* Documents, 121/93, supplement to No. 11562. Liaisons Sociales, Paris.

Coll. (1992) Où sont passés les parents? *Le Nouvel Observateur,* **1457** (October), 4–13.

Debré, R. (1974) *L'Honneur de vivre.* Paris: Stock.

Durand, G. (1983) Oui, la gauche peut être nataliste, *Le Nouvel Observateur,* **949,** 46–7.

Eurostat. Luxembourg: Office for the Official Publications of the European Communities (annual publication – 1989, 1990, 1992, 1994).

Ferrand, M. (1982) L'appel au désir d'enfant dans la pratique et le discours des médecins, *Les Temps Modernes,* **38**(426), 1284–97.

Festy, P. (1993) XXIIème rapport sur la situation démographique de la France, *Population,* **6,** 1572.

Fournier, T. (1980) Contraception, l'état s'en moque, *F Magazine,* **12.**

Girard, A. (1986) *L'Institut national d'études démographiques: histoire et développement.* Paris: Editions de l'INED.

Girard, A. and Roussel, L. (1980) Dimension idéale de la famille, fécondité et politique démographique, *Population,* **6,** 1010.

Interview with Michel Valadier, of Renaissance catholique, 22 August 1995.

Kraeger, P. (1992) La démographie et l'émergence d'un dilemme moderne, *Population,* **6,** 1639–56.

Lamy-Festy, M. (1994) La démographie française des trois dernières années, *Cahiers de Sociologie et de Démographie Médicales,* **4.**

Le Bras, H. (1991) *Marianne et les lapins.* Paris: Olivier Orban.

Le Pen, J.-M. (1995) Presidential Election Manifesto.

Lenoir, R. (1985) Transformations du familialisme et reconversions morales, *Actes de la Recherche en Sciences Sociales,* 3–47.

Leridon, H. (1982) Stérilité, hypofertilité et infécondité en France, *Population,* **4–5,** 807–36.

Lettre de la CAF (August 1994) *Europe, des politiques sous influence.* **47**, 9.

Lettre de la CAF (November 1994) *Allocution d'Edouard Balladur.* **49**, v.

Lévy, M. (1990) *Alfred Sauvy, compagnon du siècle.* Paris: La Manufacture.

London School of Economics (1993) *Population Investigation Committee Annual Report 1992.*

Louguy, R. and Larue, J. (1950) 'Cerisier rose et pommier blanc', Hortensia, sung by Tino Rossi.

Monnier, A. (1981) La reprise de la natalité dans quelques pays d'Europe occidentale, *Population,* **4–5**, 897–922.

Odent, M. (1987) *Primal Health.* London: Century Paperbacks.

Pressat, R. (1980) Le relèvement de la fécondité au Royaume-Uni, *Population,* **1**, 189–94.

Prioux, F. (1990) Fertility and family size in Western Europe, *Population – English Selection,* **2**, 141–61.

Ragot, B. (1984) Mouvements de consommateurs, où en est-on? *Après-demain,* **268–9**, 10–12.

Raymond, G. (1994) Les droits de l'enfant, le droit français de l'enfance, *Problèmes Economiques et Sociaux,* **669**, 27–8.

Rossillon, P. (1993) Editorial, *Population et Avenir,* **611**, 1.

Royal Commission on Population (1949) *The Royal Commission on Population Report,* HMSO, 185–96.

Sauvy, A. (1981) *La Vie en plus, souvenirs.* Paris: Calmann-Lévy.

Steck, P. (1994, 2nd edn) *Les Prestations familiales.* Paris: Presses Universitaires de France – Que sais-je?

Stewart-Richardson, E. (1995) Les idéologies qui sous-tendent l'approche de l'accouchement, unpublished MA thesis, University of Portsmouth.

Unsigned (1983) La France veut susciter un néonatalisme européen, *Le Matin,* 2–3.

Unsigned (1980) Histoire des modes de garde, *Office Social et Culturel Rennais,* **9**, 7–8.

Unsigned (1995) Tout sur la pension de réversion, *Bonheur,* **3**, 13.

Venner, F. (1993) Le militantisme féminin d'extrême-droite, *French Politics and Society,* **11**(2), 33–54.

Zola, E. (1899) *Fécondité.* Paris: Charpentier.

2.

The demographic argument in France: coherence, reference and metaphors

HERVÉ LE BRAS

TRANSLATED BY CHRISTOPHER DE LUCHI

Adolphe Landry, the great French demographer of the inter-war period, who was a minister of the Front Populaire in 1936, published a treatise on secular ethics in 1906. This first statement sums up the ambiguous position of demography in France for the last hundred years: between power and republican ethics in the guise of an exact science. These ingredients are still found today, for example, in the appeal *SOS Jeunesse*, made in February 1996 by five French people working in the field of population studies, to prevent 'le suicide de la France par la dénatalité' (the suicide of France by a falling birth-rate). (The appeal was made by E. Sullerot, sociologist, J. C. Chesnais, demographer, J. Dupâquiez, demographic historian, M. Godet, re-searcher, and P. Rossillon, president of the Alliance population et avenir.) The signatures they collected come from the entire political spectrum (Pierre Messmer, a Gaullist ex-prime minister, Jean-Pierre Chevènement, a Socialist ex-minister close to the Marxists, and Philippe De Villiers, a country squire from the Vendée, close to the extreme Right and head of a moral order party). Alongside the signatures of politicians appear those of various moral personalities, such as J.-M. Domenach, the former director of the left-wing religious review *Esprit*, J.-C. Casanova, a disciple of Raymond Aron and president of the scientific council of the INED, J. Lesourne, former editor of *Le Monde*, and Henri de Jouvenel, editor of the review *Futuribles* founded by his father Bertrand, who introduced the discipline into France.

In the eyes of any foreigner, be they British, American or Chinese, such an alliance of these demographic scientists and politicians of all persuasions and personalities seems strange. What common convictions do they share which unite them on the theme of population when they oppose each other on most other subjects? What is it that mysteriously causes their divergent philosophical, religious and political conceptions suddenly to converge when it is a question of *la démographie*? Perhaps there is no mystery, but merely a blinding truth such as two plus two equals four. After all, these people no doubt think that the earth is round and revolves around the sun. Why should they not adopt the same attitude towards elements of demographic evidence?

This then is the first question to ask: are these items of evidence justified and how are they connected? They are mentioned regularly in a number of works published each year in France. In order to throw light on the discussion, an example of this literature has been sought which contains the principal items and links them up. A short passage in a recent book written by a candidate for a place on the board of directors of the INED will serve to illustrate it as a typical account. Because of the objective he was aiming at, the demographer in question had to provide proof of technical competence and to rally in support of his application the politicians and moral authorities upon whom his nomination depended, whilst speaking the language they expected. This chapter will analyse a characteristic passage from his work, upon which to base the discussion of natalist policy, its instruments and its functions which are implied by the possibility of a population decrease broached by the author. Here is what he writes:

> Bien que nous n'en soyons pas là aujourd'hui, posons crûment la question: l'Etat pourrait-il assister impassible à un déclin rapide de la population française, se contentant d'en gérer les conséquences au jour le jour (on lui souhaite, d'ailleurs, bonne chance dans ce cas de figure, le vieillissement accéléré qui accompagnerait une telle évolution n'étant pas de nature à lui faciliter la tâche . . .)? Ce serait, pour notre société, un aveu d'échec terrible: on admettrait, en somme, que notre type de civilisation a fait complètement fausse route, et qu'il vaut mieux laisser la place à une autre, puisque l'espace libéré ne resterait pas vide très longtemps! Mais objectent certains, une telle réponse ne doit-elle pas être envisagée dans une vision mondialiste des questions démographiques? Notre civilisation occidentale n'est-elle pas de fait, déjà usée et de moins en moins efficace face aux nations plus jeunes du tiers-monde?[1]
>
> (Leridon, 1995: 78)

Let us first examine the validity of this text. Have the suggested causes and consequential effects been observed in the recent or distant past or have they a scientific basis using sound theoretical demographic knowledge?

Searching for empirical and logical proof

To start with the first question posed in the text: could the state witness impassively a rapid decline of the French population? This is an improbable hypothesis. In the last 50 years the French population has in fact increased sharply and regularly from 40 million people in 1946 to 58 million now, a growth of almost 50 per cent. This is the highest growth in the space of half a century found in all French history since records began, that is, since the reign of Louis XIV (Le Bras, 1992). The population is at present increasing by about 300,000 per year. Can this trend be reversed in the next few years? The projections of the United Nations and the INSEE, although cautious as to the volume of future immigration, foresee a continuance of growth at best until 2025 (*Perspectives démographiques*, 1993; 'World Population Prospects 1988', 1989). Beyond that date, the lowest estimates indicate only a fairly slow population decrease. The 'rapid decline' is thus a fiction, a hypothetical school problem used to set the stage for the 'accelerated ageing' which the author then goes on to talk about.

It would, he tells us, be a 'terrible admission of failure'. Does this value judgement refer to the drop in population or to the ageing? If it is the former, it is difficult to understand since most developed countries pray for such a development. Many scientists in England, the Netherlands and even in the United States consider that their countries have overtaken their optimum and perhaps even their maximum population, their 'carrying capacity' (Le Bras, 1994a; Cohen, 1996). Are the rules different in France? Does what is right on one side of the English Channel or the Rhine become wrong on the other? On what empirical observations does the author of the text base his judgement? What reasoning leads him to speak of 'terrible failure'? Is the latter term a scientifically defined demographic concept? Is it one of the objectives of demographic research? The answer to all these questions cannot be in the affirmative.

The 'terrible failure' is then a consequence of the 'accelerated ageing'. The ageing of the population is, however, a relative term: it designates an increase in the proportion of the population that has passed a certain age. What age? No one knows. Some put it at 60, others at 65. Before the war it was taken to be 50, and 75 may be chosen in a few years, because of the improved vigour and health of old people. The adjective 'accelerated' is in any case wrong. It means that the proportion of old people would increase more and more rapidly from one year to the next, rising, for example from 16 per cent to 17 per cent then 18.2 per cent, 19.5 per cent and so on. Now whatever the age taken to define old age, the projections show that the proportion of old people will increase more and more slowly from the time when the generation born in 1946 reaches it, for example from 2006 if it is taken to be 60. The author should therefore have spoken of 'decelerated ageing', which sounds less 'terrible'. How can such an ageing be bad? The real problem is that of financing pensions. It is of economic and above all social importance. At what age should people give up work and with what pension? What proportion of the allowances will be borne by the working population? What proportion of the capital will be represented by the capitalization of pension funds and patrimony? Complex questions, widely debated, without any 'terrible failure' being detected. To reduce them to the inevitability of respective proportions of different age-groups wipes out their economic, social and political stakes.

In reality the failure is made clear by the end of the sentence: our civilization 'should make way for another since the space vacated would not remain empty for very long!' Upon what empirical data and scientific reasoning does this assertion rest? Upon nothing other than an analogy with the behaviour of liquids and gases in communicating chambers. The idea that migrations are the result of a 'population pressure differential' is pretty reductionist. If it were true, Russia, the least densely populated country in Europe, would rapidly be invaded by its neighbours. More generally, throughout history, scattered peoples have invaded and dominated dense populations as many times as the converse. In fact, no risk or causality can be drawn from a variable as condensed as density on a national scale. Moreover, if the theory of communicating chambers were applicable to migrations, the countryside would fill up instead of becoming deserted, and cities would decentralize because of their greater population pressure. In reality, migrations obey rules of logic and social, economic and military relationships of force which the population pressure argument obscures by naturalizing them.

Let us accept for a moment the scenario of the disappearance of the French population and its replacement by another: in what way has 'our civilization completely taken the wrong road'? Is a civilization defined by the permanence of a given population in a given place, or by its contribution to the whole of humanity? Are the Greek and Roman civilizations characterized by the continuing presence of Greeks and

Romans on the same soil since antiquity or by the art, science and philosophy which were developed at a certain period in these countries and spread throughout the whole world? Biology and culture are not synonyms. A civilization cannot be reduced to the biological population that supports it, nor the converse. The difficulty of empirical proof resides here in the vagueness of the concepts used. We go from 'the French population' to 'our society', then to 'our Western civilization'. These concepts embrace very different meanings. By definition, reasoning in the course of which the concepts change their content is not valid. Moreover, it may be that the function of the reasoning is not of a logical nature, but is intended to establish an equivalence between the different terms used, between, therefore, 'population', biological, and 'civilization', cultural.

There are no bad answers, only bad questions, said Wittgenstein. Starting from an improbable hypothesis, the text we have just examined has effectively arrived at conclusions that are without empirical or logical foundation. The issue is not the truth of each proposition. For the author there is no doubt of it and it does not need to be established empirically or demonstrated, since eminent French demographers have accepted these propositions for more than a century. He considers them therefore to be axiomatic that is 'undemonstrable', 'atomic' first propositions from which the demographer constructs his reasoning and interprets the present circumstances. An examination of the conditions in which each of these axioms appeared makes it doubtful, however, whether they are more acceptable today than they were formerly.

Archaeology of demographic common sense

The text we have studied takes up almost word for word several leitmotifs of French natalists (advocates of a higher birth-rate) from the beginning and middle of this century, Bertillon, Leroy-Beaulieu, Sauvy and Chaunu in particular. Let us start with the 'rapid decline':

> Il s'agit d'une population déclinante et dont le déclin serait appelé à s'accentuer d'une manière progressive et rapide,[2]

wrote Leroy-Beaulieu (1913) on the subject of the French population. 'L'inaction est stupide et criminelle' (Inaction is stupid and criminal) stressed Bertillon in 1897, and he went on to comment on the programme of the Alliance nationale pour l'accroissement de la population française (National Alliance for Increasing the French Population) whose present-day heir is the Alliance population et avenir (Alliance for Population and Future):

> Contre un mal aussi grave, certains sages professent qu'il n'y a rien à faire! Ils disent que la France est perdue et se résignent à assister à sa mort avec autant de sérénité qu'un physiologiste étudie les convulsions d'un petit lapin empoisonné.[3]
>
> (Bertillon, 1897: 31)

This same Bertillon started his work dated 1911 with:

> Un problème angoissant devrait seul occuper toute la pensée des Français: comment empêcher la France de disparaître? Comment maintenir sur terre la race française?[4]
>
> (Bertillon, 1911: introduction)

and he recommended in capital letters the slogan:

> Tout homme a le devoir de contribuer à la perpétuation de sa patrie exactement comme il a le devoir de la défendre.[5]
>
> (Bertillon, 1911: 265)

More recently, Chaunu (1979) echoed this phobia of disappearing and this appeal to the public authorities when he wrote:

> La liberté de refuser la vie n'est qu'une liberté secondaire, elle n'a de sens que si existe concrètement organisée par la société civile et l'Etat, la liberté principale qui est de choisir la vie. Toute la richesse de la nation doit être mobilisée au service de la vie.[6]
>
> (Chaunu, 1979: 157)

Depopulation appears in the 'accelerated ageing', the second theme of the text we have analysed. It is also a classic of demographic literature. The term ageing has, however, undergone a remarkable change (Le Bras, 1994b). Whereas, before the First World War, it was used to denote a phase of civilization, after the Second World War it designates the increase in the proportion of old people. So, Leroy-Beaulieu wrote in 1913:

> Il a semblé aux observateurs et aux historiens que les nations, quoique leur carrière soit prolongée, ne sont pas éternelles, qu'elles connaissent comme les individus, la vieillesse et la mort.[7]
>
> (Leroy-Beaulieu, 1913: 179)

for

> L'insuffisance de la natalité paraît bien témoigner du vieillissement des nations; la stérilité est l'une des caractéristiques les plus manifestes du vieillissement chez les individus; elle l'est aussi chez les peuples.[8]
>
> (*ibid.*: 183)

The ageing of the nation (for which, moreover, Leroy-Beaulieu held the spirit of democracy responsible) brings about the drop in fertility. Sauvy reversed this causality in his works: it is the low birth-rate which now leads to the ageing of the population:

> La France est un vieux pays, dit-on; certes, mais la France est surtout un pays vieux, un pays de vieux. La population de la France est la plus vieille du monde que l'on considère son âge moyen ou bien la proportion de vieillards . . .[9]
>
> (Sauvy and Debré, 1946: 54)

There follows a comparison, interesting for 1946, between age pyramids in France and in the Soviet Union:

> L'accroissement de la proportion de vieillards est l'aboutissement fatal de la baisse des naissances et de l'allongement général de la vie.[10]
>
> (*ibid.*: 55)

The confusion between these two forms of ageing allows a link to be made between demographic decline and decline of civilization, and to bring the two together so that they seem to point to the decay or even the disappearance of France, which can be described in both senses. The biological sense gives us:

> Un organisme qui vieillit, c'est un organisme qui se laisse envahir par des cellules inutiles, par des éléments incapables d'aucun travail différencié. Plus il y aura dans la nation de vieux, incapables de se reproduire, plus baissera la natalité. C'est à ce cercle vicieux qu'il nous faut échapper.[11]
>
> (*ibid.*: 58)

and the cultural sense:

> Cette baisse de natalité a automatiquement provoqué le vieillissement. Nous avons donc chronologiquement: baisse de natalité, vieillissement, décadence politique et soumission.[12]
>
> (Sauvy, 1979: 95)

Demography is thus immersed in the vast theme of the life cycle of civilizations, such as it has, for example, been set down by Spengler (1947). Sometimes, as in Leroy-Beaulieu, ageing is one of the consequences of sterility, sometimes it is the efficient cause of it, as in Sauvy.

How will the decay of France end? 'By making way for another, since the space vacated will not remain empty for very long' is the reply in the text commented upon, which once again joins a long tradition, that of the fear of invasions. Leroy-Beaulieu, Bertillon and Sauvy devoted a number of studies to *la dénationalisation* (denationalization), *la colonisation par les étrangers* (colonization by foreigners) or *l'Europe submergée* (Europe submerged). Two factors combined to veer in this direction in France at the end of the last century – the fear of Germany and colonial imperialism (Le Bras, 1994c; 1995). It was a Frenchman, Alfred Pernessin, author of a famous forgery in German under the name of Doctor Rommel (1882), who best expressed the first fear:

> Quand une nation grossissante en côtoie une plus clairsemée qui, par suite forme centre de dépression, il se produit un courant d'air, vulgairement appelé invasion, phénomène pendant lequel la loi et la morale sont provisoirement mises de côté.[13]
>
> (Rommel, 1882: 27)

Bertillon quoted him several times and added the fear of an invasion which is at first peaceful:

> Qu'ils [les étrangers en France] soient plus nombreux encore et plus riches, et il deviendra possible que leur nation d'origine prétende faire valoir les droits (illusoires ou réels) qu'ils auront acquis dans le pays. C'est l'histoire de la lice et sa compagne ... Il vaudrait incomparablement mieux que l'agriculture et l'industrie n'eussent pas à attirer chez nous l'étranger, c'est à dire le rival, l'ennemi, et au jour du danger, l'espion.[14]
>
> (Bertillon, 1911: 47)

Leroy-Beaulieu considered for his part that the large foreign communities would never be assimilated, so that:

> La France ne pourra éviter la dépopulation qu'en subissant la dénationalisation, et cette dénationalisation peut s'effectuer très rapidement en quatre ou cinq générations.[15]
>
> (Leroy-Beaulieu, 1913: 387)

The second fear comes from a reversal of colonial hopes. Surprising though it may seem today, men at the beginning of the twentieth century believed in the populating mission of Europe, which they linked to its surplus population. Leroy-Beaulieu is particularly explicit:

> Si la race blanche et la civilization occidentale ont pu prendre la prédominance dans le monde, c'est qu'elles ont produit régulièrement un excédent de population qui a pu se déverser sur l'Amérique et l'Océanie. Autrement, la race blanche eût pu être subalternisée et l'eût même été certainement à la jaune.[16]
>
> (*ibid.*: 280)

or again:

> Si, par la baisse du taux de natalité, l'Europe ne maintient pas son émigration, elle manquera manifestement à sa mission et elle risquera de voir détruire à son préjudice, l'équilibre des races humaines.[17]
>
> (*ibid.*: 487)

This idea is often found outside France. As late as 1936 the British Chancellor of the Exchequer was lamenting the fact that the fall in the birth-rate prevented England from supplying the Dominions with people 'of the right breed' (cited in Glass, 1936: 12). After the Second World War, we again find a nostalgia for emigration in Sauvy:

> Ainsi, la vieille Europe va vieillir encore. Son élan pour peupler le monde est bien fini.[18]
>
> (Sauvy and Debré, 1946: 22)

These opinions were not unusual in Europe at the beginning of the twentieth century. Germany represented a military threat, especially as war was waged with large battalions and not with electronic equipment or nuclear missiles. Colonialism kept pace with populationist doctrine because the colonizers had technical superiority (Le Bras, 1994d). It is more curious that these ideas should persist in the very different present-day conditions: the theory of colonization has simply been turned into a theory of invasion, as if population growth alone explained imperialism. It is as if the North African immigrants corresponded to the European colonists and the Algerian conscripts took the place of German soldiers. It is a further example of concealing social, economic and political conditions, and of reducing them to the biology of a population dynamic.

These ideas can retain their impact on old people who were impressed by them in their youth. That they should be taken up by a contemporary researcher suggests that they are back in service fulfilling new functions. To discover them we must come down a notch in the analysis and study the vocabulary used, the connections it creates and the metaphors which unify it.

Metaphors and changes of scale: the mythological role of demography

The vocabulary of the text quoted is composed of tropes concerning population which politicians and the press have been using for decades. Instead of using exact terms, it resorts to expressions full of imagery. Thus, the word 'decline' is used in place of decrease, 'ageing' instead of increase in the proportion of old people and 'the space vacated' to mean a lower density. Colourful adjectives and hackneyed expressions especially prepare a decor instead of directing the line of argument: 'crudely', 'impassive', 'rapid', 'accelerated', 'terrible', 'empty', 'worn-out', 'young', 'one wishes him good luck', 'make way for another', 'take the wrong road', 'from day to day'. A climate is being created by means of two artifices, the similarity of the terms used, which actually connects them and then keeps them linked in the memory, and in particular the effect of perspective or scale, which is seen in two of the most frequent tropes in rhetoric, synecdoche and metonymy, that is, taking the part for the whole and vice versa (Fontanier, 1977).

The state, for example, is put into the position of an individual who might 'witness impassively' or 'deal with day to day' the whims of Madame Population, who would age more particularly because Monsieur State did not attend to her. Civilization and even our 'type of civilization', like a thoughtless traveller, would take the 'completely wrong road' and would then have to 'make way for another one'. The 'younger' nations of the Third World would be more 'effective' than the 'worn-out' developed countries. Let us remember that the state, civilization, population, 'society', are not independent beings each inhabited by a little autonomous spirit, but wholes constructed and closely linked to one another, for, in the final analysis, they all come down to countless individuals who make them up, to their relationships, aspirations, choices and to their voluntary associations.

The confusion of scale is not limited to the comparison between the individual and the nation. It extends to nations. In the text quoted, the term 'French population', which at first seems to restrict the argument to one country, gives way to 'society', 'Western civilization' opposed to the 'Third World', in a 'global perspective', all in fifteen lines. Is Japan part of this 'Western civilization', or of this 'type' of civilization? Is it Korea and the little dragons, or Mali and Zaire that are ranked amongst these 'younger, more-effective Third World countries'?

It is of little importance, because the mixing of scales is a rhetorical device which has a more general aim: to connect the individual with the world in general. The triteness of the language and the jumps from the nation to the continent and then to the planet serve this purpose. Stretching time performs the same function: from 'day to day', then the next few years which constitute our personal horizon, we jump in a 'rapid' then 'accelerated' way to the life cycle of 'civilizations' and to their 'types' which reflect Spengler. Everyone suddenly finds the problems of this existence transposed to the time and space scale of the planet and thus finds himself in a world which he has difficulty imagining. Demography here becomes a modern or degraded version of ancient mythologies. They too seek to unite the one and the many, the individual and the world as we find in the fine works of Otto (1984) or Hornung (1984). But instead of art and religion which favour such an association, our disenchanted age now uses science and in particular demography.

It is doubtless for the same reason that politicians and the popular press are fond of demography. They too must establish in a practical way links between the individual and the nation or the planet, explain to every citizen their place in and their effect on the world and report on the disturbing effects of the exterior human world, of humanity, on the individual in the very depths of their being. In this way the mysteries of the globalization which is taking place intensify the mythical use of demography.

Throughout the analysis we have used the methods of present-day hermeneutics from which we find several results. For example, there is the contention that holds that every conception of the world rests upon received ideas which were absorbed during childhood and in the course of education. There is doubtless no other way to construct a model of the world. To question it, it is necessary to practise what H. G. Gadamer calls a *Verfremdungserfahrung*, taking a person out of their usual surroundings, such as occurs with the contact with other cultures past and present, in particular through works of art, history and anthropology.[19] This is also one of the principal functions of science, which questions common sense by producing paradoxes, that is truths which are not obvious or intuitive. In France demographic science does not follow that road. It is fascinating to see the same clichés, the same simplistic metaphors, the same syllogisms used for a hundred years unchallenged. The positivism of Demography serves as a shield to repel all criticism of the natalist doctrine and strengthen received ideas. Its moral and political functions also encourage conservatism.

Conclusion

This is a curious situation which is not without danger for democracy. It has been shown in a previous work that natalist policy probably prevented eugenics from having an influence between the two world wars (Le Bras, 1981). Not that one is opposed to the other, but rather because they occupy neighbouring institutional positions. Depending on the country, either one or the other prevailed: natalist doctrine in Communist countries and France, eugenics in the Axis countries and the English-speaking world. It was held that natalist doctrine led to xenophobia, whereas eugenics veered towards racism (Le Bras, 1981). Small consolation, but it was important at the time. Today eugenics is more or less kept in check if only because of its use by the Nazis. Natalist doctrine, which has not been associated with that kind of horror, may then turn out to be equally dangerous. It shares with eugenics a morality by which the group prevails over the individual, by which geneticists, demographers and others can impose irreversible courses of action on the population, sterilization in one case, unwanted births, obtained by handing out rewards, in the other.[20] But one should not cry wolf too soon. With the disappearance of its military justification on account of atomic weapons, then of its economic justification because of the rise of unemployment, natalist doctrine has lost its principal arguments. There remains the defence of the family, which emphasizes its moral commitment, but which risks alienating several sectors of opinion: few French people consider, for example, that 'second' families following divorce, widowhood and remarriage are rotten and breaking down as they are said to be by *SOS Jeunesse*, the last resort of the natalists, as mentioned earlier in this chapter. Holy matrimony, which had constituted one of the most important concrete arguments of natalist doctrine, may thus be demolished. More precisely, it seems to be transforming itself at present around the theme of integration. This blend of morality, politics, nationalism and expertise which characterized natalist doctrine is indeed found there, but the scientific underpinning, which studies in fertility drew from biology through eugenics and social Darwinism, is missing.

Notes

1. Although we have not yet arrived at this situation, let us put the question crudely: could the state witness impassively a rapid decline of the French population, contenting itself with dealing with the consequences from day to day (one wishes it luck, moreover, in this hypothetical case, since the accelerated ageing that would accompany such a development is not of such a nature as to facilitate its task ...)? It would be, for our society, a terrible admission of failure: we would be admitting, in short, that our type of civilization has taken the completely wrong road, and that it is better to make way for another, since the space vacated would not remain empty for very long! But, some object, should not such a response be considered within a global view of demographic questions? Is our Western civilization not in fact already worn out and less and less effective compared with the younger nations of the Third World?

2. It is a question of a declining population and one whose decline is destined to become progressively and rapidly accentuated.

3. Certain sages claim that nothing can be done against such a serious predicament! They say that France is lost and resign themselves to witnessing her death with as much serenity as a physiologist studying the convulsions of a little rabbit that has been poisoned.

4. One alarming problem alone should occupy entirely the thoughts of the French: how to prevent France from disappearing? How to maintain the French race on the earth?

5. Every man has the duty to contribute to the perpetuation of his country just as he has the duty to defend it.

6. The freedom to refuse life [that is, abortion in his language] is only a secondary freedom, and only makes sense if the fundamental freedom, which is to choose life [that is, to reproduce], is concretely organized by the civil society and the state. The entire wealth of the nation must be mobilized in the service of life.

7. It has seemed to observers and historians that nations, although their careers may be long, are not eternal, that, like individuals, they experience old age and death.

8. The insufficient birth-rate does appear to bear witness to the ageing of nations; sterility is one of the most obvious characteristics of ageing in individuals; it is in peoples as well.

9. France is an ancient country, it is said; indeed, but France is above all an old country, a country of old people. The population of France is the oldest in the world whether one considers its average age or the proportion of old people.

10. The increase in the proportion of old people is the inevitable outcome of the drop in births and the general increase in lifespan.

11. An organism which ages is one which is taken over by useless cells, by elements which are incapable of any differentiated work. The more old people who are incapable of reproducing there are in a nation, the more the birth-rate will drop. It is from this vicious circle that we must escape.

12. This drop in the birth-rate has automatically brought about ageing. We have therefore in chronological order: drop in the birth-rate, ageing, political decay and submissiveness. (Sauvy was discussing the subject of ancient Greece, and applied the same list to the case of Rome with the suggestion that it was applicable to modern France.)

13. When an expanding nation borders on one that is more sparsely populated, which subsequently forms the centre of a depression, a current of air is produced, commonly called an invasion, a phenomenon during which laws and morality are temporarily set aside.

14. That they [the foreigners in France] are still more numerous and richer, and their nation of origin might try to enforce the rights (illusory or real) that they have acquired in the country. It is the story of *La Lice et sa compagne*... It would be far better if agriculture and industry did not draw the foreigner to our country, that is, the rival, the enemy and, in times of danger, the spy.

    * *The Bitch and Her Friend* – a fable by Jean de la Fontaine in which the bitch of the story takes over the home of her too-trustful friend.

15. France will only be able to avoid depopulation by undergoing denationalization and this denationalization may take place very rapidly in four or five generations.

16. If the white race and Western civilization have been able to predominate in the world, it is because they regularly produced a population surplus which spilled over into America and Oceania. Otherwise the white race might have been overwhelmed and would certainly have been so by the yellow race.

17. If, by a fall in the birth-rate, Europe does not keep up its emigration, it will plainly be failing in its mission and might see the balance of the human races destroyed to its detriment.

18. So, old Europe is going to become older again. Its impulse for populating the world is indeed finished.

19. In *L'Universalité de l'herméneutique*, Archives de philosophie, **33** (1970), H.G. Gadamer shows how our conception of the world is constituted of and rests upon received ideas. He lays stress upon the fundamental role of language in the solidity of this construction, therefore upon the importance of rhetoric. The term 'myth' is preferred here to conception of the world because the procedures of inclusion promoted by demography are close to the role of myths, such as analysed by C. Levi-Strauss in his *Anthropologie structurale*.

20. In *Le Savant et le philosophe* (Plon, Paris, 1959) (translation of part of the work of 1919), Max Weber stresses the differences between the two points of view, the scholar limiting himself to examining social hypotheses and the path which leads to their formulation without issuing injunctions or recommendations which fall within the province of the politician. Another article could be written with other quotations by other writers on demography, present-day or of former times, lavishing advice and injunctions of the kind: 'the state should' or 'it is necessary'. This confusion of practices is dangerously close to anti-democracy: from a political point of view any recommendations mean that the demographer as expert places himself or herself above mere citizens.

References

Bertillon, J. (1897) *Le Problème de la population.* Paris: Armand Colin.

Bertillon, J. (1911) *La Dépopulation de la France.* Paris: Félix Alcan.

Chaunu, P. *et al.*, (1979) *La France ridée.* Paris: Hachette-Pluriel.

Cohen, J. (1996) *How Many People Can the Earth Support?* New York: Norton.

Fontanier, P. (1977) *Les Figures du discours*. Paris: Flammarion. (first published 1746)

Glass, D. (1936) *The Struggle for Population*. Oxford: Clarendon Press.

Hornung, E. (1984) *Les Dieux de l'Egypte: l'un et le multiple*. Paris, Flammarion (published in Germany in 1971).

Landry, A. (1906) *Traité de morale laïque*. Paris: Girard.

Le Bras, H. (1981) L'histoire secrète de la fécondité, *Le Débat*, **5**, 76–101.

Le Bras, H. (1992) *Marianne et les lapins: l'obsession démographique*. Paris: Hachette-Pluriel.

Le Bras, H. (1993) *La Planète au village*. Paris: Editions de l'Aube/ DATAR.

Le Bras, H. (1994a) *Les Limites de la planète*. Paris: Flammarion.

Le Bras, H. (1994b) Le vieillissement de la population: de la rhétorique à l'idéologie, *Revue Française des Affaires Sociales*, **48**(1), 157–77.

Le Bras, H. (1994c) *Le Sol et le sang*. Paris: Editions de l'Aube.

Le Bras, H. (1994d) Guerre et population. In P. Boniface (ed.), *La Puissance internationale*. Paris: Dunod, pp. 41–59.

Le Bras, H. (1995) Migrations internationales: de la colonisation à l'invasion ou la rhétorique des vases communicants, *The Toqueville Review*, **16**(1), 83–111.

Leridon, H. (1995) *Les Enfants du désir*. Paris: Julliard.

Leroy-Beaulieu, P. (1913) *La Question de la population*. Paris: Félix Alcan.

Otto, W. (1984) *Les Dieux de la Grèce*. Paris: Payot (first published in Germany in 1929).

Perspectives Démographiques (1993). Paris: INSEE.

Rommel, Dr (1882) *Le Pays de la revanche*. Paris: published by author.

Sauvy, A. (1979) Les conséquences du vieillissement de la population. In P. Chaunu *et al.*, *La France ridée*. Paris: Hachette-Pluriel, pp. 61–118.

Sauvy, A. and Debré, R. (1946) *Des Français pour la France*. Paris: Gallimard, Ch. V: 'Un corps qui vieillit, l'envahissement des vieillards' (An ageing body, the invasion of the old people), pp. 54–9.

Spengler, O. (1947) *Le Déclin de l'occident*. Paris: Gallimard. 2 vols. (translated by Tazerout).

World Population Prospects 1988 (1989) *Demographic Studies*, **106**. New York: United Nations.

3.

Marianne and the mother rabbits: feminism and natality under the Third Republic

CHRISTINE BARD

TRANSLATED BY ANABEL TAYLOR

The falling birth-rate in France was a serious political problem during the Third Republic: what had begun as a cause for concern developed into a major obsession after the defeat of France by Prussia in 1870 (Dupâquier, 1988). Pro-family and pro-natalist pressure groups were formed (Talmy, 1962) which, during and, above all, after the First World War, gained increasing support from both the Left and the Right, and secured the passage of repressive and provocative legislation. The feminist movement shared this fear of depopulation, which undoubtedly hindered the progress of women's emancipation, and partly accounts for France's late development in the field of equal rights (Klejman and Rochefort, 1989; Bard, 1995; Cova, 1994). The majority of feminists proposed or accepted measures designed to bring a halt to declining fecundity. They devised a theory of feminist pro-natalism which was seen as heresy in the eyes of the radical militants. It should be remembered that the feminist movement was made up of groups with very different political and sociological identities. From the 1920s, the reformists, politically associated with the Radical Party, had to compete with the moderates, who represented the bourgeoisie and the Roman Catholic aristocracy. The hegemony of these two groups was challenged by a minority of radical feminists who demanded 'free maternity'.

The ideological foundations of pro-natalism

Women were directly affected by the debate about the causes of the falling birth-rate. According to Arsène Dumont (1990), author of an authoritative demographic study published in 1890, *Dépopulation et civilisation*, France's oliganthropy was the result of social capillarity, the falling birth-rate being a consequence of the desire for excessive individualism instilled in young couples by the progress of democratic civilization. Morally, it was necessary to condemn and fight against the ambition and egotism of the 'new' women, who devoted themselves to study, work and leisure. This intellectual, a 'chaste celibate' who lived only for his work, was not a reactionary. Like Adolphe Landry (1982), the great demographer of the next generation, he was a freethinker, an anti-clerical and a democrat. In Landry's book, *La Révolution démographique*, first published in 1934, he also attributed the falling birth-rate to a fundamental change in mentality, which began with the French Revolution. To explain this new 'rationalization of reproduction', he made a distinction between altruistic motives, such as the desire to raise one's children well and to see them move up in society, and selfish motives, in particular the aspirations of the new women:

> N'y a-t-il pas, chez certaines femmes, une répugnance à la maternité, dans laquelle elles voient une sorte d'asservissement attentatoire en même temps qu'à leur indépendance, à leur dignité?[1]
>
> (Landry, 1982: 41)

He also mentioned the not insignificant effect of the propaganda spread by eugenicists, feminists, humanitarians and pacifists, particularly in the English-speaking nations, in favour of restriction or, to use their own terminology 'control' of the number of births (Landry, 1982: 43). It is no coincidence that the decline in the birth-rate was contemporaneous with the growth of the feminist movement. The opponents of feminism, lacking Landry's delicacy, had no hesitation in identifying the enemy: emancipated women, the bluestockings who were disfigured by the scars of their voluntary sterility. For the majority of the population, the emancipation of women was part and parcel of the demographic peril that threatened the nation's very existence.

The rise of nationalism went hand in hand with the rise of pro-natalism:

> Il faut quatre naissances par ménage bien portant pour que la France puisse vivre.[2]
>
> (Bovérat, 1913: 167)

insisted Fernand Bovérat, who demanded that the 'duty of paternity' be regarded in the same way as military service (Bovérat, 1913: 181). Only then would it be possible to repel 'foreign invasion' and stem 'the daily tide of immigration' (368). Many pro-natalists, without going so far as nationalism or xenophobia, were simply 'patriots' who were concerned about the decline of their country. The chronology of pro-natalist politics is clear: the most important measures were taken by the Chambre bleu horizon, the overwhelmingly right-wing Parliament elected in 1919, in the immediate post-First World War era and, 20 years later, on the eve of the Second World War.

In spite of its bellicose and anti-feminist appearance, pro-natalism was not a male monopoly. Many feminists subscribed to the saying of Alexandre Dumas junior: 'La maternité est le patriotisme des femmes' (Maternity is the patriotism of women). They willingly accepted that women should pay a tax of blood, even going so far as to compare the number of women who died in childbirth with the number of men who died in the execution of their military duties. As ardent partners in the Union sacrée (the wartime coalition government, see Chapter 10) during the First World War, they experienced patriotism on an intense level, and this strengthened pro-natalist convictions. There were empty cradles to be filled: they applied themselves to the task and in return asked for recognition of their citizenship.

Pro-natalism was closely linked to a vigorous campaign against *l'indiscipline des moeurs* (lack of moral discipline) (Bureau, 1919), inspired by the War and conducted by organizations such as the French League for the Revival of Public Morality. The League's President, Paul Bureau, believed that, in order to fight effectively against depopulation, it was necessary to:

> supprimer le célibat, le concubinage, l'égoïsme des jeunes mariés, et surtout le travail de la femme dans l'industrie et le commerce, car seul le rétablissement de la vie familiale comme elle existait jadis pourra redonner vigueur au pays.[3]

(Bureau, 1916)

Even if the militants did not support the whole populationist programme, they did share the concern about the *survie de la race française* (survival of the French race) (de Witt-Schlumberger, 1916) and condemned *l'égoïsme des célibataires* (the selfishness of celibates).[4] Do they deserve, because of this, to be labelled puritans? Such a label would imply the somewhat anachronistic revival of the traditional contempt of the historians of the sexual revolution for bourgeois feminism, and would disregard both the importance of ethics in feminist culture and the objectives of the militants. Their battle against state-controlled prostitution shows that they were quite capable of brazenly denouncing sexual exploitation. It is not surprising that their struggle focused on the issue of morals, a subject on which women were considered to be experts. One set of morals for both sexes was their constant cry against the hypocrisy of the double standard where women were always the victim. In the West, including France, Protestant women in particular distinguished themselves in the battle for feminist reform, and duly left their mark. They combined support for the emancipation of women with an unshakeable commitment to secular and Republican values. Their campaign had the characteristics of a moral crusade, and they were less conservative than the Catholics who joined the moderate feminist groups in the 1920s. For them, the family was the indispensable core of society. A large family was testament to its own success, and to the authority of the head of the household, who was not on trial.

In order to gain such influence in the political arena, pro-natalist ideology needed to build on the support it enjoyed in secular and Republican circles by seducing Catholic opinion. The Roman Catholic Church had always been suspicious of prolific reproduction, the evidence of, doubtless excessive, sexual activity. In addition, it had always preached the superiority of chastity. In the inter-war period, however, concern about the declining population produced important changes. In 1918, Abbé Jean Viollet created l'Association du mariage chrétien (the Association of Christian Marriage), which aimed to prepare young Catholics for marriage and re-establish the conjugal moral code. The following year, he founded la Confédération générale des familles (the General Confederation of Families). From that time on, fecundity was seen as a virtue, a development which was confirmed by the *Casti Connubii* encyclical of 1930, which formally condemned contraceptive practices (Sévegrand, 1995).

Finally, the value which feminists in France placed on their own 'femininity' and motherhood cannot be understood without considering the influence of the anti-feminist movement. The war had exacerbated concern about a lack of sexual differentiation. By insisting on the difference between the sexes, feminists contributed to a collective need for reassurance. They developed a concept of modern femininity which lay half-way between the traditional role of women and their recent new experiences. They sought respectability, and feared scandal. In 1922, for instance, they condemned the novel, *La Garçonne* (The Bachelor Girl), and abandoned its author, Victor Margueritte, who for years had been their comrade-in-arms, to his fate as an outcast, expelled from the Légion d'honneur for his explicit description of the troubled sexual emancipation of a young French girl.

The strength of the dominant ideology explains to some extent the attitude of the majority of feminists. The pro-natalists could claim the authority of science, thanks to the new, politically highly influential, demographic findings. In addition, Adolphe Landry, who was appointed minister several times between the wars, and who set up the Groupe parlementaire de la famille et de la natalité (the Parliamentary Group for the Family and Natality), was the brother of Marguerite Pichon-Landry, president of the leading feminist organization, le Conseil national des femmes françaises (the National Council of French Women). Such family ties between the moderate and reformist feminists of the élite and the government were common. Rooted in the same culture, based on the same moral values, the potential for autonomous feminism was limited, and the means of protest restricted. The pro-natalist argument also had the support of the medical profession. Professor Pinard, the 'father of childcare', became the spokesman of the pro-natalists, and ended up in Parliament. Lastly, the pro-natalist lobby was supported by a number of groups with feminist links. The most important of these was l'Alliance nationale pour l'accroissement de la population française (the National Alliance for the Growth of the French Population), led by Jacques Bertillon (Thébaud, 1985). Founded in 1896, this organization was recognized as a public body in 1913, thus gaining a status which was coveted by the feminists, who longed for such official recognition. The Alliance called for state intervention: the politics of repopulation should concentrate on women rather than men. The role of fathers was not neglected, however, as shown by the existence of la Ligue des pères de familles nombreuses (the League of Fathers of Large Families), or even the demand for a family vote, which would benefit only prolific fathers, and also the demand frequently voiced by nationalists that the duty of paternity should be put in the same category as military service.

The implementation of pro-natalist policies

The first convincing results of pro-natalist pressure were seen at the end of the First World War. In addition to state measures, many private initiatives contributed to the pro-natalist cause. Employers' Compensation Funds paid out family allowances, called bonuses, which were subject to stringent moral conditions. They were eliminated in the event of a strike, and were paternalist in nature, aimed at securing a docile workforce. The upper middle classes were affected by the fate of large families. The most famous example was that of the director of the

Samaritans, Ernest Cognac-Jay, who in 1920 instructed the Académie Française to award a prize for large families.

After winning the elections, the Right introduced a series of measures inspired by the proposals of the first Congress on Natality, organized by the Nancy Chamber of Commerce with the support of the government, the Académie Française, the Academy of Medicine and the Academy of Moral and Political Sciences. Three feminists took part: Doctors Clotilde Mulon, Augusta Moll-Weiss and Marguerite de Witt-Schlumberger, President of the French Union for Women's Suffrage. The call, at this Congress, for a moral revival in France made an impact. On 27 January 1920, Le Conseil supérieur de la natalité (the Higher Council for Natality) was set up, chaired by Auguste Isaac, the President of a group called La Plus Grande Famille (The Largest Family). Of 31 members, two were women: Marguerite de Witt-Schlumberger and Marguerite Bérot-Berger, who, like their colleagues, were committed to:

> rechercher toutes les mesures susceptibles de combattre la dépopulation, d'accroître la natalité, de développer la puériculture et de protéger et d'honorer les familles nombreuses.[5]
> (*Journal Officiel*, 28 January 1920; Cova, 1994: 427)

The Council came under the auspices of the newly created Ministère de l'hygiène, de l'assistance et de la prévoyance sociale (Ministry of Hygiene and Social Welfare), which was expected to play an important role. On 30 April 1920, it was decided that subsidies would be paid by local authorities, assisted by the state, to families with three or more children. On 26 May 1920, the Medal of the French Family was created for families with at least five legitimate children. It is still awarded today. The celebration of Mother's Day, which was apparently inspired by the American custom, and would be both politically and commercially significant, became official in 1926.

The most important decision was of a repressive nature. On 31 July 1920, a law was passed which severely penalized abortion and prohibited neo-Malthusian propaganda, such as the sale of all means of contraception apart from the sheath, which was useful for the prevention of venereal disease. In 1923, a new law was introduced placing abortion under the jurisdiction of summary courts, so that the penalties could be systematically and uniformly applied, without consideration of mitigating circumstances which might influence a jury. Reformist feminists approved of these measures, which they had been advocating for several years. Nevertheless, they thought that the 'criminal' should also be seen as the 'victim' of both the moral outrage against unmarried mothers and of the poverty which led to the 'crime'. Prevention should be encouraged by, for example, setting up asylums where women could go to have their babies in anonymity. In addition, they called attention to the responsibility of the male partners who pushed women to commit the crime of abortion in spite of their fear that it could cost them their lives. They called for these men, who would be the legal fathers if the pregnancy went to term, to receive the same punishment as the women who had the abortion.

Pro-natalism was the politics of maternity, the feminists argued. They supported developments in child welfare, adopting the view expressed by Professor Pinard:

> La puériculture seule peut relever la natalité française aussi bien au point de vue de la quantité qu'au point de vue de la qualité.[6]
> (Speech in the Chamber of Deputies on 2 December 1920; Cova, 1994: 442)

They campaigned in favour of breastfeeding as a means of combating infant mortality, which was particularly high during the first year, due to gastroenteritis, and supported a law passed on 24 October 1919 granting a supplementary allowance to new mothers, already eligible for childbirth benefit, who breastfed their infants during the first twelve months. This measure applied only to French nationals, and excluded certain categories of destitute women. Moreover, the law was neither effectively nor uniformly applied, since it could be interpreted according to the politics of the local municipality or council.

The number of maternity homes, usually run by the municipality, multiplied during the 1920s. They offered women a refuge before, during and after the birth, and the right to remain anonymous. Feminists wanted such homes to become universal, but proposals to this effect in parliament came to nothing. They opposed reliance on charity, defended women's right to assistance and campaigned for nursing centres, which would act as 'de vraies écoles populaires de puériculture contre les préjugés et l'ignorance' (popular centres for child welfare education, overcoming ignorance and prejudice) (Clotilde Mulon (1921) La protection de la maternité, *La Française*, 16 April, cited in Cova, 1994: 504). Above all, it was this systematic support for mothers' rights which distinguished the feminists from the pro-natalists. They were also active in the Committee for the Medical and Moral Prevention of Disease, which incorporated a Women's Education Committee run by a feminist doctor, Germaine Montreuil-Strauss. They were particularly interested in the issue of social health, and welcomed the new service provided by district nurses, who assisted mothers in their own homes (1922), as well as the general process of increased social control over working-class families.

Equally important to the feminists was the issue of maternity benefit, introduced because of the number of mothers in paid employment. It was established under Article 9 of the National Insurance Legislation which was finally passed in 1928 after years of difficulty due to opposition from employers, trade unions and the health and agricultural sectors. Under this legislation, the state assumed responsibility for the payment of pharmaceutical supplies, doctors' or midwives' fees, and part of the cost of maternity leave during pregnancy and for six months after the birth. Members of the insurance scheme received daily compensation of half their normal salary for twelve weeks; a special allowance existed for housewives:

> Par l'extension de la protection à toutes les femmes mariées ou salariées, l'augmentation de la durée de repos et des allocations correspondantes et l'élévation du taux des primes d'allaitement, l'assurance-maternité dans la loi de 1928–1930 est un grand pas en faveur de la protection de la maternité.[7]

writes the historian Anne Cova (1994: 517). It was effectively the most important measure affecting mothers since the Paul Strauss law of 17 June 1913 on women's entitlement to rest after childbirth. However, the law was not efficiently applied, and was severely criticized by the pronatalists, who saw it as a *prime à la stérilité* (sterility benefit) (Cova, 1994: 682), and the Communist Party, which regarded it as *une loi bourgeoise d'hypocrisie et d'esclavage* (a law of bourgeois hypocrisy and slavery) (Cova, 1994: 684). Feminists argued that women's contributions to the costs of childbirth went against the Washington Convention, and felt that the daily allowance was paltry. Unemployed mothers not married to a wage earner were disadvantaged. Moreover, France lagged behind Britain (1911), the Netherlands (1913), and Denmark (1915).

The Law on Family Allowances introduced on 11 March 1932 was, by contrast, a pioneering measure in Europe. Family allowances would be introduced in 1935 in Germany, 1936 in Italy, 1938 in Spain, 1945 in Britain, 1946 in Norway, 1947 in Sweden and 1952 in Denmark. Until 1932, allowances were paid out by Employers' Compensation Funds and covered less than half the workforce, usually those in heavy industry. The law passed on 22 July 1923 on national encouragement for large families only provided an annual allowance after the birth of the fourth child. The aim of the Poincaré law was to promote natality and encourage women to resume their traditional domestic role: it was inspired by the legal proposals of social Catholics, who were influenced by the *Quadragessimo Anno* and *Casti Connubii* encyclicals. All employees in trade, industry, agriculture and the liberal professions were eligible for these allowances, which were not means-tested, and excluded illegitimate children.

On the eve of the Second World War, and as a direct response to the threat of conflict, Edouard Daladier and Adolphe Landry set up, on 23 February 1939, the Haut Comité de la population. Five months later, the *Code de la famille* was adopted, becoming law on 1 January 1940. As part of the policy of providing incentives, family allowances were made universal, and were paid from the first birth. Repression of abortion, on the other hand, intensified with the introduction of five- to ten-year prison sentences for abortionists, and six-month to ten-year sentences for women who had undergone an abortion. Doctors were permitted to disregard the rules of patient confidentiality and denounce women seeking abortion. This Code was the result of pro-natalist and pro-family pressure, and was also expected to strengthen the Republican cause in the face of obvious government instability. Without actually opposing it, the feminists pointed out that the allowance for first-born children was insufficient and unjust, noting the absence of assistance for unmarried mothers. With regard to abortion, their opinion had not changed: they did not protest against the severity of the measures, but did call for the introduction of preventative measures. Above all they deplored the fact that the Code had been drawn up without consulting them. Their complaints carried little weight compared to the declarations of approval by the Catholic women's groups, such as the Catholic Women's Action League, which were growing in popularity.

By the eve of the Second World War, reformist feminists were disillusioned. Not one woman was appointed to the Haut Comité de la population. Women were still excluded from the political decision-making process. Their unsuccessful demands for better maternity welfare were part of a larger campaign for suffrage. In order to win over the opponents of votes for women, who were manifestly unimpressed by arguments concerning women's rights as citizens, they stressed women's specific contribution to politics, and developed a political programme which concentrated on child and maternal welfare, in order to combat depopulation. The struggle turned out to be too great, and ended in failure in 1940. The Radicals, whom they had considered their closest political allies, had turned their noses up at them. The pro-natalists, to whom they had promised their co-operation, had disappointed them. They had disrupted the debate on women's suffrage with numerous proposals in favour of family suffrage, forcing a split between the two groups. The feminist movement's slow growth of political awareness accelerated during the 1930s. They condemned the pro-natalist and eugenicist measures taken in Italy and then Germany, and were concerned about the development of a similar trend in France. 'La famille, pas plus que l'Etat, n'est une fin en soi',[8] wrote Cécile de Corlieu (Corlieu, 1936), a Christian-Democratic feminist who was outraged to see German women treated 'comme des pouliches dont le pedigree attesterait de la pureté de la race'[9] (Courlieu, 1933). Pro-natalists and pro-family groups launched an unprecedented campaign to restore women to their traditional domestic role. The rapidly expanding Catholic social groups glorified the 'sublime mission' of mothers, arousing an enthusiastic response from syndicalist and pro-family militants and young Christian workers – members of the JOC (Jeunesse ouvrière chrétienne, Christian Youth Workers), founded in 1927, and the JOCF, its women's branch. The feminist groups decided therefore to form a united front in defence of the right of every woman to work. They were supported in this fight by the same demographic trend that they had deplored. In truth, it was economic realism which prevailed: it was simply not possible to exclude one-third of the active population. Laval's government tried to keep the wives of civil servants out of public service, but the Popular Front made women's employment part of its political agenda. In the end, the crisis had little impact on women's employment. However ineffectual it turned out to be, the debate about the politics of the family during the 1930s should really be seen as a debate about female employment, which is still a point of contention today. It soon became clear that behind the pro-natalist rhetoric lay a very traditional vision of the role of women.

Neo-Malthusian resistance

A number of feminists rose up against the wave of repopulationist fervour to defend 'sexual liberation' and even the right to abortion. Often freethinkers, revolutionaries and anti-militarists, they attacked on several grounds the *lapinisme* (pro-reproduction ideology) espoused by the Church and the nationalists. Under the flag of neo-Malthusianism, radical feminists favoured the argument of *libre-maternité* (freely chosen maternity), and the *droit de disposer librement de nos flancs* (right to do what we like with our own bodies) (Roussel, 1920). They disputed the very cornerstone of pro-natalism, saying that depopulation was a myth, and 'la plus énorme des sottises dont on farcit le cerveau du pauvre peuple'[10] (Roussel, 1920). In effect, the decrease in mortality and immigration would ensure that the population of France continued to grow. Rejecting all national arguments, they were on the contrary concerned about *le redoutable fléau* (the dreadful scourge) of world overpopulation. They denounced the consequences of pro-natalism, which they identified as an increase in female mortality due to illegal abortions or repeated pregnancies, restriction of the right to work and domestic slavery. Amongst these militants, Madeleine Pelletier and Arria Ly were notable for their radicalism: they preached and practised chastity, believing it to be the only guarantee of independence and the only way in which they would be able to use their talents to the full, free from male restrictions.

Not many feminists ventured into the highly politicized, anarchistic and very masculine world of neo-Malthusianism (Ronsin, 1980), which shared with socialism the rejection of bourgeois and puritan feminism. The lecturer Nelly Roussel and Madeleine Pelletier, a doctor, were the exception: otherwise, the relationship between the feminists and the neo-Malthusians could be seen as a missed opportunity. The embryonic movement for birth control did not progress. The World League for Sexual Reform launched in London by Norman Haire, and in Berlin by Magnus Hirschfeld, found no real support in France, in spite of the efforts made by the President of the League of the Rights of Man, Victor Basch, and Eugène Humbert and Bertie Albrecht, whose magazine *Le Problème Sexuel* folded after a few editions due to lack of readership. Humbert's magazine, *La Grande Réforme*, however, was published regularly between 1931 and 1939. Defending neo-Malthusian politics was not without risk, and Eugène and Jeanne Humbert were sentenced to six and two years' imprisonment respectively (Guerrand and Ronsin, 1990). On the other hand, the instigators of the Feminist Secular Education Groups, who were arrested in 1927 for publishing a report entitled *La Maternité, fonction sociale* (Motherhood: a social function) in favour of birth control, were acquitted. Jeanne Humbert was put on trial in 1934 for calling for a *grève des ventres* (womb strike) at a conference, and Madeleine Pelletier, author of the first feminist plea for the right to abortion, paid a heavy price for her beliefs since, as a doctor, she chose to exercise this 'right'. In 1939, she was denounced, arrested and sent to an asylum, where she died six months later, unmourned.

The hurdles created by the law of 1920 do not, by themselves, explain the weakness of the neo-Malthusian movement, which lacked the support it might have expected from the feminists, the trade unions and left-wing parties. The Communist Party, which had voted against the 1920 *loi scélérate* (Special Powers Act against Anarchists), seemed a likely ally at the beginning. However, its members refused to associate themselves with the neo-Malthusian anarchists, who were nevertheless 'astounded' by the Communist Party proposal, tabled on 31 March 1933 by Jean-Marie Clamamus (Delpla, 1975), calling for maternity and child allowances, sexual education, the repeal of the laws of 1920 and 1923 and the legalization of abortion under certain circumstances. But one year later, in a spectacular turn around, Maurice Thorez called the falling birth-rate 'un des fléaux les plus redoutables' (one of the most dreadful scourges) (Cova, 1994: 628). The Popular Front also disappointed the neo-Malthusians: Léon Blum did not touch the 1920 law. Between the wars, electoral prudence was obligatory for the Socialists, whose opposition to voluntary birth control was long-standing. Cabet, Proudhon and Marx all objected to it, leaving Charles Fourier (1772–1837), the champion of women's liberation and sexual and emotional freedom, in splendid isolation:

> Qu'on ne s'imagine pas que cette furie repopulatrice ... soit particulière aux réactionnaires et aux religieux: les socialistes donnent l'exemple de la même incohérence de conduite.[11]
>
> (Hardy, 1914: 33)

claimed one neo-Malthusian in 1914. The ideological consensus was such that it is hard to imagine how the feminist movement could have found a sympathetic reception for a critical viewpoint.

Conclusion

The attitude of feminist groups towards the issue of natality shows that it was not a subversive movement: it sought to be reassuring rather than shocking, and to prove its sense of patriotism and civic duty. This, at least, is true of the reformist and moderate feminists who co-operated with the changes introduced by the state between the wars, such as repression of abortion, increased social control of working-class families and the glorification of motherhood (Donzelot, 1977; Marand-Fouquet and Knibiehler, 1977). Nevertheless, they broke away from the fold to fight for the reform of the Civil Code, achieved in 1938, albeit without questioning the authoritative role of the father of the family.

They opposed the pro-natalists and the pro-family groups over the issue of female employment. If, like so many others, they subscribed to the 'pro-natalist obsession' (Le Bras, 1991), they still continued to fight for the emancipation of women in the public arena. The resistance they met explains, to a large extent, their caution over the issue of morals. As a result, a split developed between reformist feminists and French women in general, who continued to limit the number of their pregnancies. This voluntary birth control, practised by means of withdrawal, abstinence or illegal abortions, was a response to the financial difficulties experienced by the majority of the population. Incentive measures, such as family benefits and a nursing allowance for the first baby, were not nearly sufficient to encourage prolific reproduction. In addition, setting material considerations aside, the overwhelming indifference with which the pro-natalist rhetoric was received can be attributed to the changing attitudes of the popular classes. While Professor Pinard spoke of biology, Bertillon spoke of patriotism (1911) and the feminists praised motherhood, most women thought only of their own happiness, and dreamed of independence. Certainly, they wanted a child, who would be all the more special for being rare (Sohn, 1993). It would none the less be a mistake to conclude that popular practice was entirely divorced from the law, the prevailing moral code and political debate. The pro-natalists sowed a seed which would flower under the Vichy Government, whose demographic policy was remarkable for its continuity. It flowered again with the baby boom that exploded in the middle of an era of economic hardship for reasons which some people consider to be obscure. Perhaps the key to the mystery lies in half a century of pro-natalist rhetoric glorifying the domestic and maternal role of women: it finally sank in.

Notes

1. Is there not, amongst certain women, an aversion to motherhood, which they see as a form of slavery that will undermine both their independence and their dignity?
2. Every healthy couple must have four children if France is to survive.
3. Put an end to celibacy, cohabitation, the selfishness of young married couples and, above all, the employment of women in industry and trade, since the country can only regain its strength if family life as it existed before is re-established.
4. In the 1920s, the anti-celibacy argument was supported by contributions from psychoanalysis. It was taken up again by the World League for Sexual Reform, as shown, for England, by Jeffreys (1985).
5. Investigating all measures for combating depopulation, increasing natality, promoting childcare and rewarding large families.

6. Child welfare is the only solution for improving the birth-rate in France in terms of both quantity and quality.
7. By extending welfare provision to all housewives and working women, increasing the duration of maternity leave and the corresponding benefit payments and raising the rate of nursing allowances, the maternity benefits introduced by the law of 1928–1930 were a great step forward for maternity welfare.
8. The family is not, any more than the state, an end in itself.
9. Like fillies whose pedigree would certify racial purity.
10. One of the greatest stupidities ever used to brainwash the poor.
11. Do not imagine that this repopulationist madness . . . is restricted to reactionaries and the Church: socialists are showing signs of the same incoherent behaviour.

References

Bard, C. (1995) *Les Filles de Marianne. Histoires des féminismes 1914–1940*. Paris: Fayard.

Bertillon, J. (1911) *La Dépopulation de la France*. Paris: Félix Alcan.

Bovérat, F. (1913) *Patriotisme et paternité*. Paris: Grasset.

Bureau, P. (1916) Report to the UFSF meeting in Paris on 20 March 1916. Police Archives, Paris.

Bureau, P. (1919) *L'Indiscipline des moeurs*. Paris: Etudes de Sciences Sociales.

Corlieu, C. de (1933) Maternité et liberté, *L'Aube*, 5 July.

Corlieu, C. de (1936) Pourrait-on s'entendre?, *L'Aube*, 25 February.

Cova A. (1994) Droits des femmes et protection de la maternité en France, 1892–1939. Unpublished thesis, European University Institute, Florence.

Delpla, F. (1975) Les communistes français et la sexualité 1932–1938, *Le Mouvement Social*, **91**, 121–52.

Donzelot, J. (1977) *La Police des familles*. Paris: Editions de Minuit.

Dumont, A. (1990) *Dépopulation et civilisation. Etude démographique*. Introduction by André Béjin. Paris: Economica.

Dupâquier, J. (dir.) (1988) *Histoire de la population française*, Vols. 3 and 4. Paris: Presses Universitaires de France.

Guerrand, R.-H. and Ronsin, F. (1990) *Le Sexe apprivoisé. Jeanne Humbert et la lutte pour le contrôle des naissances*. Paris: La Découverte.

Hardy, G. (pseudonym of Gabriel Giroud) (1914) *L'Avortement*. Paris (published by author).

Jeffreys, S. (1985) *The Spinster and Her Enemies*. London: Pandora.

Klejman, L. and Rochefort, F. (1989) *L'Egalité en marche. Le féminisme sous la Troisième République*. Paris: Presses de la Fondation Nationale des Sciences Politiques et Editions des Femmes.

Landry, A. (1982) *La Révolution démographique. Etude et essais sur les problèmes de la population.* Introduction by Alain Girard. Paris: INED.

Le Bras, H. (1991) *Marianne et les lapins. L'obsession démographique.* Paris: Olivier Orban.

Marand-Fouquet, C. and Knibiehler, Y. (1977) *Histoire des mères du Moyen Age à nos jours.* Paris: Montalba.

Ronsin, F. (1980) *La Grève des ventres. Propagande néo-malthusienne et baisse de la natalité en France XIX–XXe siècles.* Paris: Aubier.

Roussel, N. (1920) La question de la population et la guerre, *La Voix des Femmes*, 4 March.

Sévegrand, M. (1995) *Les Enfants du bon Dieu. Les catholiques français et la procréation au XXe siècle.* Paris: Albin Michel.

Sohn, A.-M. (1993) Les rôles féminins dans la vie privée à l'époque de la Troisième République. Rôles théoriques et rôles vécus. Unpublished thesis, Université de Paris I.

Talmy, R. (1962) *Histoire du mouvement familial en France 1896–1939.* Paris: UNCAF.

Thébaud, F. (1985) Le mouvement nataliste dans la France de l'entre-deux-guerres: l'Alliance nationale pour l'accroissement de la population française, *Revue d'Histoire Moderne et Contemporaine*, April–June, 276–301.

Witt-Schlumberger, M. de (1916) Speech at the UFSF meeting in Paris on 20 March 1916. Police Archives, Paris.

4.

In vitro fertilization in France: a feminist critique

MARGARET GIBBON

Having examined the question of limitations of feminist attitudes to natalist policies early in the twentieth century, we turn now to a more recent political development, that of the ethics or otherwise of the interference of modern medicine in human reproduction. This chapter aims to provide a compelling critique of in vitro fertilization in general while specifically focusing on France, arguably the IVF capital of the world. It will outline and contextualize IVF and describe the procedures involved, provide a concise history of relevant medical, juridical and political events and finally account for the specific French situation by reference to eco-feminist principles.

Development of technique

In vitro fertilization first hit the headlines in 1978 when the world's first 'test-tube baby' was born in Britain. In 1982, France became the fourth country to produce a baby born using the technique of extra-corporeal fertilization. Since that date, France has invested heavily in IVF research and provision, and today boasts the greatest number of IVF centres per capita in the world, according to CNRS researcher Françoise Laborie (Laborie, 1990: 85). Twenty-seven countries in the world, including Brazil, India and what was then Yugoslavia, had IVF centres in 1989, a year in which about 20 per cent of all IVF births occurred in France (Testart, 1993: 72). It should be noted in passing that in a number of those countries which have developed IVF technology, large numbers of children are available for adoption.

The technique was originally designed to circumvent infertility caused by absent, damaged or blocked fallopian tubes in women. Other problems of hypofertility were treated by more traditional methods. However, by 1988 in France, fewer than 20 per cent of couples taken on by French IVF centres were presenting as a result of tubal sterility. Indeed, fertile women with perfectly patent tubes were now undergoing IVF procedures – qualified by many as *un parcours de combattant* – in order to achieve a pregnancy. Thus, the number of indications for IVF was growing rapidly in France, within the legal vacuum of a hyper-liberal state. Voices of dissent began to be heard as the technology aiming to fix the problem of infertility and sterility began to engender ethical and legal problems of its own. Chief among IVF's detractors were feminists who began to question the ethics of subjecting women to medical procedures which had not been adequately tested or evaluated, while excluding certain women from the 'treatment' on social grounds. Certain religious organizations also voiced dissent over the fate of surplus embryos, a normal by-product of the technique, and over the effects of the new technologies upon our understanding of what constitutes filiation and the family.

Standard in vitro fertilization involves a number of stages. Following extensive testing of the couple, the question quickly evolves around female fertility: the woman's normal hormonal cycle is suppressed by means of hormones which induce a menopausal state. Then, women undergo a second hormone treatment, this time to hyper-stimulate the ovaries to produce more than one ovocyte or egg-cell, in order to increase the chances of producing several viable embryos. The development of the egg-cells is monitored by ultrasound scanning. When deemed large enough, an injection of another hormone is given to allow doctors to time ovulation precisely. They then puncture and extract the sacs containing the eggs by suction through the abdomen. The eggs are transferred to the laboratory where they are put in contact with prepared sperm in a culture medium (the sperm may be from a donor in the case of IVF with donor gametes). If fertilization occurs, between one and four embryos are transferred to the womb. They may or may not embed in the lining. Women continue to receive hormone supplements to support a possible pregnancy. Failure can occur at any stage: no eggs may develop; eggs may be lost or 'dropped' during suctioning; they may fail to fertilize or fail to implant or spontaneous abortion may occur.

Despite the existence of national statistics on IVF in France, figures are notoriously difficult to interpret and often contradict each other. The success rate for IVF is claimed to be at most 17 per cent, and the more circumspect quote figures between 8 per cent and 13 per cent. In 1991, Yvette Roudy claimed that in just under 85 per cent of cases, couples were unsuccessful in their attempts to conceive using IVF (Roudy, 1991: 12). This failure rate, surely a better term than success rate in the context of IVF, should cause us to question the very definition of IVF as a 'therapy', as one of the range of procreative medical procedures, *médecines de procréation* (medicines of procreation). Clearly the technique is still at the experimental stage, which makes women akin to human guinea pigs. Yet the status of IVF as a treatment, covered by the Sécurité sociale (up to five attempts), means that some of the more questionable social, legal and ethical aspects of IVF have been obscured. It is highly doubtful, for example, that IVF patients would consider themselves implicated by the Huriet law of 1988 relating to the rights of people consenting to biomedical experiments (see Chronology in Appendix 4.1).

Medically assisted reproduction enjoys a degree of prestige never before enjoyed by the gynaecology/obstetrics field, due to its association with high technology, to unscrupulous journalism and to laissez-faire politicians. It is also a speciality whose time had come due to a number of factors, which are rarely mentioned in relation to IVF. Although practitioners and politicians pay lip-service to the idea that prevention is better than a 'cure' (no one is 'cured' by IVF), little or no epidemiological research is being carried out on the causes of infertility. The developments in IVF have reduced the likelihood of such research being done. Other research areas, such as tubal transplants or artificial tubes, are now also being starved of funds.

The lack of research on the causes of infertility is especially worrisome. Longitudinal studies of European and North American men show conclusively that male sperm count is dropping rapidly in industrial countries. This reduction in male fertility has been convincingly correlated with pollution to rivers, lakes and seas caused by the plastics industry (Corea, 1988: 146 ff.). Certain aquatic species such as the crocodile are in danger of extinction due to extreme hypofertility in the males, where genital malformation and even absent genitalia have been observed. Similar malformation has been observed to be on the increase in male newborns, including in Britain. Unfortunately, the technological fix is the preferred solution in our Western culture, hence IVF and related downstream technologies such as pre-implantation diagnosis.

The patriarchal nature of our culture also means that women pay the price of male infertility too. In up to 40 per cent of IVF cases treated in

France, it is male factor infertility at cause. In other words, healthy, fertile women undergo the onerous, life-threatening IVF procedures in order that their partner's spermatic deficiency can be circumvented. This is done by concentration of sperm or by the latest technique, the micro-injection of one sperm under the egg's protective zona pellucida, a technique which is already leading to a reduction in the number of artificial inseminations by donor, a much less invasive procedure for women, but one which does not provide a man with a genetically related child.

The feminist critique of IVF technology

Whose interests are served by the new reproductive technologies? What happens to our ancient concepts of kinship when eggs, sperm and now embryos can be donated? What might the result be psychologically for individuals to learn that they began as a donated embryo and have no rights to search for their genetic parents? Is it appropriate for the French taxpayer to foot bills of 8 billion francs per annum to finance a technique with such a low rate of success, when the complaint it treats is neither life-threatening nor, strictly speaking, a disease? It seems at the very least unfair that this treatment is covered by the Sécurité sociale when spectacles for children, for example, are not.

To answer the question of whose interests are served, it is clear that among those with the most obvious economic interests at stake are the practitioners, who benefit directly and indirectly by publishing, big research grants and career enhancement, as well as media visibility for the more famous *pères scientifiques*. More important and more worrying, however, are the interests of the pharmaceutical industry, for whom IVF represents a new and growing market for their products and a willing contingent of patients upon whom to test them. Such a claim – that women are knowingly or unknowingly being used as experimental subjects for new drugs and new combinations of drugs – does not emanate from disgruntled feminists who oppose the equation woman = mother at any cost. On the contrary, practitioners, allies of the industry which finances their conferences, admit as much without qualms:

La fécondation in vitro est un instrument remarquable d'évaluation des nouveaux traitements de stimulation de l'ovulation grâce aux paramètres qu'elle permet de contrôler, au nombre de patientes qu'il est possible de traiter et à la possibilité de réaliser des séries contrôlées comparant la nouvelle thérapeutique avec les protocoles de stimulation dits 'de routine'. Il n'apparaît plus désormais possible d'envisager la commercialisation de nouveaux médicaments stimulant l'axe hypothalamo-hypophyso–gonadique sans qu'ils aient été testés dans le cadre de la fécondation in vitro.[1]

(Buvat and Bringer, 1986: 52)

Recognizing that the protocols for IVF involve the administration of unevaluated drug regimes and, in particular, of hormonal 'cocktails' or combinations of drugs, does cause concern to feminists with long memories. The thalidomide tragedy of the 1950s has not been forgotten, any more than the long-term side effects of the drug diethylstilboestrol (DES) upon the daughters and sons of women given the drug during pregnancy. Ironically, 'DES daughters' are now among the candidates for IVF, the drug their mothers took having damaged their own reproductive tracts during their foetal development. It does not augur well for the reproductive future of their own potential offspring when we learn that the main drug used to stimulate ovulation in IVF routines – clomiphene citrate – is structurally similar to DES and has been shown to cause cancer in cultured foetal reproductive tissue (Klein and Rowland, 1988: 257 ff.).

Responsibility for regulation of technology

To turn to legal and political aspects, the most interesting point to note is that developments in IVF (including cryopreservation of sperm, egg and embryo; sperm, egg and embryo donation; embryo research and destruction) went unchecked and unregulated in France until 1994 when a law was finally passed stating what was and what was not legally possible. This was almost ten years after the British introduced licensing, inspection and national ethical guidelines. Why was there such reluctance to introduce legislation in France and what finally prompted it?

It would be no exaggeration to say that French doctors between 1982 (the first IVF birth in France) and 1994 were given *carte blanche* with regard to the new procedures. As the chronology appendix shows (Appendix 4.1), public concern or in some cases outcry, and media attention in 1990, eventually led to the parliamentary bill, *projet de loi numéro 67*, discussed and passed in late 1992. Jacques Testart, *biologiste repenti* (repentant biologist), was largely instrumental in initiating a public debate by his call in 1986 for a moratorium on the IVF down-stream developments of embryo research, his numerous anti-IVF publications (Testart, 1984; 1986) and the declarations he co-signed and published in the press (Testart, 1988a, 1988b, 1989). Many of the criticisms Testart and others had levelled at the medical and political establishments went unheard, however.

The *projet de loi numéro 67* was passed and became law after a number of modifications in July 1994. Although there is evidence in the law of a degree of statutory control over IVF and related practices by the state, the doctors' prerogative to decide remains paramount. It emerges clearly that the political inertia of the early years led to a situation where politicians and the ethics committees advising them felt it was impossible to turn back the clock. Professor Jean-François Mattei, member of the French parliament and author of an official report to Edouard Balladur in 1993 on the application of previous legislation (see Chronology in Appendix 4.1), began the section dealing with IVF by drawing attention to government inaction and its deleterious effects:

> Concernant la légitimité de la FIVETE, il faut d'emblée noter qu'il s'agit typiquement d'une technique qui, si des dispositions législatives avaient été adoptées précocement, aurait évolué différemment dans un cadre contrôlé, selon des modalités maîtrisées au regard des exigences sociales et des bonnes pratiques médicales. La mission attire l'attention sur le fait que les dispositions qui sont proposées ne correspondent pas toujours aux convictions intimes qui auraient pu s'imposer il y a vingt ans, mais prennent en compte l'évolution des pratiques qu'on a laissé se développer sans réagir et qu'on a tacitement admises en ne légiférant pas.[2]
>
> (Mattei, 1993: 88)

Criticisms by Testart of the *projet de loi numéro 67* of 1992, the draft version of the current law, which he expressed in his 1993 book *La Procréation médicalisée*, included an attack on IVF practitioners' deceitful use of the terms sterility and infertility. He argued that amongst themselves they distinguished between the two states, but deliberately confused the public and the authorities by using the term *stérilité* systematically in submissions to drafting bodies, in order to disguise the fact that numerous couples being treated by IVF methods were not in fact sterile. Describing them as sterile permitted doctors to prescribe the now favoured but not necessarily the most appropriate treatment, IVF. By law, since 1978, all medical treatments for sterility are reimbursed by the Sécurité sociale.

Between the draft version of 1992 and the final version of 1994 a number of subtle differences occur. Regarding the application of IVF we read in the 1992 draft:

> La procréation médicalement assistée est destinée à répondre au projet parental d'un couple. Elle a pour objet exclusif de pallier la stérilité dont le caractère pathologique a été médicalement constaté ou d'éviter la transmission à l'enfant d'une maladie particulièrement grave et incurable.[3]
>
> (art. L 671–2, *projet de loi numéro 67*, 1992)

The final version of the 1994 law reads:

> L'assistance médicale à la procréation est destinée à répondre à la demande parentale d'un couple. Elle a pour objet de remédier à l'infertilité dont le caractère pathologique a été médicalement diagnostiqué. Elle peut aussi avoir pour objet d'éviter la transmission à l'enfant d'une maladie d'une particulière gravité.[4]
>
> (art. L 152–2, Loi no. 94–654, 2917/94)

The omission of the word *exclusif* would appear to permit the use of PMA for other reasons. The notion of *projet parental* (literally 'plan to be parents'), criticized so radically by collaborators of Testart in the collective work *Le Magasin des enfants*, has been more accurately rendered. Most significantly, the term sterility has been dropped and replaced by infertility. This is possibly a case to comfort those on the side of the linguistic political correctness debate who argue that changing the words does not change the reality. Testart's critique has been met, with the net result that hypofertility and idiopathic infertility can legally be treated with IVF techniques.

Medical responsibility

What the law in draft and final form fail to do, however, is to protect the patients. Apart from stipulating that licensed centres must submit annual reports and be staffed by competent personnel, the law does not provide for access to information or for strict supervision of protocols; it does not specify the criteria for the use of IVF, i.e. which symptoms will qualify patients for IVF treatment; moreover, it fails to give guidelines regarding the number of embryos to be transferred, despite the clear evidence that multiple pregnancies are pathogenic. In other words, the law still permits doctors to define what is meant by *les procréations médicalement assistées* (medically assisted reproduction) and by sterility or infertility. Doctors determine what *l'âge de procréer* (child-bearing age) might be, they judge *la motivation d'un couple* (the couple's motives) and decide what might be meant by the phrase *à titre exceptionnel* (in exceptional cases). In the 1994 law, apart from surrogate motherhood and the practice of requiring IVF couples to find an egg donor for another, anonymous patient, in order to procure eggs for their own treatment (*don d'ovocyte avec anonymat croisé*) (Mandelbaum and Plachot, 1991, 168–9),[5] which are both categorically prohibited, we find numerous examples of articles forbidding a practice, only to permit it in the next line *à titre exceptionnel*. For example in Article L 152–8 we read

> Toute expérimentation sur l'embryon est interdite. A titre exceptionnel, l'homme et la femme formant le couple peuvent accepter que soient menées des études sur leurs embryons.[6]

The state abdicates responsibility for ensuring adequate information of patients by ruling that doctors themselves (who, as we have seen, are hardly disinterested parties) must provide information on the techniques, their rates of success and failure and on alternatives such as adoption. Given the wildly differing success rates quoted and the extreme complexity of their presentation (Humeau and Arnal, 1994: 184), it is incumbent upon the state to provide figures, both for use by consumers, who could thus compare hospitals, and for taxpayers, who might consider that the funds devoted to this still-experimental technique might be better spent.[7] After all, being childless is not a disease, the desire to have a child should not be allowed to become the right to have a child at any cost and, most importantly, we should remember the low success rates of IVF and the documented evidence of serious, potentially lethal, side effects, such as ovarian and uterine cancer in the patient and damage to the foetus (Henriet *et al.*, 1984: 114).

Feminist criticisms of IVF and related technologies in genetics, which cannot be covered in a chapter of this scope, are not widely shared by the French public. A 1993 SOFRES poll found that 72 per cent of the French consider 'qu'il faut aller toujours plus loin, car c'est la façon de sauver des vies humaines'[8] (Mattei, 1993: 36). Asked who should decide on such matters, only 10 per cent favoured legislation brought through parliament. This reluctance to give power to government needs to be explained.

Conclusion

In the postmodernist age in which intellectuals sow doubt and in which grand narratives are suspect or debunked, the scientific and medical communities continue to proclaim certainty, mastery and control. In this sense, they are the new priesthood whose growing power is now extending to the definition of what it means to be human, to deciding which babies may or may not be born, which women may or may not give birth. These powers are social and political in nature and reflect their specific cultural and ideological positions, often at variance with the needs and expectations of clients (for example, Muslims or Jews, whose views on kinship differ from those of a Christian or lay persuasion, and homosexuals, who have been refused access to the technologies, a position inconsistent with the presentation of the techniques as a therapy for a medically diagnosed illness).

Finally, from an eco-feminist perspective, it makes sense to question a technique which is available largely to women in the northern hemisphere while the vast majority of infertile Third World women go untreated with far more serious social consequences for them. In vitro fertilization is part of a global population strategy which legitimates the birth of ever more white babies (who will consume on average 30 times more of the world's resources than their Third World counterparts) while attempting to reduce population in the developing countries. It is, moreover, a failed and expensive technological fix to a problem with a partially environmental cause. It is dangerous to the health of women and their babies and further increases the control of a largely male obstetrical and gynaecological élite over women's bodies and reproductive capacity, an aim to which some happily admit:

> Où donc nous aura entraînés la conjonction aujourd'hui faite des moyens d'interventions sur la génétique humaine avec les méthodes qui permettent de vaincre la stérilité et de toujours mieux maîtriser l'emprise qu'ont les femmes sur leurs destinées procréatrices?[9]
>
> (Cohen and Lepoutre, 1989)

Appendix 4.1 Chronology

1973 First CECOS (Centre d'étude et de conservation des oeufs et du sperme humains) for the study and preservation of human gametes set up in France.

1976 The Caillavet law made every French citizen a potential cadaveric organ donor.

1982   Birth of 'Amandine', first French *bébé-FIV*. The 'lab-father' was Jacques Testart and the doctor was René Frydman.

1983   Creation of the CCNE (Comité consultatif national d'éthique pour les sciences de la vie et de la santé – National Consultative Committee on Ethics in Health and Life Sciences). The committee has produced 45 *avis* (recommendations) between 1983 and 1995, which often had force of law in the legislative vacuum.

1986   A moratorium called on embryo research, due largely to the *biologiste repenti* (the self-proclaimed repentant biologist), Jacques Testart.

1988   The Huriet law (loi 88–1138) permitting experiments on people unable to give consent (e.g. children, the comatose) and protecting the rights of those taking part in biomedical experiments without benefit to themselves. Law revised in 1990 (*Loi* Huriet-Sérusclat). The (Braibant) *avant-projet de loi* (draft bill) implicitly condones all *de facto* biomedical procedures in place, claiming reversal is impossible.

Michèle Barzach issues a decree (no. 88–327) which licences 76 IVF centres, out of a total of 400 applicants. The decree meets with wide-scale opposition, and is thrown out by the Conseil d'Etat. The centres continue in the interim to practise without a licence.

Barzach also sets up a Commission nationale de médecine et de biologie de la reproduction et du diagnostic prénatal (National Commission on Reproductive Medicine and Prenatal Diagnosis), a toothless commission whose recommendations are largely ignored. Unlicensed IVF centres continue to flourish.

1990   Laboratory fees for IVF are covered by the Sécurité sociale system and reimbursed up to a ceiling of 3500 francs per attempt. Four attempts are allowed (this has since been increased to five).

Prime-time television programmes and debates on IVF and embryo research intensify public concern. Major disagreements between 'stars' Testart and Frydman hit the headlines.

Testart edits and introduces a collective book vehemently critical of IVF: *Le Magasin des enfants*. He is excluded from the IVF laboratory at Antoine Béclère maternity hospital and resigns as president of the Groupe d'étude de la fécondation in vitro en France (French IVF research group).

1992   *Projet de loi* (bill) no. 67 'relatif au don et à l'utilisation des parties et produits du corps humain, à la procréation médicalement assistée et au diagnostic prénatal' (relating to the donation and use of human body products and organs, to medically assisted reproduction and to prenatal diagnosis) passed on 25 November by the Assemblée nationale.

1993   SOFRES poll on French attitudes to the new reproductive technologies finds the French largely in favour.

Edouard Balladur commissions a report on the application of the Huriet-Sérusclat law and other matters relating to bioethical issues. *Député* J.-F. Mattei produces report, later published by the Documentation française.

Destruction of embryos in an unlicensed laboratory in July. Minister for Health circular on preservation and transfer of gametes and human embryos. The circular remains largely a dead letter due to absence of legislation.

1994   Law no. 94–654 passed on 29 July. For the first time in twelve years, since the birth of the first IVF baby in France, reproductive technology is now a subject of state regulation and malpractice can result in criminal proceedings. The law, however, remains silent on a number of issues. As the IVF and related fields change, specific decrees will need to be passed to fine-tune legislation.

Notes

1. In vitro fertilization is a remarkable tool for the evaluation of new methods of stimulation of ovulation thanks to the number of variables which can be controlled, the number of patients it is possible to treat and the possibility of carrying out a series of experiments which compare the new therapy with other 'routine' methods of stimulation used on control groups. This means that it is now no longer feasible to market new drugs for stimulation of ovulation without testing them in in vitro fertilization protocols.

2. As far as the legality of IVF goes, it must be pointed out that typically this involves techniques which would have developed differently if there had been a legal framework set up in advance and if they had been carried out in a controlled setting, in line with proper social criteria and good medical practice. The committee draws attention to the fact that our proposals do not always correspond to the deeply held beliefs which might have regulated the situation 20 years ago. Proposals are now predicated which have developed by default and which have been tacitly allowed due to a legislative vacuum.

3. Medically assisted procreation is intended to respond to a couple's desire to become parents. Its sole aims are to rectify medically diagnosed sterility of a pathological nature or to avoid the transmission of a serious untreatable illness.

4. Reproductive medicine aims to respond to a couple's request to become parents. It aims to overcome medically diagnosed pathological infertility. It may also be used to avoid transmitting a very serious disease to the child.

5. This is prohibited by the 1994 law.

6. Embryo experimentation is forbidden. In exceptional cases, however, a couple may give their consent for tests to be carried out on their embryos.

7. Wagner and St. Clair argue that IVF costs are underestimated, as they do not reflect the downstream costs of IVF pregnancies, which are atypical. Costings should

include the treatment of patients with high-risk, multiple pregnancy, the increased rate of Caesarean sections, longer hospital stays and increased use of neonatal intensive care. See 'La FIVETE bénéficie-t-elle à tous' in J. Testart, *Le Magasin des enfants*, pp. 107–13, originally published in English in *The Lancet*, October 1989.

8. 'That it is necessary to carry on doing research because it is the way to save lives.' This, and subsequent references to the poll, are taken from J.-F. Mattei, 1993: 36–48.

9. Where will today's situation lead us when we have the possibility of genetic engineering along with methods of overcoming sterility and of further controlling women's reproductive destiny?

References

Buvat, J. and Bringer, J. (eds) (1986) *Induction et stimulation de l'ovulation, Progrès en gynécologie*, 1. Paris: Douin.

Cohen, J. and Lepoutre, R. (1989) 10 ans déjà, *Gyn Obs (La Médecine et la Femme)*, 1 November.

Corea, G. (1988) *The Mother Machine*. London: The Women's Press.

Henriet, B., Henriet, L., Hulhove, D. and Seynave, V. (1984) The lethal effect of super-ovulation on embryos, *Journal of in Vitro Fertilisation and Embryo Transfer*, 1(2).

Humeau, C. and Arnal, F. (1994) *Les Médecines de procréation*. Paris: Odile Jacob.

Klein, R. and Rowland, R. (1988) Women as test-sites for fertility drugs: clomiphene citrate and hormonal cocktails, *Reproductive and Genetic Engineering*, 1(3), 251–73.

Laborie, F. (1990) D'une banalisation sans évaluation et de ce qui peut s'ensuivre. In J. Testart (ed.), *Le Magasin des enfants*. Paris: François Bourin, 83–106.

Mandelbaum, J. and Plachot, M. (1991) *Génération éprouvette*. Paris: Flammarion.

Mattei, J.-F. (1993) *La Vie en questions*. Paris: La Documentation Française.

Roudy, Y. (1991) Preface to C. Ramogida, *Bébés éprouvettes*. Paris: Plon, 11–14.

Testart, J. (1984) *De l'éprouvette au bébé-spectacle*. Paris: Editions Complexes.

Testart, J. (1986) *L'Oeuf transparent*. Paris: Flammarion.

Testart, J. (1988a) Maîtriser la science, *Le Monde*, 19 March.

Testart, J. (1988b) *Nature*, 333 + 390.

Testart, J. (1989) Pour les états généraux de la biomédecine, *Libération*, 3 February.

Testart, J. (1993) *La Procréation médicalisée*. Paris: Flammarion.

5.

Men, women, work and family size in France: a feminist perspective

JAN WINDEBANK

Most women researchers in France, and indeed many women in general, view pronouncements on the problem of the falling birth-rate by politicians with suspicion and concern. Women's employment outside the home is often cited as the major cause of declining fertility rates, particularly by the Right. The often implicit, and sometimes explicit, conclusion is that a return to a more Parsonian family model – man the breadwinner and woman the homemaker – would assist in the rejuvenation of the population. An historical reading of fluctuations in the birth-rate in industrialized countries does lend some credence to this argument since birth-rates have been falling as women's employment rates have been rising over the last 30 years. However, a cross-national reading of the current situation in Western nations suggests that no simple causal relationship exists between women's employment and the decline in the birth-rate. This is because some of the most fecund countries are those with the highest rates of women's employment – France being the prime example of this – and vice versa. Differences in the material and ideological environment created by family policy in various countries are said to explain this finding.[1]

The aim of this chapter is therefore to investigate the relationship between women's employment, fertility rates and family policy in France and, more specifically, to investigate it from a feminist perspective. This will be done in a number of ways. Firstly, much research into the effects of social policy on family size assumes that the policy environment created in a particular country influences fertility rates, but that this influence will always be limited because the state cannot intervene directly into this most personal of decisions within the private sphere. There is a tendency to abandon analysis at this point, suspended between, on the one hand, a list of possible structural determinants of fertility and, on the other hand, the assertion that couples' decisions concerning whether to have children and how many to have are so personal and embedded in emotion that they elude rational explanation. This chapter attempts to reconcile the individual and the structural within discussions of family size, women's employment and family policy in France from a feminist perspective by employing the notion of 'strategy'.[2] A 'strategy' is taken here to mean a set of actions which have been informed by a general aim without being consciously organized in relation to an explicit goal (Commaille, 1993: 12). Therefore, using the concept of 'strategy', individuals' actions can be interpreted as being the product not only of external forces over which they have no control but also as the product of their own aspirations and desires as these encounter the constraints which the current organization of society brings to bear on them. However, in contrast to neoclassical theory, these aspirations are taken to be socially constructed and therefore influenced by ideologies, whether these be dominant or subversive ideologies. In consequence, the number of children in a family is interpreted in this chapter neither as the pure product of certain structural determinants (including family policy), nor as a predominantly emotional decision, but as a facet of the 'strategy' that women in France adopt to chart a course between motherhood and employment.

Secondly, the perspective embraced in this chapter can be termed 'feminist' in that it seeks to identify the effect of the role played by men in the family in determining women's strategies *vis-à-vis* employment and motherhood. Most policy, and indeed most research, in France focuses on how women do or do not cope with having a job and a family. The role of men, and the possibility of targeting policy at men if the state wishes to increase the birth-rate, is scarcely ever discussed seriously. However, it will be argued here that gender equality will only be achieved when men's relationship to the family and to employment changes, and it may be that such a transformation in gender relations would be conducive to larger families.

Thirdly, the chapter asks a question rarely posed by studies of fertility rates: namely, is the declining birth-rate a problem for women? This question is answered from the point of view of competing feminist approaches.

The chapter will therefore commence by outlining the current situation *vis-à-vis* family size and women's employment in France. Next, it will discuss how women's aspirations to free themselves from their domestic shackles coupled with an economic requirement for their labour in France, which encouraged the state to provide childcare facilities, has produced a situation in which a large number of women can combine motherhood and a full-time job, provided that family size remains limited to a maximum of two children. The chapter discusses the ideological and material constraints which come to bear on French women as they attempt to negotiate a path between motherhood and employment and which make it very difficult, if not impossible, for the majority of women to remain in full-time activity with three children. Finally, and in conclusion, the chapter discusses the way forward for men, women, work and family size in France from a feminist perspective.

Birth-rates and women's employment in France

As stated above, France has followed a general twin trend apparent in all Western countries of increases in women's employment rates and falls in the birth-rate over the last 30 years.[3] However, it should be noted that the birth-rate in France has scarcely changed since 1975, despite a massive increase in the number of mothers working.[4] Indeed, France is one of the most fecund countries in the European Union 'despite' having some of the highest levels of women's employment.

It can be seen from Table 5.1 that there is very little correlation between countries' rankings in terms of birth-rate and in terms of women's employment rate, with the exception of Ireland. Moreover, French women are more likely than most of their European Union

Table 5.1 Women's employment and fertility rates in the European Union

Total period fertility rates, 1989 (average births per woman), ranked from least to most fecund		Employment rates for women aged 25–59, in 1990, as % of total in employment (ranked from highest to lowest employment rate)	
Italy	1.27	Denmark	87.9
Spain	1.33	France	73.2
Portugal	1.43	UK	72.7
Greece	1.45	Portugal	69.9
Germany (West)	1.48	Belgium	65.5
Luxembourg	1.61	Germany (West)	63.4
Belgium	1.62	Netherlands	58.2
Netherlands	1.62	Italy	55.8
Denmark	1.67	Greece	54.3
France	1.80	Luxembourg	51.6
UK	1.85	Spain	47.9
Ireland	2.18	Ireland	45.0

Source: For fertility rates: Monnier and de Guibert-Lantoine, 1991: 55; for employment rates: Eurostat, 1991, Table 03, col. 5, 55

counterparts to work continuously through their childbearing years and to work full-time.[5] Thus, French women show a high attachment both to motherhood and to employment.

However, despite France's relatively good position on these twin comparative indicators, the success which eludes pro-natalist French policy-makers is the production in a majority of families of the 'third child', in other words, the golden child who ensures the rejuvenation of the population. Although French family policy has been geared to the production of the 'third child' (for example, most benefits increase with the rank of the child and pay for parental leave is only mandatory for the 'third child'), the average family size remains lodged at two children, with childless or one-child couples outstripping the number of three or more child families. Indeed, evidence of a link between women's employment and their refusal to produce a third child is convincing since, in France, it is the presence of a third child which causes the most significant fall in women's employment rates across all social strata.[6] It can be posited, therefore, that a major component of French women's strategy to stay in the labour force is to limit the number of children which they produce to two or fewer.

Charting a course between motherhood and employment: the experience of French women[7]

The notion of 'strategy' implies, as stated before, that behaviour is intentional, if not rational in a neoclassical sense, and that social actors have certain albeit socially constructed aspirations, which they attempt to fulfil through their strategies given certain circumstances. In keeping with this perspective, French women's engagement with the labour market and their attachment to motherhood must therefore be seen in the light of both material and ideological factors. This section will ask what the factors are which have led to such high levels of women's employment in France, and particularly mothers' employment, and what the factors are which help to explain why women employees pursue a strategy of limitation of family size in order to keep their place in the labour market. We begin with a discussion of 'women as employees', followed by a discussion of 'women as mothers' and end with a discussion of 'men as fathers'.

Women as employees

In the 1970s, a debate grew up between different schools of Marxist-feminist thought concerning the way in which women's exclusion from the sphere of production should be explained.[8] Some argued that women remaining in the home both to reproduce male labour power and as a possible reserve army of labour was in capitalism's best interests. Others interpreted this state of affairs as the result of a contradiction between capitalism and patriarchy. According to this line of argument, capitalism should have put women's labour power into competition with that of men to lower wage costs. Thus, the exclusion of women from the labour market, and their continued dependence on men for economic survival within capitalism, can only be interpreted as the triumph of patriarchal relations over capitalist relations.

However, in response to these rather monolithic views of the capitalist relations of production, other theorists and researchers began to notice cross-national differences in the use of women's labour power, France representing a country where women had never been completely and purposefully excluded from the labour force. Indeed, Lewis (1992) terms France a 'modified male breadwinner' state since there has been an underlying current in French family and employment policy which has not consistently assumed that women will be dependent on a male breadwinner. Jenson (1986: 12) interprets this state of affairs as the result of French capital needing female wage labour due to France's weak demographic position at the end of the nineteenth century which forced the state to use women both as producers and reproducers of the labour force. For example, France introduced paid maternity leave as early as 1913. Jenson asserts that:

> The French state was ... called upon to find a workable balance between motherhood and French capitalism's employment of women. The emphasis on [paid maternity] leave clearly reflected a widely-shared assumption that women's participation in the paid labour force even after marriage and childbirth was widespread, inevitable and even desirable.
>
> (1986: 18–19)

It should be remembered that the 'ideal' of the mother at home held as much sway in France as elsewhere, particularly during the 1950s.[9] However, when a new era for women's labour force participation dawned at the end of the 1960s, combining women's aspirations for a place in the public sphere with a need for new workers by the burgeoning service sector, there was already in place a tradition of women's employment, and full-time employment at that, supported by a relatively extensive network of nursery education.

Even though in more recent times mass unemployment would appear to mean that the need for women's labour power has diminished to some degree, other economic factors have played a part in maintaining women's participation in the labour force. The same processes which have brought about mass unemployment – namely, the globalization of world trade and subsequent increase in competition and productivity – have also led to a downward pressure being put on the male 'family' wage. Consequently, to attain a 'desired' standard of living, most French families perceive a need for two incomes. Moreover, women increasingly have to envisage a future where they will need to look after themselves and their children financially as divorce rates rise. They therefore need to keep their place in the employment market.

Nevertheless, as mentioned above, French women's employment should not be seen purely in economic terms. As Commaille (1993: 19) asserts, French women increasingly see working as a conduit to the social world. Going out to work is a way of escaping the isolation of domestic labour and a means of contact with people outside the family (Bloch, Buisson and Mermet, 1989: 105). It is also a means of social and individual recognition for one's contribution to society (Pitrou, Battagliola and Rousier, 1984: 88). Therefore, Commaille concludes that

> Le sens spécifique du travail pour les femmes ne se réduit plus alors à la compatibilité entre activité professionnelle salariée et vie familiale. Ce qui est en jeu aussi, c'est la construction d'une identité, d'un statut qui ne passe plus exclusivement par les fonctions assumées au sein de la famille.[10]
>
> (Commaille, 1993: 20)

Thus, in France we can see that there has been a coming together of a material need for women's participation in the labour force (in terms of both a demand for women's labour from the service sector and industry and from families' need for two incomes), and women's aspirations to have a life separate from the family and not to be dependent on a man. Family policy provision, discussed below, has enabled them to combine these aspirations with motherhood, but the scope of this assistance is limited, therefore explaining women's 'strategy' of limiting family size.

Indeed, a number of factors still prevail within the realm of production which constrain women, and particularly constrain mothers, in their employment opportunities, and help to explain why French women limit their family size in order to be able to participate in employment. These factors primarily concern the requirement for employees to be ready to respond to the demands of their job without reservation, particularly if they want to be well remunerated and/or if they want promotion. This requirement stems from the model of a male worker whose family responsibilities are met by a wife. Although some concessions are being made in the French public and private sectors in terms of the availability of part-time work, the acceptance of this by women when they can secure it is often at the expense of career chances and earning potential.

Furthermore, even when French women are prepared to limit their career horizons, a relatively long working day and inflexible use of part-time staff compound the spatial and temporal difficulties of combining motherhood and employment. These difficulties are multiplied by the number of children in the family. Rigid work hours, particularly when combined with inflexible childcare arrangements, lack of help from husbands and the complexities of commuting and taking children to and from childcare, make it unsurprising that what can be achieved with two children cannot be achieved with three. Furthermore, and as will be discussed in more detail below, ideological influences which determine the parameters of what constitutes a 'good mother' exacerbate these material problems.

Women as mothers

The ideology of motherhood in the sense of women feeling the need to have children in order to be 'fulfilled', even if not in the sense of staying at home to look after them, still holds strongly in France. This is a state of affairs to which the relatively strong birth-rate testifies. Women may no longer find that it suffices to devote themselves entirely to home and family, but neither is a childless life of employment perceived as an ideal by French women. Women's 'strategies' will therefore usually involve the attempt to combine motherhood and employment. Indeed, there are material factors which assist women in France to fulfil these dual aspirations in terms of the country's supportive family policy. As indicated above, Lewis (1992) identifies France as a 'modified male breadwinner' state in which women have benefited indirectly from the horizontal redistribution of resources from families without children to families with children. As Hantrais (1994: 149) notes, the founders of the French welfare state were concerned with demographic issues, and more specifically with the falling birth-rate allied in recent years to an ageing population. This pro-natalism, combined with a situation in which French capitalism needed women's labour power, has meant that family policy has developed in such a way so as not to make women choose between motherhood and employment.

It should be noted that there was no explicit attempt to help women combine motherhood and child-rearing until the 1980s in France. Indeed, until that period, particularly in terms of family benefits, single-earner families were favoured over dual-earner families.[11] However, particularly during the 1970s, it was the services in kind, namely, the provision of free nursery education for a large proportion of three-year-olds and a steadily increasing number of state-run and subsidized crèches, which assisted French mothers to participate in the labour market by making it more financially viable for them to balance childcare costs against wages (Grignon, 1993: 51). Present-day support for dual-earner parents is fairly extensive with childcare allowances, tax relief on childcare (introduced in 1972) and parental leave[12] (Haut Conseil de la population et de la famille, 1987). Since the early 1980s, the Caisse des allocations familiales has increased the number of assistance schemes to help local authorities provide more childcare services. In 1984, the *contrats-crèches* were put in place and in 1988 the *contrat-enfance* was implemented to extend the help available to *haltes-garderies* (playgroups), support for *assistantes maternelles* (childminders) and *accueil péri-scolaire* (pre-school reception classes) for 3- to 6-year-olds. These measures have vastly increased the number of childcare places available (Commaille, 1993: 80). In addition, children are going to nursery school at an ever earlier age. In 1980, it was at the age of four that a 100 per cent school participation rate was reached for an age cohort. In 1991, nearly 100 per cent of 3-year-olds were attending nursery school. Moreover, in 1992 the *aide aux familles pour l'emploi d'une assistante maternelle agréée* was introduced, which subsidized families using childminders and nannies.

In addition to this material assistance, various researchers have pointed to the important ideological message that these policies give out to women, namely, that is it acceptable to be a working mother. As Fagnani states:

> Les différentes formes et le niveau des aides dont peuvent bénéficier les familles ne déterminent pas seulement les possibilités objectives dont peuvent disposer les mères pour concrétiser leurs aspirations: elles contribuent également à plus ou moins légitimer aux yeux des femmes ces aspirations.[13]
>
> (Fagnani, 1992: 130–1)

It should not be thought from this discussion that the measures implemented by the French state solve all of the childcare problems of all mothers. There remain a number of difficulties which French women attempt to overcome partially at least by limiting their family size. First, state provisions and the market-subsidized private arrangements which complement them are not sufficient to cater for the needs of all French working mothers for all their childcare. For example, Leprince (1991) asserts that of the 41 per cent of under-threes reported in his study not looked after by their mother, 11 per cent were in nursery school, 5 per cent in other publicly funded services, 8 per cent with registered childminders and 11 per cent with family members, usually grand-mothers, and 6 per cent with unregistered minders. In other words, 24 per cent were in state-regulated, sponsored or provided care and 17 per cent in unregulated and unsubsidized care. Moreover, many children of nursery school age and above are cared for between school hours and parents' work times by childminders, friends or family members on an informal basis rather than left in school-based forms of care.

Indeed, as a general rule, it could be said that French women, despite the network of crèches and before and after school collective facilities, show a preference for forms of care, on the one hand, which imitate most closely the home environment and which are consequently seen as the best 'quality' care, and, on the other hand, which provide the most flexibility for parents. It is not surprising, therefore, that members of the extended family, or a 'mother substitute' such as a *nourrice* (childminder or nanny), are often preferred over a crèche or school-based facility which closes its doors at a given hour. Although the existence of state subsidies and collective forms of childcare can explain to a certain degree the high participation rate of mothers in employment in France alongside their relatively high fertility rate, such policies cannot meet all the needs for flexibility and the requirements for quality of care demanded by women. The more children in the family, the more conflicting school, work and childcare timetables become a problem. The more children in the family, the more arrangements the mother has to make to ensure not only that her children's material needs are being catered for, but that they are all receiving the emotional and educational attention which they are perceived to require.

The whole question of quality of care, and the importance to mothers of ensuring this, is a part of the ideology of motherhood which prevails in France and elsewhere which expects mothers to provide more and more emotionally and materially for their children. That is, parents, but more particularly mothers, are expected to expend much time and effort on each child. For example, Pitrou and Gaillard (1989: 424–5) assert that, in France, giving a child 'all that it needs' means providing multiple leisure activities for its development. Not only do these activities have to be paid for, but also managed and fitted into already hectic schedules. Pitrou and Gaillard note that, given the amount of effort that is expected on the part of parents, and particularly mothers, it is not surprising that there is a strict limitation of fertility: 'Réussir l'avenir d'un enfant est une aventure qu'il ne faut pas multiplier' (Successfully preparing a child's future is an adventure which should not be multiplied).

If these were the expectations of 'parenting', the whole discussion would be very different, but they are not. These are essentially the expectations of 'mothering'. Distinguishing and separating mothering and gender is probably the hardest task of all in liberating women from patriarchal constraints, but, we could add, the most necessary if gender relations are to be challenged. As Glenn argues:

> Mothering and gender are closely intertwined: each is a constitutive element of the other ... Perhaps because the gendered allocation of mothering appears to flow inevitably from the division based on reproductive function, mothering – more than any other aspect of gender – has been subject to essentialist interpretation: seen as natural, universal and unchanging.
>
> (Glenn, 1994: 3)

Although the ideology of motherhood may be moving away from the idea that women have to spend every waking moment with their children, 'mothering' still entails constant responsibility for the welfare of the child.

Men as fathers

As shown, the majority of studies of demography and fertility rate centre on the question of women's employment and women's 'double burden'. The role of fathers, particularly as regards their work commitments and their degree of participation in the home, is rarely discussed in any depth as a factor in allowing families to move, for example, from having two children to having three, since it is almost taken for granted that men do not and will not participate more in the home. Indeed, in its synthesis report on female activity and fertility, the European Commission states:

The domestic division of labour is an implicit theme in all [individual country] reports [for this survey] and in some reports the major responsibility borne by women for children, their care and development is left unstated. It is seen to be so obvious.

(Commission of the EC, 1991: 52)

However, this chapter asserts that it is precisely the lack of participation of fathers which makes it too difficult for a woman to have a job and more than two children, given the time and effort which she will be expected to devote to each, whatever the state assistance in terms of monetary benefits or benefits in kind for child-rearing. What, then, is the evidence concerning French men's participation in child-rearing?

General research on fathers has shown that men tend to intensify, rather than reduce, their labour market participation in order to maximize their rewards when a child is born into the family, despite the extra domestic burden that this entails (Rosenfeld, 1980). Neither fatherhood in general, nor the number of children in the family, appear to make much difference to men's relationship to their employment.

This does not only mean that men do not give up work or go part-time on the birth of their children. It also means that men less

Table 5.2 Mothers' and fathers' domestic labour and childcare by number of children and employment status

	Professional work	Domestic work	Childcare
Employed mothers			
with one child	5h15	4h20	0h40
with two children	5h	4h40	0h50
with three or more children	4h40	4h50	0h50
Fathers with employed wives			
with one child	6h20	2h20	0h15
with two children	6h10	2h25	0h20
with three or more children	6h20	2h05	0h15
Mothers at home			
with one child	0	7h15	1h25
with two children	0	7h35	1h40
with three or more children	0	8h	1h55
Fathers with wives at home			
with one child	6h20	2h	0h20
with two children	6h40	2h05	0h20
with three or more children	6h10	2h05	0h15

Source: INSEE, Enquête 'Emploi du temps' 1986, in Chaudron (1991: 140).

frequently disturb the regular pattern of their employment for child-care needs. Take the example of time taken off work to look after sick children (a question that becomes very important for working parents of larger families). In his study of the arrangements made by working parents to look after their children when they are ill, de Singly (1993) found that of all the cases of illness reported in his sample, 51 per cent were looked after by their mother and only 13 per cent were looked after by the father.[14]

The fact that men's participation in the labour market is left relatively undisturbed by the onset of fatherhood is obviously connected to men's lack of participation in the home and in childcare. The 1986 INSEE French time-budget study (see Table 5.2) shows that fathers spend much less time on domestic work and childcare than do mothers; that this time does not increase when their wives are employed rather than at home; and although the time spent by mothers on domestic work and childcare increases with the number of children they have, regard-less of whether or not they are in employment, the time spent by men on these activities does not increase with the size of their families (see Table 5.2). Moreover, studies have found that the nature of the involve-ment of fathers with their children differs from the involvement of mothers in that fathers are more likely than mothers to concentrate their time with children in passive and less demanding 'secondary childcare activities' (Barnett and Baruch, 1987; La Rossa and La Rossa, 1984) and not to take responsibility in organizing the life of the child. In all aspects of domestic life, men 'help out'. They do not take responsibility. Indeed, Lemel (1990) notes that women's strategies as far as work and family are concerned must proceed on the basis that the weight of family life will fall on their shoulders alone. Furthermore, when children are present, according to Glaude and de Singly (1986: 24–6), the inequality between men and women in the household becomes more accentuated rather than less.

Perhaps more than anything else, therefore, limiting family size to two children or fewer in France on the part of women is a strategy to compensate for the lack of participation of men in this aspect of life, legitimated by the commitment which men are supposed to give to employment. Indeed, it should be noted that, for example, in contrast to countries such as Sweden, the French state in its family policy has never made an explicit effort to get men more involved in the family. Pitrou (1994: 126), for example, remarks that in the recent debates in France concerning the reduction of the working week to 32 hours, there has been no mention of men reinvesting the time thus liberated to family commitments. Rather, it is assumed that men will indulge in more leisure, training, participation in associations and so on. Conversely, all discussion about part-time work for women has concerned the 'conciliation' of work and family life.

Therefore, in summing up this part of the discussion, it can be seen that economic and ideological factors have enabled French women to aspire to join the labour force and partially facilitated their entry into it. Alongside this insertion into the world of employment, a new ideology of motherhood has started to emerge in France whereby it is acceptable for a woman to want a job and a family, but less acceptable for her to want either the one or the other alone. This echoes Commaille's notion of the tension that women face in contemporary France between *familialisme* and *féminisme* (1993: 92). A principal factor in the strategy which women employ in this negotiation process is to limit the number of children they have, and equally to postpone motherhood and/or to space out births.

Conclusion

In conclusion, and on the basis of the findings outlined above, this chapter will attempt to further the debate on fertility rates and women's employment from a feminist perspective. It is safe to say that no feminist would see the falling birth-rate as a problem in a 'traditional' sense, in other words, as a problem whose resolution should take precedence over women's liberation from dependence on men and from confinement in the domestic sphere. Indeed, it is perhaps for this reason that very little explicitly 'feminist' scholarship has been undertaken in the field of population and demography. However, the degree to which the falling birth-rate is evidence of women breaking free from the confines of motherhood in order to take part in the public domain or a sign of an increasing domination of 'male' culture and values over 'women's' culture and identity varies in accordance with a basic fault line running through feminism. This fault line, according to Glenn (1994) and Descarries and Corbeil (1992), divides those who regard motherhood as the source of women's oppression from those who see motherhood as the source of women's identity, culture and power. For example, Firestone (1970) argues that women's biological function as childbearers led to the first division of labour, which was the basis for excluding women from all but domestic concerns. Men's relative freedom in this regard allowed them to participate in larger-scale organizations that transcend the household. In the same vein, Ortner (1974) contends that women's role in procreation led to them being associated with nature, which has always been deemed inferior to the male domain of culture. In contrast, in Rich's (1976) view, it is precisely the power ensuing from women's role in biological reproduction that men attempted to limit because they feared it. Furthermore, some argue that it is women's biological role as nurturers which shapes their culture, making it more co-operative and caring than that of men, and thus 'superior'.

In agreement with the first theoretical position, it must be said that women would not have made the progress which they have in terms of gender equality if they had not had the means to control their fertility. In so doing, they made themselves more available for employment and thus less financially dependent on men. As has been argued throughout this chapter, the limitation of family size is an important aspect of French women's strategy to combine motherhood and employment. However, it cannot be denied either that the resistance to change on the part of men regarding their domestic responsibilities and the continued domination of traditionally male patterns of employment in the workplace and the values that accompany these have turned this triumph into a treadmill for many women. Seen in this light, the limitation of family size by French women is symptomatic of the larger problem that women face. This problem is that they have become the family workhorse: they are expected, and expect of themselves, to bring home a full-time, or near full-time, wage, to bring up children to an ever-increasing standard of education and emotional well-being and to take responsibility for the running of the household. If male work patterns, and the values associated with them, are not challenged, there is little prospect that the domestic division of labour will change for most households. Much political rhetoric concerning demographic decline centres on the notion of allowing families to have the number of children they wish, free from financial worries. It should perhaps centre more on the question of the division of family responsibilities and the accommodation of work patterns to family responsibilities not just for men as well as women, but for men more than women. This would entail a much more all-embracing shift in cultural values towards those normally associated with the 'feminine'.

Notes

1. See, for example, Fagnani (1992) for a discussion of France and the former West Germany and Hantrais (1994) for a discussion of France, Germany and Britain.
2. The notion that individuals are active in shaping their own destinies, and thereby in bringing about social change, albeit within material structural constraints and

existing power relations, was pioneered in sociology by such figures as Giddens (1984) in Britain and Bourdieu (1980) in France.

3. In 1965, the fertility rate in France was 2.8 children per woman and three-child families were the norm (Pitrou, 1994: 99). In 1961, 33.9 per cent of all women were economically active whereas the percentage had risen to 42.5 per cent by 1988 (Artinian and Boccara, 1992: 13).

4. Pitrou (1994: 99) notes that the fertility rate was 1.9 births in 1975 and 1.8 births in 1992.

5. In 1991, 68 per cent of all mothers of children under 18 were economically active. Approximately 25 per cent of all women working in France worked part-time and 40 per cent of all women with children under 10 worked full-time (14 per cent of mothers with children under 10 work full-time in Britain) (Artinian and Boccara, 1992: 13).

6. In 1991, of all women with one child under 18, 77.6 per cent were economically active; of all women with two children, 71.4 per cent were economically active; and of all women with three or more children, 41.7 per cent were economically active (Artinian and Boccara, 1992: 66).

7. There are two caveats concerning this discussion. First, it focuses on women's strategies rather than on the strategies of the couple because it is considered that women have the 'ultimate' decision on whether to have children and how many to have. Furthermore, in reality, the major share of the domestic burden remains with women. The role of men will therefore only be considered as it impacts on women's strategies. Second, because of time and space constraints in this chapter, French women will be considered as a homogeneous group. However, social class, education and position in the life cycle will make a difference both to women's aspirations and to the constraints and enabling factors which come to bear on them.

8. See Windebank (1991), Chapter 5, for a more in-depth discussion of this debate.

9. Duchen (1994) discusses this idealization of the housewife in the 1950s.

10. The particular meaning of work for women can no longer be reduced therefore to the compatibility between employment and family life. What is at stake also is the fact that identity and status for women are no longer constructed exclusively around the role they play in the family.

11. For example, the *allocation de salaire unique* and the *salaire de la mère au foyer* were introduced in the 1950s and persisted into the 1980s.

12. In 1984, *congés parentaux* were required of companies with more than 100 employees for up to three years, in principle for both parents, but with no legal requirement for payment.

13. The different forms and the level of assistance from which families can benefit do not only determine the objective possibilities open to women to realize their aspirations: they contribute as well to justifying these aspirations to women themselves.

14. De Singly studied 55 families with children under 12 where both parents were in employment. In the remaining cases of illness mentioned above: 23 per cent were looked after by a member of the extended family, 13 per cent by a friend or housekeeper, 7 per cent by the child itself, 7 per cent in the school or crèche and 6 per cent by a friend or neighbour.

References

Artinian, A. and Boccara, L. (1992) *Femmes au travail.* Paris: Hatier.

Barnett, R. and Baruch, G. (1987) Determinants of fathers' participation in family work, *Journal of Marriage and the Family*, **49**, 29–40.

Bloch, F., Buisson, M. and Mermet, J.-C. (1989) *Dette et filiations. Analyse des inter-relations entre activité féminine et vie familiale.* Report of the CNAF.

Bourdieu, P. (1980) *Le Sens pratique.* Paris: Minuit.

Castelain-Meunier, C. and Fagnani, J. (1988) *Avoir deux ou trois enfants: contraintes, arbitrage et compromis (Le cas des nouvelles couches moyennes).* Report of the CNAF.

Chaudron, M. (1991) Vie de famille, vie de travail. In M. de Singly, *La Famille: l'état des savoirs.* Paris: La Découverte, pp. 133–44.

Commaille, J. (1993) *Les Stratégies des femmes: travail, famille et politique.* Paris: La Découverte.

Commission of the European Communities (1991) *Study on the Relationship between Female Activity and Fertility.* Luxembourg.

Descarries, F. and Corbeil, C. (1992) Penser la maternité: les courants d'idées au sein du mouvement contemporain des femmes, *Recherches Sociographiques*, **32**(3).

Duchen, C. (1994) *Women's Rights and Women's Lives in France 1944–1968.* London: Routledge.

Eurostat (1991) *Labour Force Survey: Results 1989.* Luxembourg: Office for Official Publications of the European Communities.

Fagnani, J. (1992) Les Françaises font-elles des prouesses? Fécondité et travail professionnel et politiques familiales en France et en Allemagne de l'Ouest, *Revue Française des Affaires Sociales*, **46**(2), 129–45.

Firestone, S. (1970) *The Dialectic of Sex.* New York: Bantam Books.

Giddens, A. (1984) *The Constitution of Society: An Outline of the Theory of Structuration.* Cambridge: Polity.

Glaude, M. and de Singly, F. (1986) L'organisation domestique: pouvoir et négociation, *Economie et Statistique*, **187**, 1 April.

Glenn, E. (1994) Social constructions of mothering: a thematic overview. In E. Glenn, G. Chang and L. Forcey (eds), *Mothering: Ideology, Experience and Agency.* London: Routledge.

Grignon, Michel (1993) Conceptualising French family policy: the social actors. In L. Hantrais and S. Mangen, *The Policy Making Process and the Social Actors.* Cross-National Research Papers, Third series: Concepts and Contexts in International Comparisons, Loughborough University.

Hantrais, L. (1994) Comparing family policy in Britain, France and Germany, *Journal of Social Policy*, **23**(2), April, 135–60.

Haut Conseil de la Population et de la Famille (1987) *Vie professionnelle et vie familiale, de nouveaux équilibres à construire.* Paris: La Documentation Française.

Jenson, J. (1986) Gender and reproduction: or, babies and the state, *Studies in Political Economy*, **20**, Summer, 9–41.

La Rossa, R. and La Rossa, M. (1984) *The Transition to Parenthood.* Beverly Hills, CA: Sage.

Lemel, Y. (1990) Indifférenciation progressive des modèles de rôles féminins et masculins. In L. Dirn (ed.), *La Société française en tendances.* Paris: Presses Universitaires de France.

Leprince, F. (1991) Day care for young children in France. In P. Moss and E. Melhuish (eds), *Day Care for Young Children.* London: Routledge.

Lewis, J. (1992) Gender and the development of welfare regimes, *Journal of European Social Policy*, **2**(3), 159–74.

Monnier, A. and de Guibert-Lantoine, C. (1991) La conjoncture démographique: l'Europe et les pays développés d'Outre-Mer, *Population*, **46**(4), 941–61.

Ortner, S. (1974) Female to male as nature to culture. In Rosaldo and Lamphere (eds), *Woman, Culture and Society.* Stanford: Stanford University Press.

Pitrou, A. (1994) *Les Politiques familiales: approches sociologiques.* Paris: Syros.

Pitrou, A., Battagliola, F. and Rousier, N. (1984) De l'invisibilité à la reconnaissance: travail de la femme et stratégies familiales, *La Revue Tocqueville*, **6**(1).

Pitrou, A. and Gaillard, A.-M. (1989) Familles de France et de Suède: à la recherche de nouveaux modèles, *Cahiers des Sciences Humaines*, **3**, 415–28.

Rich, A. (1976) *Of Woman Born.* New York: Norton.

Rosenfield, R. (1980) Race and sex differences in career dynamics, *American Sociological Review*, **45**, 583–609.

Singly, F. de (1993) *Parents salariés et petites maladies d'enfant.* Paris: La Documentation Française.

Windebank, J. (1991) *The Informal Economy in France.* Aldershot: Avebury.

6.

In search of the missing female subject: comments on French migration research[1]

ELEONORE KOFMAN

The inclusion of immigrants as an integral element of the formation of the French nation is a recent development in historical studies (Lequin, 1988; Noiriel, 1988), although there have been many such studies in demography and sociology. Yet, on the one hand, the presence of women in this history of immigration has been ignored (Lequin, 1988) or limited to their role in the household or stabilization of immigrant groups (Noiriel, 1988). Any large-scale studies centred on men were designed without thought to the specific position of women (Girard and Stoetzel, 1953: 71). On the other hand, contemporary studies of women immigrants (first- and second-generation) construct what could be termed an *année zéro*, whereby their presence and history begin to be significant from the 1970s onwards. It will be argued in this chapter that this separation, producing a synchronicity largely devoid of temporality or historical depth, together with an increasing tendency for a cultural-ist interpretation of women's integration in French society, poses a number of serious problems, theoretically and in policy terms. As we shall see, the theme of women and integration has been taken up at the highest level, by the Haut Conseil à l'intégration and by Simone Veil, who, as Minister for Social Affairs in 1994, stressed the need for immigrant women to acquire as much autonomy as possible. Will we then be able, in introducing gender into the history and contemporary study of immigration, to treat the female immigrant as a subject and player in society, rather than as having an invisible or subordinate role as the stabilizer of families and ethnic communities?

A critique of the commonly accepted story about the presence of women in immigration flows, particularly in the post-war period, will be presented first. This situation is not unique to France, for women are largely absent, except in a secondary role, in our understanding of the processes of immigration in France in general (but see Tapinos, 1992) and especially in Europe (Boyd, 1991; Campani, 1991). Secondly, we shall consider the interest that has been shown in the potential women hold for integration, a subject that has begun to generate a substantial literature by academics, politicians and policy-makers.[2] Over the past 20 years a large amount of material on this theme has accumulated, primarily focused on North African groups, and more recently on African populations establishing polygamous households in France.

The absence of history in her story

The discovery of women's presence in migratory flows and the emergence of studies about them, albeit generally concerned with their problems and living conditions as Taravella (1984) notes, dates from the growing significance of family reunification after 1974. The shift towards this type of migration resulted in an increasing feminization of the foreign population, which was aided by a disproportionate return of single men to their country of origin. Other reasons contributing to the interest in women and immigration in this period were the increasing participation of women in the formal labour force, the impact of feminist movements, the implementation of policies for the social management of immigrant populations and the increase in the population originating in Muslim countries.

The simplified version of the process of immigration for most European states, including France, is that in the post-war years and until the economic crisis of 1973 and 1974, when labour migration was more or less halted and family reunification took its place, immigration involved solitary males who were either unmarried or had left their wives and children behind. The rotation of men, in which members from the same family or village would replace one another, ceased and from the 1970s they began to bring in wives and children. The standard account of family reunification also places it in this latter phase. One should ask why this account has constituted an orthodoxy amongst many, though by no means all, researchers.

A more detailed examination of changes of immigration flows from the 1960s to the mid-1970s shows that the proportion of women amongst the foreign population had already begun to increase. In 1962, 38.8 per cent of the foreign population was female, in 1968 39.2 per cent and in 1975 40.1 per cent. Between the two census periods the number of foreign women increased from 16.6 per cent of the foreign labour force in 1968 to 18.8 per cent in 1975. The nature of their work changed, in that those employed in domestic service fell from 36.3 per cent in 1968 to 27.7 per cent in 1975. Furthermore, family reunification also occurred before 1974 (Lebon, 1978: 8). Michèle Tribalat (1991) shows too, as does Gérard Noiriel (1988) for earlier periods, that it was merely a matter of time before family reunification gained pace. For some groups, such as the Portuguese, it was rapid and in fact had already begun to slow down by 1974. There had also been considerable family reunification amongst Algerians before the mid-1970s. On the other hand, Moroccans, whose immigration took place at a later date, have taken longer to participate in this process, but even so it was already evident before 1974. Probably the most significant date in this respect was 1960, when family reunification was allowed for those who regularized their status after their entry into the country.

One cannot make a clear-cut division between labour migration and family reunification: the one contained the other. For example, when a woman came in as a single person, the man often joined her as a labour immigrant; for women, however, it was even at that time easier to enter on the basis of family reunification than for labour purposes. Women were associated almost exclusively with children, the home and the family (Morokvasic, 1975b). It was the preoccupation with labour migration which shrouded the significance of family reunification. The classic model of migration that was applied for statistical purposes was the married man coming to work in France and later bringing in his family, which had already been established in the country of origin. On average 55,000 immigrants entered under the category of family re-unification in the period 1965 to 1969, rising to 76,000 from 1970 to 1974 (Haut Conseil à l'intégration, 1992: 13) with a peak of 85,000 entrants in 1971. This was, of course, less than the official labour migration of over 100,000 (men and women) per annum (see Table 6.1).

The standard portrait of family reunification is very much wide of the mark for a number of the immigrant groups of that earlier period, namely the Portuguese, Spanish and Yugoslavs. The Portuguese often migrated with their husbands, a substantial minority leaving their children behind. For the Spanish and Yugoslav groups there was a considerable immigration of women on their own. Furthermore, we should not assume that family reunification implies lack of intention to work. Yugoslav women came specifically to work, often in small and medium-sized factories in France (Morokvasic, 1975a). The 1968 census revealed a higher participation in the work force than the French

Table 6.1 Family reunion, 1960–89 (mean yearly number of persons entering)

1960–64	41,000
1965–69	55,000
1970–74	76,000
1975–79	48,000
1980–84	43,000
1985–89	30,000
1990–93	34,000

Note: These yearly totals are rounded to the nearest thousand and do not include non-French persons entering to join French citizens or refugees who have brought in family members.

Source: Haut Conseil à l'intégration, 1992; Lebon, 1994

average (36.1 per cent) amongst Yugoslav women (57.4 per cent) and Portuguese (38.8 per cent) (Lévi, 1975). By 1977 Portuguese women constituted 40.2 per cent and Spanish 33.1 per cent of the active immigrant population who either entered legally or were subsequently regularized. For Moroccan women this percentage, though much lower, had increased from 4.4 per cent in 1968 to 15.9 per cent in 1975 (Lebon, 1978: 10).

Nevertheless, how do we explain the neglect of the experience of immigrant women from southern and eastern Europe in the recent history of immigration? In one of the first major post-war studies of French attitudes to immigration and adaptation by Italian and Polish immigrants (conducted by INED), Girard and Stoezel (1953) state that they know far more about men than women, due to the way that the questionnaire had been constructed, and that a study of women would be necessary to unravel their role in the household in its new environment. Gérard Noiriel, whom many would consider as the foremost advocate of the study of immigration as a constituent element of French history and the formation of the nation, also limits women's role to the stabilization of immigrant groups. His thesis (1988, 1990) is that the three major periods of immigration in the 1880s, 1920s and the period from 1945 to 1975 were followed by economic crisis and stabilization and settlement of immigrants. Thus, in periods of crisis the percentage of women increased, as in the 1930s and in the second half of the 1970s, during which the problem also switched to integration in contrast to immigration (Noiriel, 1990: 14). Although Noiriel briefly notes the use of women workers in the textile industry in the north, part of his blindness to the economic activity of working-class women is not just a lack of feminist history (and this is more than he admits to) but because of his emphasis on the same groups as in the INED study, that is Italians and Poles, who were concentrated in heavy industrial regions, especially mining areas, where there was little formal employment for women, and agriculture, where women's work is taken for granted and not considered work at all.

Yet several pioneering studies by Lévi (1975) on Portuguese women and Morokvasic (1975a) on Yugoslav women sought to understand the complexity of immigrant women's presence in France, and their different trajectories, and to go beyond the stereotype of the uneducated mother of a large family who encountered serious problems of adaptation to her new society (Taboada-Léonetti and Lévi, 1978). They treated women not primarily through the focus of the family, but as social actors in the workplace, in unions, neighbourhood and political associations, and included a wide range of groups – Portuguese, Spanish, Algerian, Moroccan and Tunisian. Women's engagement with French society took diverse forms; they argued that options other than assimilation or segregation must be made available and that modernization should not be simplistically associated with assimilation. By the time that immigrant women's presence began to generate a more substantial number of studies in the early 1980s, the largest and most problematic immigrant groups were North Africans, with Algerians as the earliest established, followed by Moroccans and Tunisians. The closest approximation to the orthodoxy, as has been described, occurred with those groups which initially had very high proportions of male immigrants who brought in their wives, or those whom they were to marry, a number of years after they first settled in France. In addition, the participation of women in the formal labour force was low, especially amongst Algerians and Moroccans, and was probably not high in the informal sector either. The women who immigrated, then, were often uneducated and culturally most distant from French society.

The studies in the 1980s came to adopt a culturalist approach, dividing women according to the cultural distance from French society of their society of origin. Although the dichotomy of tradition (associated with the unchanging values of the society of origin of the Other) and modernity (conceived as that which Western society has to offer for women's emancipation) was strongly criticized by feminists (Morokvasic, 1975b), it has continued to structure much of the research, implicitly if not explicitly. To some extent the shift in the focus on women, family reunification and identity was accompanied by a shift from the world of men and work. Immigrant women are relegated to the private sphere as the guardians of tradition or their female qualities of mediation are vaunted in the public sphere (Costa-Lascoux, 1994).

Thus the construction of the object of immigration was derived from a static and uniform portrait of groups whose entry and existence in France seemed to correspond most closely to the orthodox model. Mahé (1992) ascribes this tendency towards a holistic approach to cultures in anthropology, though this has been strongly criticized by anthropologists, to a methodology which removes conflicts within the group, and also to the neglect of emigration as the complementary and necessary process of immigration. The latter is a point worth stressing; it is also a component of what has been termed the *année zéro* tendency, whereby men and women somehow begin their journey into modernity upon entry into European society. The changes that have occurred in the societies from which they have emigrated are largely ignored, as if education, urbanization, globalization, communications and so on had left them in a time warp, and as if the groups from which emigrants came had not altered. Dubet (1989) has also highlighted the synchronicity or static nature of studies and the lack of historical depth, which reinforces the absence of a migratory trajectory applicable to both men and women (but see the Boulahbel-Villac (1989) study of a group of Algerian women mostly living in the Parisian suburbs). It is not at all surprising that the value of a biographical approach, which recognizes the complexity of the society which emigrants leave, and with which they frequently retain many contacts, is not appreciated, given the almost total concern with integration into French society.

The divisions between women of the same nationality, who increasingly came from diverse backgrounds, were often lost in these studies (for an exception see Costa-Lascoux, 1994). Former urban dwellers became dominant after the mid-1970s, and their backgrounds differed according to educational level, length of residence in France, the stage of their life when they came to France and their relationship to a husband, if that was the case. Tribalat (1995) not only adopts a biographical approach within a large-scale study of 13,000 people undertaken by INED and INSEE, but includes the seven main immigrant groups. She is concerned, as she had been previously (1991, 1993), with demonstrating the extent of assimilation achieved by immigrants and their children.[3] Some of the ethnographic studies of Algerian women reveal quite clearly that in the 1980s many of them have been more educated than the men they marry. Furthermore, family reunification no longer conforms to the orthodox version, if it ever did so for many groups. The most common situation since the 1980s, though by no means the only one, has been the man or the woman bringing in a partner either recently married or to be married (Silberman, 1991).

Tribalat (1995) notes the development of an ethnic marriage market, especially prevalent amongst Turkish girls, whose value is particularly high.

However, it was the focus on North African women of Muslim origin (Jazouli, 1992; Jelen, 1991) which was to provide the background to the political and policy-making concerns about women's potential role in integration and the problems they encountered in adapting to French society. To this was added in the late 1980s a preoccupation with polygamous unions amongst African populations (Barou, 1994; Gaspard, 1992a). Recent groups, such as Filipinos and Thais, who have migrated for labour market purposes, for example domestic labour, seem to receive no attention from researchers. It is as if they did not exist, possibly because they are not considered to be significant in terms of integration into French society.[4]

Women and integration

In outlining a contract of integration, Michel Rocard, the Socialist Prime Minister in 1990, affirmed that 'France does not intend to accept within its territory practices that are incompatible with its fundamental principles, particularly in relation to women' (Haut Conseil à l'intégration, 1992: 27). He then goes on to stress that certain principles are fundamental and cannot be abrogated by other legal systems. These are, firstly, the equality between the sexes and rejection of discrimination against women and, secondly, protection of the child and what is in its best interest. Both are particularly relevant for a whole series of practices in the private and public spheres.

The following quotation taken from a glossary of terms relating to immigration in the journal *Passages* (1989) expresses succinctly the reasons for the interest in women's role in integration:

> Grandes oubliées de tous les discours de l'immigration, bien que le processus d'acculturation dépende d'elles, l'accès des femmes aux services sanitaires et sociaux, celui des filles à l'école et l'université, formes modernes de l'égalité républicaine, jouent aujourd'hui le rôle de 'creuset' qu'avait naguère joué l'armée. La réussite scolaire des 'beurettes' devrait apaiser les relations interethniques en France, et contribuer à la 'modernisation' des familles musulmanes. Il est vraisemblable que le futur major de l'X s'appellera Cherifa, Fatima ou Djamila avant de s'appeler Ahmed ou Mustapha.[5]
>
> (Moreira, 1989)

We see quite clearly here the dominant themes associated with women and integration by the end of the 1980s. The significance of women in the process of integration and the relevance of familial and generational conflicts and relations were not, however, suddenly discovered in the 1990s, although in the past few years a spate of official studies (Bentaieb, 1991; Darius and Fayman, 1987; Gaspard, 1994), special issues of journals (*Accueillir*, 1992; *Diplomées*, 1992; *Hommes et Migrations*, 1991; *Migrants-Formation*, 1991), ethnographic accounts (Lacoste-Dujardin, 1992) and reports of local initiatives (Bonvicini, 1992) have been produced. It had been preceded by over a decade of studies and professional interest.[6] Why? This interest developed in the 1980s for a number of reasons: the creation of a Ministère de la femme (Ministry for Women) encouraged studies on women and links with international organizations (EU, UNESCO) which were also beginning to turn their attention to immigrant women; there was an expansion of associations permitted after a change in 1981 in the regulations pertaining to immigrant organizations, especially those which were concerned with women's issues or in which women participated to a large degree (Haut Conseil à l'intégration, 1992; Mahé, 1992); and increasing contacts amongst largely feminized professions such as teachers and social workers made women immigrants more visible. It has been commented that the immigrant has displaced the worker as the object of social policy. A crisis in social work and in the image that social workers have of themselves and their function, as well as an acute sense of conflict between universal values and respect for specific cultures (*Migrants-Formation*, 1992a), have played a part. The change was also linked to the development of a localized urban policy in disadvantaged areas. Hence women were very much the target of much social intervention. They have increasingly become the clients of national agencies working at local levels, such as the Service social d'aide aux emigrants, originally set up in 1926, for whom women represented 41 per cent of individual clients in the early 1990s and more than 50 per cent (46 groups) of collective actions through associations (Roux, 1992: 22). Educationally, the idea took hold that North African girls performed better than boys (Schnapper, 1991); they were more closely supervised and so did not spend time outdoors hanging about in gangs. It was their ticket to greater independence.

It would be unwise to ascribe this interest solely to the headscarf affair (a conflict between the republican principles of secularism and racial tolerance over Muslim girls wearing religious dress to state lay schools), in late 1989, although the orientation of the debate has certainly been modified by it. The headscarf affair, given fresh impetus by the Bayrou circular in September 1994 (Farne, 1994),[7] and in conjunction with the deteriorating situation in Algeria since the late 1980s, has kept the spotlight on Algerians. This was despite the existence of groups, such as other Africans, of whom Jean-Pauvel Tauvel, the editor of *Migrants-Formation*, asked whether they were about to replace North Africans in the French perception of the problematic and strange outsider (*Migrants-Formation*, 1992b). Polygamous practices have produced a spate of studies (Poiret, 1992; Rude-Antoine, 1992) and put African families in the limelight (Barou, 1992; Jelen, 1993; Quiminal, 1995).[8] Legislation in relation to family reunification was altered as part of the package of Pasqua laws passed in August 1993, so that men cannot use this to form a polygamous union in France (Farne, 1994). The Turkish population, another group which has grown substantially in the past two decades, shares the same familial conflicts and rules for protection of women and, as studies have shown, Turks tend to live amongst their own communities, that is, making little effort to integrate into French society (Todd, 1994; Tribalat, 1995). Though all of these groups are largely Muslim, when this term is employed it usually conjures up the image of a North African.

The other constant theme, which has become more prominent as a result of the headscarf affair, was the familial and generational conflicts that young girls faced and their attempt to steer a balanced course between family and community traditions and the modernity of French society. In the 1990s, the themes of generational conflict and familial relations, especially in disadvantaged suburban neighbourhoods, have hit the media headlines and been taken up by academics such as Françoise Gaspard (Gaspard, 1992a; and Gaspard and Khrosrokhavar, 1994). The same theme has also figured in personal accounts such as Soraya Nini's *Ils disent que je suis beurette*, and cinematic representations, as in *Rai* directed by Thomas Gilou, the successful film *La Haine* by Mathieu Kassowitz and *Douce France* by Malik Chabine.

One could easily draw a composite portrait of the average North African family from these sources – father is an unskilled worker, mother does not work but pins her hopes on the educational success of her children, boys are allowed freedom. The theme of the absent father, more in a metaphorical than a real sense, emerges (Mongin, 1995), and in *Rai* we actually witness both. By this is meant loss of the paternal authority, which the brother attempts to reclaim by the surveillance of his sisters – a means of reasserting the parental pride and position (Leveau, 1994). The mother, as the guardian of traditions, upholds the restrictions of girls going out and often invokes traditional spells.

Conclusion

Now that women have been propelled into the limelight of integration, it is on them, or rather we should specify North African young women of the second or even third generation, that hopes for successful integration are being pinned. It is likely that this emphasis will continue, even more so when immigration control is repressive and the demonization of the suburbs proceeds relentlessly. Simone Veil announced in December 1994 that the integration of immigrant populations should focus on measures to welcome new families, with integration of the young and a place for women among them.[9] FAS has launched a large-scale research programme on families and integration (Mayeur, 1994). Whether any of these measures will address the diverse needs of different generations of women of immigrant origin remains questionable. So far, the culturalist interpretation and associated policies directed towards adaptation to French society, such as literacy programmes and domestic management in France, have tended to dominate. Much less common have been training programmes which recognize women's desire to work and gain qualifications or the discrimination immigrant women face.

Notes

1. The research for this chapter was made possible by a British Academy Small Personal Research Grant for a month's fieldwork in Paris on gender and familial relations, immigration and integration in France. Thanks are also due to the librarians at the Agence pour le développement des relations interculturelles (ADRI), the Direction de la population et des migrations (DPM) and the Fonds d'action sociale (FAS) in Paris for their assistance. Given the vast amount of literature on this topic, this chapter concentrates more on women's presence in the process of immigration and leaves to a subsequent article a more detailed discussion of the current research and debates on women and integration, the state and associations.

2. Recently a number of wide-ranging reports (Chaib and Chaib, 1994) have been produced and conferences held, for example, by research centres at the Université Paris VII (16–17 November 1995) on *Femmes en migration* and the Observatoire régional de l'intégration on *Femmes de l'immigration: images et réalité* (29 November 1994). Fortunately, these surveys are beginning to recognize the diversity of experiences.

3. Tribalat deliberately uses the term 'assimilation', which was severely criticized in the 1970s and increasingly replaced by 'insertion' and subsequently 'integration' (Gaspard, 1992b). Tribalat argues that assimilation is more easily operational,

clearer and cannot be undone, but that is precisely the kind of neat positivist solution which fails to take into account the complex ideological and political overtones of these terms and the changing relationship of populations of immigrant origin and French society.

4. Annie Phizacklea and Rekha Narula brought the significance of these groups to the attention of the author.

5. Although the process of acculturation depends on them, women have been the forgotten ones in the debate on immigration. Today the access of women to health and social services, and of girls to school and university, are the modern forms of republican equality which the army, in a previous era, played in creating the 'melting-pot'. The educational success of the *beurettes* [a term used for a second-generation girl of North African origin] should improve inter-ethnic relations in France and contribute to the 'modernization' of Muslim families. It is likely that a future major [top-placed student] of the Polytechnic will be called Cherifa, Fatima or Djamila sooner than one called Ahmed or Mustapha.

6. For a critical review of the literature and its depiction of immigrant women see Chaib and Chaib (1994).

7. The clarification published on 20 September 1994 stated that ostentatious religious signs could not be worn in schools. Just before the All Saints holiday of 1 November 1994 there were 1000 outstanding cases to be resolved about whether girls should be expelled.

8. It is difficult to come to a firm conclusion on the number of polygamous households in France. Estimates range from about 3000 to 15,000 in 1992 (Quiminal, 1994). Tribalat (1995) tends to underestimate the phenomenon because her method is based on an even geographical distribution for France, whereas polygamous households tend to be heavily concentrated in the Paris region.

9. The priority policies are:
   Women acting as mediators.
   Emergency refuges in four regions for young girls or women who have had to leave their family environment.
   Prevention of sexual mutilations (female circumcision), which remains a permanent objective.
   Participation of African women's associations.

References

Barou, J. (1992) Familles, enfants et scolarité chez les Africains immigrés en France, *Migrants-Formation*, **91**, 12–23.

Bentaieb, M. (1991) *Femmes immigrantes et intégration: bilan et propositions*. Paris: Haut Conseil de la Population et de la Famille.

Bonvicini, M.-L. (1992) *Immigrer au féminin, les 'femmes du lundi'*. Paris: Editions Ouvrières.

Boulahbel-Villac, Y. (1989) L'intégration des femmes algériennes, *Espaces et Familles*, **16**. Paris: Caisse nationale des allocations familiales.

Boyd, M. (1991) *Les Femmes immigrées et les politiques d'intégration*. Paris: OECD.

Campani, G. (1991) La condition des femmes immigrées. In D. Lapey-ronnie (ed.), *L'Intégration des minorités immigrées en Europe*, **2**, 81–102. Paris: Centre National de la Fonction Publique.

Chaib, S. and Chaib, Y. (1994) *L'Insertion socio-professionnelle des femmes d'origine étrangère*. Paris: Agence pour le développement des relations interculturelles.

Costa-Lascoux, J. (1994) Femmes immigrées: de l'oubli à l'action, *Femmes de l'immigration: images et réalités*. Strasbourg: Cahiers de l'Observatoire, **14**, 10–18.

Darius, F. and Fayman, S. (1987) *Les Réseaux associatifs et l'insertion socio-professionnelle des femmes étrangères d'origine étrangère et issues de l'immigration*. Paris: Fonds d'Action Sociale.

Dubet, F. (1989) *Immigrations: qu'en savons-nous? un bilan des connaissances*. Notes et Documents. Paris: La Documentation Française.

Elles ... Femmes en mouvement(s) (1991) *Hommes et Migrations*, **141**, whole issue.

Familles africaines (1992b) *Migrants-Formation*, **91**: whole issue.

Farne, P. (1994) Des lois Pasqua à l'affaire du voile, *Migrations Société*, **36**, 33–8.

Femmes et sociétés multiculturelles (1992) *Diplomées*, **162**: whole issue.

Gaspard, F. (1992a) La société française confrontée à la polygamie: quelques éléments de réflexion, *Revue Française des Affaires Sociales*, **46**, hors série, 181–97.

Gaspard, F. (1992b) Assimilation, insertion, intégration: les mots pour 'devenir Français', *Hommes et Migrations*, **1154**, 14–23.

Gaspard, F. (1994) *Obstacles in Society to Equality of Opportunity for Immigrant Women. The Situation in France, Belgium, Italy and Spain.* Joint Specialist Group on Migration, Cultural Diversity and Equality of Women and Men, Strasbourg: Council of Europe.

Gaspard, F. and Khrosrokhavar, F. (1994) La problématique de l'exclusion de la relation des garçons et des filles de culture musulmane dans les quartiers défavorisés, *Revue Française des Affaires Sociales*, **48**(2), 3–27.

Gaspard, F. and Khrosrokhavar, F. (1995) *Le Foulard et la république*. Paris: La Découverte.

Girard, A. and Stoezel, J. (1953) *Français et immigrés, l'attitude française. L'adaptation des Italiens et des Polonais*. INED Travaux et Documents, cahier 19/Presses Universitaires de France.

Haut Conseil à l'Intégration (1992) *Conditions juridiques et culturelles de l'intégration*. Paris.

Jazouli, A. (1992) *Les Années banlieues*. Paris: Seuil.

Jelen, C. (1991) *Ils feront de bons Français. Enquête sur l'assimilation des Maghrébins*. Paris: Robert Laffont.

Jelen, C. (1993) *La Famille, secret de l'intégration. Enquête sur la France immigrée*. Paris: Robert Laffont.

Khellil, M. (1992) *L'Intégration des Maghrébins en France*. Paris: CIEMI.

Lacoste-Dujardin, C. (1992) *Yasmina et les autres, de Nanterre et d'ailleurs. Filles de parents maghrébins en France*. Paris: La Découverte.

Lebon, A. (1978) Présentation. In I. Taboada-Léonetti and F. Lévi, Femmes et immigrées. L'insertion des femmes immigrantes en France, *Migrations et Société*, 4. Paris: La Documentation Française, pp. 4–10.

Lebon A. (1994) *Situation de l'immigration et présence étrangère en France 1993–1994*. Paris: Ministère des Affaires Sociales.

Lequin, Y. (1988) *La Mosaïque France. Histoire des étrangers et de l'immigration*. Paris: Larousse.

Les femmes au coeur de l'intégration (1992) *Accueillir*, **185**: whole issue.

Les femmes et jeunes filles d'origine étrangère (1983) *Migrants-Formation*, **54**: whole issue.

Les travailleurs sociaux et les populations immigrées (1992) *Migrants-Formation*, **88**: whole issue.

Leveau, R. (1994) Les beurs dans la cité, *Vingtième Siècle*, **44**, October–December, 65–71.

Lévi, F. (1975) L'évolution des femmes portugaises immigrées à Paris et dans la banlieue parisienne, *L'Année Sociologique*, **26**, 153–77.

L'intégration au féminin (1991) *Migrants-Formation*, **84**: whole issue.

Mahé, A. (1992) Remarques critiques à propos de quelques postures dominantes dans les recherches sur l'immigration maghrébine en France, *Migrants-Formation*, **90**, 54–67.

Mayeur, L. (1994) *La Place des familles dans l'action du FAS*. Paris: Service documentation, Fonds d'action sociale pour les immigrés et leurs familles.

Mongin, O. (1995) Regarde-les tomber. A propos de la haine de Mathieu Kassovitz, *Esprit*, August–September, 172–86.

Moreira, P. (1989) Où va l'argent de l'Etat? *Passages*.

Morokvasic, M. (1975a) Les femmes yugoslaves en France et en RFA, *Hommes et Migrations*, **915**, 4–17.

Morokvasic, M. (1975b) L'immigration féminine en France: état de la question, *L'Année Sociologique*, **26**, 563–75.

Noiriel, G. (1988) *Le Creuset français. Histoire de l'immigration XIXe–XXe siècle*. Paris: Seuil.

Noiriel, G. (1990) L'histoire des femmes immigrées. In GREC (ed.), *Femmes immigrées. Quelles chances pour quelles insertions sociales et professionnelles*, pp. 11–25.

Poiret, C. (1992) Le phénomène polygame en France, *Migrants-Formation*, **91**, 24–43.

Quiminal, C. (1994) *Mode de constitution des ménages polygames et vécu de la polygamie en France*. Paris: Direction des Population et de la Migration.

Roux, S. (1992) Action sociale du SSAE. Des passerelles vers l'intégration, *Accueillir*, **185**, 22–5.

Rude-Antoine, E. (ed.) (1992) *L'Immigration face aux lois de la République*. Paris: Editions Kalhaln.

Sayad, A. (1994) Le mode de génération des générations immigrées, *Migrants-Formation*, **98**, 6–20.

Schnapper (1991) *La France de l'intégration. Sociologie de la nation en 1990*. Paris: Gallimard.

Silberman, R. (1991) Regroupement familial: ce que disent les statistiques, *Hommes et Migrations*, **1141**, 13–1.

Taboada-Léonetti, I. and Lévi, F. (1978) Femmes et immigrées. L'insertion des femmes immigrantes en France, *Migrations et Société*, **4**. Paris: La Documentation Française.

Tapinos, G. (1992) Immigration féminine et statut des femmes étrangères en France, *Revue Française des Affaires Sociales*, **46**, Special issue, 29–60.

Taravella, L. (1984) *Les Femmes immigrantes, bibliographie analytique (1965–1983)*. Paris: L'Harmattan.

Todd, E. (1994) *Le Destin des immigrés*. Paris: Seuil.

Tribalat, M. (1991) *Cent Ans d'immigration*. Paris: INED.

Tribalat, M. (1993) Les immigrés au recensement de 1990 et les populations liées à leur installation en France, *Population*, **48**(6), 1911–46.

Tribalat, M. (1995) *Faire France. Une enquête sur les immigrés et leurs enfants*. Paris: La Découverte.

7.

Sexual and racial boundaries: colonialism and Franco-Algerian intermarriage (1880–1962)

NEIL MACMASTER

Historians, with few exceptions (Todd, 1994), have neglected a key feature of colonial Algerian society, the extraordinary degree of sexual segregation between Europeans and the indigenous people. Marriages between Algerian men and European women averaged four per year between 1891 and 1900 and eight per year between 1905 and 1914 (Meylan, 1933: 32; Meynier, 1981: 195).[1] This was at a time when the two populations stood at 4,740,000 and 752,000 (1911 census). Approximately 0.05 per cent of Algerian marriages were with a European. This is of considerable interest since the extent to which ethnic groups are willing or able to marry with other peoples (exogamy) or only with their own kind (endogamy) is the most sensitive indicator of boundary maintenance, especially of a hierarchical and racialized kind (Poliakov, 1980: 7). Colonial Algeria practised a *de facto* level of segregation as absolute as that in apartheid South Africa, a fact that has gone unnoticed since it was less overt and not enforced by racist laws and a police apparatus. A ban on intermarriage did not have to be institutionalized simply because it was largely unthinkable; segregationism was so rooted in everyday cultural and social practice that it did not require conscious articulation or legal reinforcement.

Segregation

There are two major explanations for this pattern. The first emphasizes the role of Islam and the general intolerance shown towards marriage with a non-Muslim. In principle, Islam permitted marriage between a Muslim man and a non-Muslim woman, provided she belonged to a 'religion of the Book' (Christianity, Judaism), but strictly forbade marriage between a Muslim woman and a non-Muslim man. Since a woman was expected to assume the religion of her husband, the latter was regarded as an act of apostasy.[2] However, low levels of intermarriage cannot be explained by religious factors alone and other colonial Muslim societies such as Indonesia showed high levels of mixing.

Emmanuel Todd emphasizes the key importance of North African family structures and high levels of endogamy, particularly cousin marriage, in the opposition to alliance with outsiders (Todd, 1994: 284–92, 317–20). The Algerian family also became a centre of resistance to colonial domination. After the long phase of armed resistance to French conquest, which finally ended in the crushing of El Mograni's rebellion in 1871, Algerian society opposed further cultural erosion by retreating into the inviolable and private space of the family (Berque, 1967: 44, 72–6, 353–7; Colonna, 1974: 233–52; Merad, 1967; Turin, 1971). Here, in the locus of biological, religious and cultural reproduction, women played a vital role in the socialization of children and the transmission of traditional values. Algerians protected the integrity of the family from European onslaught by spatial segregation, the isolation of women from contact with foreign men and the retention of Muslim family law (Charnay, 1991: 20).

The second explanation for the barrier to intermarriage lies with the deepening racism of settler society. Since the 1840s French policy had been to create a colony of settlement, one in which European men and women would be encouraged to migrate on a sufficient scale to achieve domination through natural increase and the displacement or Social-Darwinian extinction of the *indigènes* (Heffernan, 1989: 382; Rouissi, 1983). From the 1840s onwards European population had achieved sufficient size and gender balance to enable all settlers to find marriage partners solely within their own ethnic group (Prochaska, 1990: 90–1, 142–3).[3] The ethnic endogamy of settler society was reinforced between 1890 and 1930 by a deepening racism. The growing insecurity of the great mass of poor Europeans, outnumbered by a rapidly increasing Algerian urban population, translated into aggressive racial superiority and a cult of masculine physicality not unlike that of the Afrikaner Boers. Racist terms like *bic(s)*, *ratons*, *melons* and *bougnoules* became generalized (Sivan, 1979; Berque, 1961; Nora, 1961). Social distance between Europeans and Algerians was maintained through deepening spatial segregation in urban centres, a process in which the Algerians were increasingly concentrated in *bidonvilles*, so-called *villages nègres*, or inner-city slums like the Kasbah of Algiers (Descloitres *et al.*, 1961; Yacono, 1955–6: 250–6; Prochaska, 1990: 156–65). The opportunities for men and women of different ethnic groups to meet one another and to strike up friendships that could mature into stable relationships or marriage were almost non-existent.[4]

However, racism did not exclude all sexual relations across the divide. While European males felt repugnance towards the idea of stable or legitimate relations with Algerian women, the latter were still regarded as fair game for sexual exploitation, particularly through prostitution. Such exploitation, as in most colonies, was one of the most manifest forms of racial power and domination. As Jacques Berque notes, 'relations [between Europeans and Algerians] were only possible on the horrible fringes of the two worlds', in the red-light districts of the Algiers Kasbah, the Busbir in Casablanca or the streets of oasis and garrison towns inhabited by the girls of the Ouled Naïl tribe,[5] known to the French army as *alouettes naïves* (Berque, 1967: 304–5). Sexual exploitation of Algerian women was sustained by orientalist fantasies of tearing aside the veil, of access to the forbidden, the harem and exotic dancing girls (Alloula, 1986; Marchand, 1954).[6]

More regular liaisons with Algerian women were regarded with hostility by European society, particularly if they involved senior officials or army officers, who thus affronted respectability and undermined the status and power of the colonial race. Official pressure was brought to bear on any functionary who began to show signs of a serious attachment, and most chose to terminate such relationships rather than see their career jeopardized (Baroli, 1967: 80, 256). Lorcin (1995: 211) notes that in the early decades of conquest, when there was a shortage of European women, officers and civil servants were able, without social stigma, to marry indigenous women.

Only the exceptional person like Isabelle Eberhardt, who was ready to break the conventions of bourgeois society, would 'cross over' and marry a Muslim. But even her relationship with her future husband, the Algerian officer Slimène Ehni, was the subject of a secret military investigation.[7] Such marriages could be dismissed as the choice of highly eccentric, literary, romantic or aristocratic individuals for whom it was 'normal' or even admirable that they should defy convention.

In reality, most European males who tried to establish liaisons with Algerian women ran the risk of Arab vengeance and the knife (Charnay, 1991: 29, 372). The absence of Algerian women from the public colonial space, their seclusion and veiling, ensured that conflict between settlers and colonized was essentially inter-masculine and that violence was suffused with a strong sexual element (Nora, 1961: 174–6). Camus's *L'Etranger* provides a penetrating insight into the psychological malaise of the *pied-noir* (white settler) and the street-level threat of anonymous and silent Arabs seeking to revenge a dishonoured sister (Haddour, 1993; Nora, 1961: 190–2).

Among the *pieds-noirs*, an amalgam of mainly French, Spanish, Italian and Maltese people, the classic double standard of the Mediterranean society of honour ensured that, while an ability to seduce the women of other groups was seen as a sign of masculine pride and virility, an inability to protect 'their' women from the sexual advances of outsiders was the ultimate disgrace. In Algeria this structure was reinforced by racism, so that any move by an *indigène* to have a sexual relationship with a European woman was experienced as a defiling transgression, the ultimate insult to French male superiority and power. Intermarriage between Algerian men and European women, apart from a very small number involving native aristocrats and educated élites, were almost unknown.

However, after 1910 appeared a new development which presented a major challenge to the pattern of racial and sexual segregation, the growing number of relationships between Algerian migrants and European women in France. Algerian migrants in France married both French women and immigrant women from Spain, Germany, Italy and elsewhere.

It is the French response to this breakdown of sexual barriers that is now to be examined in more detail, since it reveals the racist sexist attitudes that were generalized in colonial Algeria but which were normally unspoken or rarely elaborated as theory.

Colonial attitudes to sexual relations

During the First World War some 300,000 Algerians travelled to France as soldiers or workers and after 1918 the number of migrant labourers resident in France increased to about 130,000 in the 1930s. Inter-war migration involved single males: in 1930 out of 60,000 men in the Paris region only about 20 were resident with their wives. However, single-male migration increased the possibilities of cohabitation or marriage to European women. Of the 60,000 migrants in Paris in 1930 700 were legally married to French women, while 5000 were cohabiting (Massignon, 1930: 168). The most reliable data exists for the *Commune mixte* of Fort-National, a zone of high emigration in the heart of the Kabyle mountains. Between 1910 and September 1937 there was a total of 266 mixed marriages registered in France, increasing through time from one or two per year (1910–18) to 28 in 1936 (Duplessis-Kergomard,

1938: 111–12). Massignon's figures suggest that nearly one in ten Algerians were living in a stable relationship with a European woman by the 1930s, a level that is confirmed by a detailed study of Gennevilliers in 1936 which found that 14 per cent of Moroccans and 11 per cent of Algerians were married or cohabiting (Ray, 1938: 197–201).

One reason for this practice was simply the desire among Algerians, who were frequently away from home for years at a time, for emotional warmth, affection and stable sexual relations.[8] Intermarriage was also possible because working-class French women were less racist and escaped the social pressures that made such liaisons impossible in the *pied-noir* community. During the First World War North African soldiers and workers frequently commented on the warmth and friendliness of European women towards them (Meynier, 1981: 436–9). It may also have helped that a number of migrants, especially the Kabyles, had been educated in French schools and were relatively Westernized. Intermarriage was particularly common among a petit-bourgeois strata of Algerians who were traders or proprietors of small cafés, shops and hotels that catered for a North African clientele. Many of these men were to become nationalist militants (Stora, 1986, 1992).

The French colonial élite (administrators, politicians, academics, journalists and so on) responded to intermarriage/cohabitation as a fundamental threat to colonial hegemony. As in so many other European colonies during the twentieth century, segregation, and in particular the 'protection' of women from natives, was seen as a key component of white prestige and authority (Stoler, 1989; Hyam, 1992). Robert Fonville attacked North African migration and intermarriage in 1924: 'la pureté de notre race serait en danger ... Notre prestige en Europe serait gravement compromis de ce fait' (Fonville, 1924: 10).[9] What particularly worried the colonial élite was that migrants returning to Algeria were boasting of their sexual conquest of French women and had come to lose all 'respect' for the wives of officials. Joanny Ray remarked, 'l'ex-émigré n'a plus pour ses chefs européens, pour l'officier des Affaires indigènes de son bureau – *et surtout pour la femme de celui-ci* – le respect qu'il avait au départ' (1938: 283).[10]

In 1919 the Gouvernement général carried out a major survey of the psychological and social impact of life in France on returning migrants. Local administrators reported that former migrants were insolent and showed a total 'manque de réserve vis-à-vis des femmes françaises' (lack of reserve towards French women). They had come to believe that all French women were prostitutes and that 'le dévergondage est une caractéristique de notre race' (licentiousness is a characteristic of our race). Algerians now thought they were on the same level as Europeans and 'ils se croient tout permis' (thought everything was permitted) (Archives d'Outre-Mer (AOM) A.D.A 2149, cited in G. Massard-Guilbaud, 1988: 64–6). Octave Depont, an ex-colonial native administrator, wrote that Algerian and Tunisian men had been flaunting photographs of French women, 'comme les images de quelques-unes de leurs innombrables maîtresses. Ces photos passeront de mains en mains dans les tribus, excitant la joie et la dérision des indigènes' (1928: 117).[11] Colonials were perfectly aware of the link between European power and sexual segregation and this led them, through a process of projection, to imbue Algerians with a desire for seduction of European women as a form of revenge on their colonial masters. In his novel *Sidi de banlieue* (1937) Jean Damase showed an obsessional preoccupation with the sexuality of the migrant Nouar who dreams constantly of French women. When he finally gains a French mistress (who is significantly sexually perverted) his migrant friends are pleased since it gave them a feeling of vengeance. The Arab had cuckolded an entire civilization (Damase, 1937: 125, 145). Marchand purports that there exists:

> la fierté pour lui [l'Algérien] . . . de pouvoir se dire uni à un représentant de la race conquérante . . . pour le vaincu une revanche dont il se délecte intimement.[12]
>
> (Marchand, 1954: 36–7)

This dubious idea, spun out of the head of the colonial as an inversion of his own power complex, continued to surface in the sociological works of Berque (1961), Charnay (1991) and Fanon (1968).

Strategy of racial and sexual oppression

The colonial élite and its lobbyists in France responded to the perceived dangers of intermarriage by five types of strategy or argument which will be examined in turn.

Firstly, the Algerian was criminalized and presented as a primitive, instinctual type who was prone to acts of uncontrollable violence. The 'Sidi' was portrayed as hot-blooded and lascivious and a perpetual danger to French women through sexual assault, rape and the transmission of venereal disease. This stereotype of the lascivious Arab had developed earlier in the colonial context (Lorcin, 1995: 65). Typical of official perceptions is the comment of an employment officer in Nancy in 1937:

Cette population des désoeuvrés livrés à eux-mêmes sans surveillance devient un danger véritable pour les femmes et les enfants qui n'osent plus s'aventurer dans les lieux déserts.[13]

(Departmental Archives Meurthe-et-Moselle, 10 M 33, cited in R. Schor, 1981: 57)

The diffusion of such stereotypes in the popular press and elsewhere served to drive a wedge between Algerians and French women and to fuel the campaign for a halt to immigration. As in the colonial context, in which fears of native assaults on white women frequently generated moral panics and a lynch-mob mentality, so Paris witnessed a wave of anti-Arab violence following on the stabbing of two women by a mentally ill Kabyle in November 1923 (MacMaster, 1995).[14]

Secondly, steps were taken to try and segregate Algerian migrants so that liaisons with French women could not develop. During the First World War the Algerian Gouvernement général and the military authorities were concerned by the friendships which developed between wounded soldiers and French nurses. It was feared that Algerian 'satyrs' would come to lose all 'respect' for French women, and in turn undermine French male authority. Letters intercepted by the military censorship revealed a 'pornographic' crudity in the preferences expressed by French nurses for the sexual skills of Arabs over Frenchmen, a classic example of the racist anxiety over the sexual potency of the Other. The response was an army circular of June 1916 which removed all female personnel from hospitals in which North Africans were recuperating (Meynier, 1981: 436–9). In February 1917 the Minister of Justice, shocked by the number of North Africans cohabiting with French women, sent a warning to mayors and insisted that they be very strict in demanding the correct documentation from couples wishing to marry, a directive which had the unintended consequence of increasing irregular unions (Ray, 1938: 278). During the inter-war period, while the government refused to encourage family migration which might have removed the need for liaisons with French women, some local authorities tried to channel Algerian sexual needs by opening segregated brothels. However, the most systematic attempt to segregate Algerians from contact with working-class life was through the establishment of a special police and welfare agency, the Service des affaires indigènes nord-africaines (SAINA), established in the Rue Lecomte in

1926. The SAINA created a network of North African hostels, medical centres, education classes, a Muslim hospital and other facilities which would facilitate surveillance, 'moral' control and separation from French women (MacMaster, 1997).

Thirdly, since such measures could not bring a halt to marriage/cohabitation, the colonial and right-wing propagandists resorted to a number of other tactics. One line was to devalue and denature such unions. If Algerians appeared to challenge or undermine colonial hegemony through their conquest of French women this was a mirage, since only the physically ugly, defective and immoral rejects of the *bas-fonds*, the dross unwanted by French men, would agree to such relationships. Baroin reported that intermarriage in Lyons in 1935 was with women who were 'defective' (1935: 177). In Jean Damase's novel, *Sidi de banlieue*, the Arab immigrant can only establish relations with the most degraded women, sexual perverts, diseased prostitutes and alcoholics. For Marchand, migrants could only relate to 'Françaises dédaignées de leurs compatriotes parce que laides ou pauvres ... [or] une femme de moeurs discutables, voire une boiteuse ou une bossue' (1954: 37, 51).[15] The historian J.-P. Charnay still repeated the stereotype in 1965: in inter-war Paris only, 'la métropolitaine, vieillie, tarée, désespérant de trouver un compagnon français, acceptera de vivre avec un Algérien' (the old, defective French woman, who had despaired of finding a French partner, would accept to live with an Algerian) (1991: 264). While Algerians did marry or cohabit with French women from the working class there is no evidence to show that they were immoral or physically defective. Military surveillance during the First World War showed Algerian soldiers involved with 'une serveuse de restaurant, une secrétaire, une fille de bonne bourgeoisie parisienne, même, mais surtout avec des infirmières' (a restaurant waitress, a secretary, even the daughter of a Parisian bourgeois family and, most often, nurses) (Meynier, 1981: 439).

Fourthly, more important was the campaign to warn French women of the great dangers which they ran in marrying North African men. The women were normally portrayed as highly gullible individuals who were won over by the deceitful and flattering charm of Algerians who spun a tissue of lies about their aristocratic background as sheiks and the oriental splendour of their homes in Africa (Marchand, 1954: 49–51). Numerous dry legal texts analysed the legal pitfalls faced by women confronted with the 'barbaric' practices of Muslim family law, including polygamy, divorce through renunciation, marital violence and a virtual absence of property rights (Charnay, 1991). In reality, polygamy was quite unusual in Algerian society and very few migrants engaged in bigamy.

What disturbed colonial officials most of all was the possible 'Arabization' of French women: conversion to Islam, wearing of Algerian clothing and adoption of North African culinary practices. This represented a dangerous blurring of the boundaries between the dominant/ civilized and the dominated/primitive. Jurists guarded against this 'descent' with the legal maxim that French women, even when married to a Muslim or converted to Islam, could not lose their essential Frenchness, their nationality (Marchand, 1954: 91).

It was considered that the worst-case scenario of this descent into barbarism arose when naïve French women moved to Algeria, only to be submerged into the primitive life of the Kabyle village. Numerous reports stressed the idea that the Algerian worker, perfectly civilized and gentle in France, would on his return home show atavistic tendencies and revert to type, treating his French wife as a slave, subjecting her to savage beatings and even driving her into prostitution.[16] Louis Chevalier reported cases of women who were no longer recognizable in the *djebels*, 'à la fontaine ou sur les routes, parmi les femmes musulmanes, chargée de paquets et désormais pliée à la dure discipline des douars' (at the fountain or on the road, among the Muslim women, loaded down with bundles and now bent to the harsh discipline of the *douars*) (Chevalier, 1947: 208). It was precisely this 'lowering' of French women to the level of the natives which Ray saw as damaging to 'le prestige de notre pays' (the prestige of our country) (Ray, 1938: 373). As Stoler notes (1991: 63–4), European colonial communities were obsessed with white prestige symbolized by the purity of women, constantly protected from native defilement by tightening of ranks, clarification of boundaries and the marking out of social space.

During the inter-war period, colonial and metropolitan officials tried to prevent mixed marriages through propaganda aimed at French women and through administrative measures to make it difficult for those that did so to move with their migrant husbands to North Africa (Correspondence of the Ministry of the Interior and the Gouvernement général (1923), AOM 9 H 13; Marchand, 1954: 61–2; Fonville, 1924: 103).

The last element in the attack on mixed marriage was the claim that miscegenation produced a flawed and deviant class of *métis* (of mixed race). For Fonville intermarriage with North Africans, unlike that with European stock, would not produce children 'de bonne qualité: la pureté de notre race serait en danger, et nous risquerions d'avoir une forte proportion d'individus abâtardis' (of good quality: the purity of our race will be in danger and we will run the risk of having a high proportion of degenerate individuals) (Fonville, 1924: 10).[17] Numerous popular inter-war novels, some written by *pied-noir* women, centred on the tragic outcome of intermarriage, particularly for the children. Torn between allegiance to Catholic or Muslim values, they ended up subject to no morality, as atheists and renegades.[18] The *métis* was an aberration, a kind of 'monstrous' being, often very clever but morally degenerate and deviant.

Contradictory as it may seem, many of those who held to the above opinions were not in principle opposed to mixed marriage. Their racism, as with the contemporary 'New Right', was in most instances based not on biological but cultural difference. Intermarriage could only work when the enormous cultural difference between Muslims and 'civilized' French had narrowed. However, the 'catching up' of Algerians and their eventual political and social assimilation were relegated to a future so distant and nebulous as to be meaningless. Through the ideology of assimilation colonial ideologues could have the satisfaction of offering Republican equality to Algerians while at the same time denying it.

The effect of migration on racial sexual relations

The post-war period saw a sudden change in the structure and scale of Algerian migration to France, particularly towards family migration, and this altered the terms of the debate. By 1952 about 3400 wives had migrated to France and soon began to overtake the number of mixed couples. By 1956 out of a total of 330,000 Algerians in France about 26,000 were women and children (Rager, 1956: 60, 100–1). The new tendency for migrants to bring over their wives, or if young and celibate to return home to seek a bride, quickly stemmed the older pattern of cohabitation or intermarriage with French women. A study of 1954 found that 95 per cent of Algerian males preferred marriage to a Muslim woman (Girard and Stoezel, 1954). The arrival in France of Algerian women, the carriers of traditional Muslim values, may have begun those processes currently referred to by Gilles Kepel as re-Islamization and redefined the boundaries between the immigrant community and French society (Kepel, 1987). The outbreak of the Algerian War, fought out with such ferocity within metropolitan France, further isolated the immigrants and reinforced ethnic endo-gamy.

The shift towards family reunification and the more pressing urgency of the Algerian War seem to have brought a sudden end to the French colonial concern with intermarriage. However, the independence struggle kept the debate open among Algerian nationalists. Nationalist opposition to intermarriage on political/Islamic grounds first seems to have developed in Tunisia during the 1930s. In 1936 Paul Azan noted:

> Les nationalistes ... font une campagne ardente contre les mariages mixtes: ils s'élèvent avec violence contre les Musulmans qui épousent des 'chiennes d'Européennes', selon une chanson récemment applaudie à Tunis.[19]
>
> (Azan, 1936: 3)

Such a position did not appear among Algerian nationalists until the 1950s. Although the evidence is fragmentary, it points towards a division over mixed marriage between the Messalistes of the MNA (Mouvement national algérien) and the FLN, the two currents that split into a bloody civil war after 1954. The MNA leadership was drawn from an older generation of migrants, many of whom – like Messali himself – had married French women. The younger generation of the FLN, in exerting an increasingly strict and all-embracing control over the moral and private lives of Algerians in France through local *Comités de justice*, including the regulation of marriage and divorce according to Muslim law, began to oppose mixed marriages (Stora, 1992: 346–51). The Algerian family was regarded as a crucial cell of religious and national identity which was resistant to French moves to undermine it since, 'Si l'on [Français] s'approche, c'est pour mieux s'infiltrer, et si l'on s'infiltre, c'est pour mieux détruire' (if the French draw close it is the better to infiltrate, and if they infiltrate, it is the better to destroy) (Saadia-et-Lakhdar, 1961: 151). Andrée Michel noted as early as 1955–6 that the Messalistes 'avaient engagé auprès des Algériens une campagne antiraciste contre la désapprobation des unions mixtes par le groupe musulman' (have engaged among the Algerians in an anti-racist campaign opposed to the Muslim group which disapproves of mixed marriages) (Michel, 1956: 202).

This position linked up in an interesting way with that of Algerian feminism which was greatly strengthened by the prominent role of women in the independence struggle. Feminists criticized mixed marriages, which were almost uniquely between Algerian men and French women, as a sign of male attraction towards European values and *la femme évoluée* and a profound repudiation of Algerian identity. In April 1950 a woman from Oran wrote to the Algiers weekly *Salam Ifrikia*:

> Je suis navrée de constater combien nos jeunes gens sont attirés par les Européennes ... Si un jour la désorganisation atteignait notre société, c'est à eux qu'il faudrait s'en prendre.[20]
>
> (Decroux, 1956: 4)

This criticism assumed its most radical and extended treatment in Fadéla M'Rabet's famous tract of 1965, *La Femme algérienne*, in which she exposed the sexual obsession for European women, viewed in comparison to Algerians as 'easily seduced tarts':

> Si l'Algérien méprise moralement l'Européenne, s'il l'assimile à une putain, s'il voit en elle, aussi, une évoluée; à cet égard, elle a bien plus de prix, à ses yeux, que sa compatriote.[21]
>
> (M'Rabet, 1983: 31)

A similar discourse of opposition to relationships with white women, not on racist biological grounds but in terms of ethnic pride and identity, was to emerge in the Black Consciousness movement of the 1960s and 1970s (Benson, 1981: 12–13).

Conclusion

Looking beyond the end of colonialism in 1962, the statistics of French-Algerian intermarriage throughout the twentieth century have followed an 'S-curve'. The phase of relatively high intermarriage in the early migration (1920–45) was followed by a rapid falling away with family emigration. This corresponded to a period of community formation and closure from the surrounding French society, partly as a consequence of the war of 1954–62. However, the growth of a 'second' and 'third generation' has seen during the last two decades a significant increase in mixed marriages among those of North African descent, a sign of integration. A study by Michèle Tribalat in 1992 found that for Algerian men arriving in France before the age of 15, 22 per cent had French wives, while for Algerian women in the same group the proportion of mixed marriages was 20 per cent (Todd, 1994: 298–302).[22] Emmanuel Todd's interpretation of integration as a process by which Algerian endogamy and resistance to intermarriage was battered down by a generous and non-racist French universalism is flawed when he states that Algerian endogamy was fundamental to the rejection of alliances, while French society was open to relationships and threw over bridges, demonstrating an 'expression de générosité plutôt que de fermeture ... C'est ici la face lumineuse de l'universalisme français qui se manifeste' (expression of generosity rather than closure ... This is the glowing face of French universalism manifesting itself) (Todd, 1994: 313). Curiously for Todd, the Algerian partners have no active role in establishing relationships but are the passive (or resistant) recipients of French 'generosity'. He plays down the extent to which colonial segregation was a product of French racism and overlooks the fact that many Algerian men were open to intermarriage where the opportunity arose, as it did in inter-war France. How this situation evolved in the more recent period is the subject of the following chapter.

Notes

1. No official statistics were kept on intermarriage in French North Africa. The most useful source, in addition to Meylan, is Marchand (1954: 12–30) and Todd (1994: 295–7). Mercier remarked on the nine marriages registered in 1879, 'La fusion ... est nulle, et pour que ce chiffre de neuf ne soit pas dépassé dans une population dont le contact est si intime, il faut que la répulsion soit complète de part et d'autre' (The fusion between the two races ... is nil, and in order for the figure to be no higher than nine for a population that lives in such close proximity there has to be a complete revulsion on both sides) (1881: 143).
2. On these rules see Arkoun, 1980: 76–8; Charnay, 1991: 265; Streiff-Fenart, 1989: 11–12.
3. The Algerian situation can be compared with colonies of 'exploitation' like the Dutch East Indies where throughout the eighteenth and nineteenth centuries the Company blocked female emigration from Europe and encouraged marriage or concubinage with Asian women. See Stoler (1991: 57–61) and Ming (1983: 65–93).
4. However, M. Meylan (1933: 30, 171) argued that 'unions irrégulières' may have been more common than generally realized.
5. Some women of the Ouled Naïl were dancing girls who engaged in prostitution to raise money for a dowry. They gave rise to a literature of erotic fantasy and were visited by tourists, among them Gide and Isabelle Eberhardt.
6. Alloula has used semi-pornographic postcards from 1900 to 1930 to show a form of colonial violence in which the body and soul of Algerian women was exposed to the gaze of the conqueror.
7. The military administrator, Gaston Cauvet, instructed to spy on Eberhardt, reported that she had 'come to El Oued principally to satisfy unhindered her dissolute tastes and her penchant for natives in a place where there are few Europeans' (Kobak, 1988: 130).
8. On the psychological and sexual trauma of migrants see Tahar Ben Jalloun (1977).
9. The purity of our race will be endangered ... Our prestige in Europe will be seriously compromised.

10. The returned migrant no longer has the respect for his European bosses, for the local officer of Native Affairs – *and particularly for the wife of the latter* [italics as in text] – that he had before leaving.
11. As pictures of some of their innumerable mistresses. These photos are passed from hand to hand in the tribes, exciting delight and derision.
12. For the Algerian there is pride in being able to say he is united with a representative of the conquering race ... for the vanquished a revenge in which he takes a profound delight.
13. This vagrant population, left to its own devices and without any surveillance, is becoming a very real danger for women and children who no longer dare to venture alone in deserted places.
14. The best study of a colonial 'Black Peril' scare is C. Van Onselen (1982: Vol. 2, 1–73).
15. French women rejected by their compatriots because they were ugly or poor [or] women of dubious morality, or even lame and hunchbacked.
16. See, for example, an official inquiry of the Gouvernement général in 1923, *Rapport sur l'émigration des indigènes* (typescript), AOM 9 H 13: 21; a further government inquiry of 1938, *Rapport de MM. Laroque et Ollive sur la main-d'oeuvre nord-africaine* (typescript), AOM 8 H 62: 90.
17. Similar racist ideas were put forward by Dr R. Martiᴌ (1931).
18. Marchand (1954: 54–5, 98–101, 164–79) analyses the tragic failure of intermarriage through the novels of the Zénati brothers, *Bou el Nouar, le jeune Algérien;* Mme Faure-Sardet, *Fille d'Arabe* (1935); Marie Bugéja, *Nos soeurs musulmanes* (1921); Rosalina Bentami, *L'Enfer de la Kasbah;* Djamila Debèche, *Leïla, jeune fille algérienne;* see also Lorcin (1995: 218–9) on the novels of Charles Géniaux, *Le Choc des races* (1911) and Ferdinand Duchêne, *Kami* (1926).
19. The nationalists ... are leading a heated campaign against mixed marriage; they protest violently against Muslims who marry 'European bitches', as they were called in a song recently applauded in Tunis [during a concert of Arab music].
20. I am sorry to remark on how much our young men are attracted by European women ... If one day our society disintegrates it will be them that you will have to blame.
21. While the Algerian man has contempt for the European woman's morals, while he likens her to a whore, he also sees in her a progressive person; in this respect she has a higher value, in his eyes, than his compatriot.
22. For a study of these mixed marriages see J. Streiff-Fenart (1989).

References

Alloula, Malek (1986) *The Colonial Harem.* Manchester: Manchester University Press.

Archives d'Outre-Mer (AOM) A.D.A 2149 cited in G. Massard-Guilbaud (1988), *Des Algériens à Lyon, de la Grande Guerre au Front Populaire.* Doctorate, Université de Lyon II.

Arkoun, M. (1980) Les unions mixtes en milieu musulman. In L. Poliakov (ed.), *Le Couple interdit. Entretiens sur le racisme.* Paris: Mouton, pp. 76–87.

Azan, P. (1936) Les problèmes de la Tunisie actuelle, *Revue des Deux Mondes*, 15 March, cited in P. Decroux (1956), Mariages mixtes au Maroc, *Revue Marocaine de Droit*, **3**.

Baroin, H. (1935) *La Main-d'oeuvre étrangère dans la région lyonnaise*. Lyons: Bosc Frères.

Baroli, M. (1967) *La Vie quotidienne des Français en Algérie 1830–1914*. Paris: Hachette.

Ben Jalloun, Tahar (1977) *La Plus Haute des Solitudes. Misère affective et sexuelle d'émigrés nord-africains*. Paris: Seuil.

Benson, S. (1981) *Ambiguous Ethnicity. Interracial Families in London*. Cambridge: Cambridge University Press.

Berque, J. (1961) Recent research on racial relations. The North of Africa, *International Social Science Journal*, **2**, 177–96.

Berque, J. (1967) *French North Africa. The Maghreb between Two World Wars*. London: Faber.

Charnay, J.-P. (1991) *La Vie musulmane en Algérie d'après la jurisprudence de la première moitié du XXe siècle*. Paris: Presses Universitaires de France.

Chevalier, L. (1947) *Le Problème démographique nord-africain*. Paris: Presses Universitaires de France.

Colonna, F. (1974) Cultural resistance and religious legitimacy in colonial Algeria, *Economy and Society*, **3**, 233–52.

Damase, J. (1937) *Sidi de banlieue*. Paris: Fasquelle.

Decroux, P. (1956) Mariages mixtes au Maroc, *Revue Marocaine de Droit*, 1–28.

Depont, O. (1928) *L'Algérie du centenaire*. Bordeaux: Caderet.

Descloitres, R. *et al.* (1961) *L'Algérie des bidonvilles: le tiers monde dans la cité*. Paris: Mouton.

Duplessis-Kergomard (1938) Mariages mixtes des Kabyles en France, *La France Méditerranéenne et Africaine*, 111–12.

Fanon, F. (1968) *Black Skin, White Masks*. London: MacGibbon and Kee.

Fonville, R. (1924) *De la condition en France et dans les colonies françaises des indigènes des protectorats français*. Paris: E. Duchemin.

Girard, A. and Stoezel, J. (eds) (1954) *Français et immigrés*. INED: Travaux et documents. Cahier No. 20, Paris: Presses Universitaires de France, 2 Vols.

Gouvernement Général (1923) *Rapport sur l'émigration des indigènes* (typescript). AOM 9 H 13.

Gouvernement Général (1938) *Rapport de MM. Laroque et Ollive sur la main-d'oeuvre nord-africaine* (typescript). AOM 8 H 62.

Haddour, Azzedine (1993) Algeria and its history: colonial myths and the forging and deconstruction of identity in *pied-noir* literature. In A.G. Hargreaves and M.J. Heffernan (eds), *French and Algerian Identities from Colonial Times to the Present*. Lampeter: Mellen Press, pp. 89–92.

Heffernan, M. (1989) The Parisian poor and the colonization of Algeria during the Second Republic, *French History*, **3**(4), 377–403.

Hyam, R. (1992) *Empire and Sexuality*. Manchester: Manchester University Press.

Kepel, G. (1987) *Les Banlieues de l'Islam*. Paris: Seuil.

Kobak, A. (1988) *Isabelle. The Life of Isabelle Eberhardt*. London: Chatto.

Lorcin, Patricia (1995) *Imperial Identities. Stereotyping, Prejudice and Race in Colonial Algeria*. London: I.B. Tauris.

MacMaster N. (1995) The *rue Fondary* murders of 1923 and the origins of anti-Arab racism. In R. Gunther and J. Windebank (eds), *Violence and Conflict in the Politics and Society of Modern France*. Lampeter: Mellen Press, pp. 149–60.

MacMaster, N. (1997) *Colonial Migrants and Racism*. London: Macmillan.

Marchand, H. (1954) *Les Mariages franco-musulmans*. Algiers: Vollot-Debacq Frères.

Martial, R. (1931) *Traité de l'immigration et de la greffe inter-raciale*. Cuesmes-lez-Mons: Imprimerie Fédérale.

Massard-Guilbaud (1988) *Des Algériens à Lyon, de la Grande Guerre au Front Populaire*. Doctorate, Université de Lyon II.

Massignon, L. (1930) Carte de répartition des Kabyles dans la région parisienne, *Revue des Etudes Islamiques*, 161–9.

Merad, A. (1967) *Le Réformisme musulman en Algérie de 1925 à 1940*. Paris: Mouton.

Mercier, E. (1881) *L'Algérie et les questions algériennes*. Paris: C. Ainé.

Meylan, M. (1933) *Les Mariages mixtes en Afrique du Nord*. Paris: Sirey.

Meynier, G. (1981) *L'Algérie révélée*. Geneva: Droz.

Michel, A. (1956) *Les Travailleurs algériens en France*. Paris: CNRS.

Ming, H. (1983) Barracks-concubinage in the Indies, 1887–1920, *Indonesia*, **35**, April, 65–93.

M'Rabet, Fadéla (1983 edition) *La Femme algérienne*. Paris: Maspéro.

Nora, P. (1961) *Les Français d'Algérie*. Paris: Julliard.

Poliakov, L. (ed.) (1980) *Le Couple interdit. Entretiens sur le racisme*. Paris: Mouton.

Prochaska, D. (1990) *Making Algeria French. Colonialism in Bône, 1870–1920*. Cambridge: Cambridge University Press.

Rager, J.-J. (1956) *L'Emigration en France des Musulmanes d'Algérie*. Documents algériens no. 49, July.

Ray, J. (1938) *Les Marocains en France*. Paris: Sirey.

Rouissi, M. (1983) *Population et société au Maghreb*. Tunis: Cérès.

Saadia-et-Lakhdar (1961) *L'Aliénation colonialiste et la résistance de la famille algérienne*. Lausanne: La Cité.

Schor, R. (1981) L'opinion française et les immigrés nord-africains (1919–1939). L'image d'un sous-prolétariat, *Cahiers de la Méditerranée*, 51–67.

Sivan, E. (1979) Colonialism and popular culture in Algeria, *Journal of Contemporary History*, **14**, 21–53.

Stoler, A.L. (1989) Rethinking colonial categories: European communities and the boundaries of rule, *Comparative Studies in Society and History*, **13**(1), 134–61.

Stoler, A.L. (1991) Carnal knowledge and imperial power. Gender, race and morality in colonial Asia. In D. di Leonardo (ed.), *Gender at the Cross-roads of Knowledge. Feminist Anthropology in the Post-modern Era*. University of California Press, pp. 51–101.

Stora, B. (1985) *Dictionnaire biographique des militants nationalistes algériens*. Paris: L'Harmattan.

Stora, B. (1986) *Messali Hadj*. Paris: L'Harmattan.

Stora, B. (1992) *Ils venaient d'Algérie*. Paris: Fayard.

Streiff-Fenart, J. (1989) *Les Couples franco-maghrébins en France*. Paris: L'Harmattan.

Todd, E. (1994) *Le Destin des immigrés*. Paris: Seuil.

Turin, Y. (1971) *Affrontements culturels dans l'Algérie coloniale; écoles, médecines, religion 1830–1880*. Paris: Maspero.

Van Onselen, C. (1982) The witches of suburbia. Domestic service in the Witwaterstrand, 1890–1914, in *Studies in the Social and Economic History of the Witwaterstrand, 1886–1914*. London: Longman, Vol. 2, pp. 1–73.

Yacono, X. (1955–6) *La Colonisation des plaines du Chélif*, Vol. 2. Algiers: E. Imbert.

8.

Families on the front line. Mixed marriage in France

YVETTE ROCHERON

The French language – via such words as *le mulâtre, l'eurasien, le métis* –
reveals a long-standing distaste for racial mixing. Between 1955 and
1987 the number of marriages including at least one foreign spouse
rose by 50 per cent, from 18,438 mixed marriages to 27,537 (Tribalat
and Muno-Perez, 1991: 116). In the past, more French women have
married foreigners: a consequence of the sex imbalance of earlier
migrations of single men. The exogamy of French women continues
with 57 per cent of all mixed marriages involving a French woman
marrying a foreigner. Said (1978) argued that the key problematic issue
is whether the union between East and West is desirable or whether they
are mutually impenetrable, given the irredeemable hostility of Islam to
Christianity and modernity. In traditional popular perception, the
answer differs according to the gender of the Oriental. Popular views
favour foreign women marrying French men but less so foreign men
marrying into the dominant culture (Streiff-Fenart, 1989, 1993). For
foreign men, it is believed, a mixed marriage would be not a marriage
of the heart but an instrumental step towards naturalization. For
foreign women, however, mixed marriage would be a way of entering
into modernity through passion and love. These popular perceptions
express, no doubt, the persistence of colonial attitudes (Marchand,
1954). But if popular representations of mixed marriages echo the
orientalists' problem, is this also the case with French social scientists
researching mixed marriage? How do they categorize forms of racial
and ethnic mixing? Are mixed marriages more desirable/regrettable
than others? If so, why?

The 1980s renewed French interest in intermarriage and several
studies which follow widely different research paradigms have been

published. This chapter focuses on the dominant neo-assimilationist interpretation which starts from a positivist premise: mixedness is attributed to the couple through demographic characteristics determined outside individuals' meaning-systems. Through such measurements, intermarriage is thought to express the dynamics of exchange and modernity. This needs to be emphasized, since the symbolic value of mixed marriage is probably greater in France than in Britain at the moment; it is certainly more confusing. With the 1993 Pasqua laws aimed at limiting immigration, marriages which include a partner from outside the EU have become a nightmare for those involved, a struggle over definitions of marriage, citizenship and foreigners' rights to family life (*Le Monde*, 'Le casse-tête des couples mixtes', 6–7 February 1994). So-called marriages of convenience have been vilified and all mixed marriages have become suspect in the eyes of law enforcers. This contradicts the optimistic, even triumphant assimilationist perspective. This chapter will seek to make sense of its optimism by examining the works of Barreau (1991, 1992), Jelen (1991, 1993) and Todd (1994) before considering in detail the role of French demography in the identification of desirable 'immigrant families'.

Mixed matrimonial strategies in general (Collet, 1991, 1993) are not dealt with here, nor is the impact of the Pasqua laws on individual couples. These laws, however, constitute a vital subtext of the interpretations under study.

Definition

The term 'mixed marriage' has been constructed, through various disciplines, as a privileged area for the study of individual and collective perceptions of otherness and self (Guyaux and Delcroix, 1992:14). There is no absolute agreement as to what constitutes a mixed marriage across the quagmire of labellings and it is, therefore, necessary to define the assumptions which frame this chapter.

Firstly, a 'mixed marriage' is a socially constructed phenomenon. From an anthropological standpoint, it is above all else an 'anomalous' arrangement that breaks away from dominant kinship patterns. Tillion (1966) noted, with regard to the endogamous structures of Mediterranean civilizations, that a mixed marriage would take place were one of the spouses to come from outside the normal pool of cousins. The 'foreigner' could live three kilometres away and share the same language and religion. This example shows that the 'anomaly', however defined, might or might not be welcomed by the community and may have very little to do with cultural differences. Secondly, the markers of the anomaly are not fixed in time, as mixed marriages are constituted through the dynamic relations between both the objective (histories of colonization, laws on sexual relationships, social divisions of power and symbols of status and so on) and the subjective (mainly interpersonal dynamics of identity). Neither are its meanings for those involved fixed. These assumptions are consistent with a definition of 'mixed marriage' which has been widely used by the relevant French literature:

> A mixed marriage is formed by a union, legal or de facto, taking place between heterosexual people belonging or having belonged to distinct nations, different religions, ethnicities or races if one of the partners feels or has felt that one or several of these differences provoke or have provoked legal, social, cultural or emotional difficulties or a reaction in the social milieu.
>
> (Philippe, 1983, cited in Collet, 1991)

Philippe's definition is, above all, relational and seeks to include different degrees of 'anomaly' which mixed marriages encompass in the contemporary institution of marriage. It is, however, not propitious for statistical comparisons over time and between countries. For these, we have to turn to demographic definitions.

French demographic sources

The statistical records of mixed marriages, unsurprisingly, reflect the well-known confusion in France about who is counted as a 'foreigner' and who an 'immigrant'. There have been two main sources of statistical information classifying mixed marriage: the marriage register and various surveys conducted by INED to complement census data.[1] All sources distort statistics about mixed marriages in different ways, especially for people moving in and out of their country of origin. However, one is able to identify general tendencies with some certainty. The figures used in this chapter rely mostly on the demographic definition of racial mixing which is limited to the marriage of a French national from birth to a foreigner. Such definitions do not include other forms of racial mixing such as cohabitation and marriages between two foreigners. In part because of such methodological problems, state institutions at the centre of French immigration policies commissioned Tribalat and her researchers from INED and INSEE to map out the dynamics of families of immigrant origin using 'ethnic' categories (place of birth and mother tongue) as indexes of origin. The turn to 'ethnicity' instead of 'nationality' as a marker of the Franco-foreign dichotomy shows a significant but limited shift in French assumptions which will be discussed later.

Prevalence

Marriages between a French national from birth and a foreigner have long been part of the phenomenon of economic immigration and have shown peaks and troughs.[2] Since 1982, the demographic structure, as well as the number, of Franco-foreign couples has altered dramatically. Whereas French marriage rates have been decreasing steadily, the proportion of mixed marriages increased sharply in the late 1980s until they peaked in 1991–92 at around 12 per cent of all marriages celebrated in France (INSEE, 1994: 32–3; Levy, 1994: 1–5; see Table 8.1).

In spite of this increase (7 per cent between 1984 and 1993), these unions still form a small proportion of all marriages in France, a proportion which is probably not much higher than in the 1930s (Tribalat and Munoz-Perez, 1991: 131–2). These points need to be stressed since there are nationalist arguments which give the impression that the French trend towards mixed unions is much larger for all groups. There is no doubt that among some of the immigrant populations, mixed marriages constitute a very large proportion of all their marriages, especially for earlier migrations (see Table 8.2).

The propensity towards mixed marriage having increased among North Africans since the late 1980s, Moroccans are now more likely than other nationals to marry French partners (see Table 8.3).

Algerian and Moroccan women now head the lists for mixed unions, before the Portuguese, who themselves overtook Spanish women in

Table 8.1 Marriages classified by nationalities of spouses

Year	Total number of marriages	French partners		Foreign partners		Mixed marriages	
		No.	%	No.	%	No.	%
1970	393,686	369,175	93.8	6696	1.7	17,815	4.5
1975	387,379	359,612	92.8	7157	1.8	20,610	5.3
1980	334,377	308,066	92.1	5696	1.7	20,615	6.2
1985	269,419	241,497	89.6	6505	2.4	21,417	7.9
1990	287,099	247,853	86.3	8703	3.0	30,543	10.6
1991	280,175	238,284	85.0	8947	3.2	32,944	11.8
1992	271,427	231,991	85.5	8469	3.1	30,967	11.4
1993	255,190	220,928	86.6	6997	2.7	27,265	10.7

Source: INSEE, *Etat civil* (1993)

Table 8.2 Estimate of mixed marriages for 1980–81 and the subsequent trends, with respect to country of birth (or geographical origin) and gender (percentages)

	Italian		Spanish		Portuguese		Algerian		Moroccan	
	Male	Female	Male	Female	Male	Female	Male	Female	Male	Female
1980–81	75	75	66	66	33	33	33	17	33	13
1980s' trend	constant		constant		rising		rising		rising	

Source: Tribalat and Munoz-Perez, 1991: 132

1978. Commentators agree that these shifts in the gender and nationality structure of mixed unions form significant social phenomena. Studies suggest that marriages including a foreigner have been sensitive to migratory flows. But in addition to demographic factors, political and cultural factors have been involved during a time when *le mythe du retour* exploded.

Table 8.3 Mixed marriages classified by nationality of foreign partner (1981 and 1992)

Nationality	Number of mixed marriages		Percentages		Gender of French partner (1992)	
	1981	1992	1981	1992	Male	Female
German	829	893	4.1	2.9	491	402
Belgian	683	711	3.4	2.3	346	365
Spanish	2385	854	11.7	2.8	373	481
Italian	2384	1171	11.7	3.8	314	857
Polish	376	417	1.9	1.3	316	101
Portuguese	3324	3382	16.4	10.9	1379	2003
British	622	814	3.1	2.6	308	506
Algerian	2568	5726	12.6	18.5	2343	3383
Moroccan	1101	5015	5.4	16.2	1833	3182
Tunisian	747	1309	3.7	4.2	223	1086
US	324	662	1.6	2.1	363	299
V, L, C*	538	652	2.6	2.1	282	370
Others	4437	9361	21.8	30.2	4739	4622
Totals	20,318	30,967	100	100	13,310	17,657

Note: * – Vietnamese, Laotian or Cambodian

Source: INSEE, *Les Etrangers en France* (1994: 33)

French singularity

Well-known commentators on the politics of post-war immigration such as Barreau (1991, 1992) and Jelen (1991, 1993, 1994) have expressed very different methodological and theoretical positions. Nevertheless, their overall ideological view is similar as they aim to defend the French melting-pot against its numerous critics. Rates of mixed marriage come on cue to illustrate their core preoccupation with 'French singularity', a key myth of all French nationalisms.

Assimilationist representations attach a major significance to marriages which include spouses of North African origin, particularly when French males marry women from Muslim backgrounds. This is a departure from past assimilationist rhetoric which rejected miscegenation in French Algeria in the name of purity and racial Darwinism. But there is also an element of continuity whenever recent trends are claimed to indicate the entrance of young, dynamic women into modernity and the destruction of 'the traditional Arab–Muslim family which always resists change' (Jelen, 1993: 128–9). One is not far here from the orientalist imagination with its images of exotic women and of walled fortresses to be conquered by Frenchmen in the name of progress. Jelen (1993:128) seizes upon the convergence between the low fertility rate of mixed couples and the rising number of middle-class families among the second generation to predict a process of differentiation between the élites and a persistent underclass. Franco-North African families belong to the élites as:

> les enfants issus de ces mariages seront incapables de définir une origine unique et séparée.[3]
>
> (Jelen, 1991: 224)

Jelen (1991: 21) mentions the need felt by some children from a mixed parentage to gallicize their names so as to succeed in companies such as Rank or IBM. As with other assimilationist representations, the 'mixed' identity of the subsequent generation is largely overlooked and deemed to be unproblematically stable. In a parallel simplification, children from foreign families are doomed to fall between two cultures, into delinquency and welfare dependency.

Barreau, who was, for a time, a key figure in the administration of French immigration policy under governments of the Left and Right, expresses an apparent ambivalence towards mixed marriage statistics. On the one hand, increased rates would signify the superiority of French assimilationist forces over, for instance, those of Islam. This is most desirable since, for Barreau, mixed marriage is more about the encounter of two religions than of two nationalities, the religious factor being particularly important for a devout Catholic. On the other hand, Barreau feared a rising tide of illegal immigrants in the wake of marriages of convenience. He estimated from the 30,000 mixed marriages per year that marriages of convenience would be in thousands and, if unchecked, would lead to the complete disappearance of French culture in 50 years. Unauthentic mixed marriages should therefore be prevented by stricter immigration controls.

The anthropologist Todd, in his deliberately provocative book (1994), celebrates the power of French civilization to destroy others. His thesis, although functionalist and marred by unsubstantiated, sweeping arguments in many places, is far from being lacklustre. Influenced by the *Annales* school, his imagination roots France in an isthmus of migrations where geographical diversity and ancestral traditions have unconsciously structured newcomers' destiny as eventual *assimilés* since neolithic times. Intermarriage is both a mechanism of assimilation and a measure of the depth of this process. Here lies Todd's originality within the positivist construction of intermarriage. It is the family structures of the host societies, not so much those of the newcomers, which determine the degree and length of the latter's segregation as measured by exogamy.

Todd correctly points out one contemporary French paradox: France has higher rates of mixed marriage than other modern democracies and yet endogamy is remarkably strong, since geographical and social proximity is the French norm. Todd seeks an answer by comparing the process of assimilation in the USA, Britain, Germany and France. He argues that the integration of new kinship value-systems are a matter of ancestral custom, values and morality with regard both to inheritance laws and to the position of women in the family. The central pillar of Todd's thesis is that, when the evolution of imported family systems corresponds to those of the host region or country, segregation has come to an end. This, he argues, has occurred with the Jewish and Japanese migrations to the USA. One of his contemporary test cases focuses on Russian Jews emigrating early in the twentieth century to the USA and France. During the 1960s, 31 per cent of the American migrants' descendants married someone non-Jewish and American-born, significantly fewer than the 42 per cent of their French counterparts marrying non-Jews during the same period:

l'échange matrimonial est plus rapide en France parce que le système anthropologique français exige moins que le système américain une réduction des différences de moeurs avant fusion.[4]

(Todd, 1994: 259)

This singularity, together with the Dreyfus Affair and anti-Semitic Vichy, are all to be explained by the notion of the two Frances. The individualist France of the nuclear family, with its egalitarian aspirations leading to exogamy and an indifference to religion and Jewishness, is usually dominant. But at the time of Dreyfus and Vichy, it had failed to contain the France of the periphery and of the Massif Central with its non-egalitarian, endogamous families which had backed an authoritarian form of differentialism. The French segregationist forces reflected the German differentialism and were revived by it:

> le problème des Juifs de France aura été la proximité géographique de l'Allemagne et non l'action spécifique des anti-sémites français.[5]
>
> (Todd, 1994: 275)

When the differentialist model fails to dominate and mixed marriage rates are low, France seems to become itself again. One sees in this example Todd's reductionism which bypasses, among other things, the centrality in anti-Semitic republicanism of the dichotomy between nationals and Jews/foreigners (Guillaumin, 1992; Silverman, 1992). Todd, oblivious to the cultural racism inherent in the Jacobin notion of a homogeneous national culture, none the less posits a critique of its model of purity by invoking the persistent dichotomy in family types. Thus, the egalitarian France may lapse into violent rejection when it is confronted with anthropologically opposed family structures – as with North African kinships.[6] Todd becomes most original when handling statistics on intermarriage in relation to Front National (FN) electoral maps. He notices that areas with high FN votes in the 1980s and in the parliamentary elections of March 1993 also show a slightly greater number of mixed marriages with Algerians. This paradox feeds Todd's view that exogamous, egalitarian family traditions facilitate assimilation through marriage, even though Algerians are demonized by the FN. He also insists that the rate of intermarriage with Algerians in the differentialist France remains relatively high compared with the German and English-speaking democracies. Putting such statistics together, Todd argues that in contemporary France universalism is at work at the level of matrimony, even in areas supporting Le Pen. Thus, mixed marriage statistics, deftly manipulated, allow Todd to defy the truth of elections and identify the persistence of assimilationist France, the only democracy where:

> la force de l'hostilité collective n'implique aucunement un niveau élevé de rejet des individus.[7]
>
> (Todd, 1994: 309)

Todd's syncretism is full of such gross oversimplifications which express a wilfully naïve political philosophy blind to the structures of exclusion embedded in the republican model of assimilation. It is also empirically most problematic to rely solely on one set of what Todd himself reports (1994: 312) as 'hardly significant' figures on regional differences in intermarriage with a view to extrapolating long-term trends.

Undesirable families

For the assimilationists, families of foreign origin should move towards greater exogamy. But contrary to what might have been implied so far, endogamy is not necessarily deemed to be undesirable. We shall deal with this conundrum first and then show in further detail, through the examination of assimilationist representations of polygamy and marriages of convenience, how mixed marriage statistics categorize and divide families of foreign origin into desirable and undesirable newcomers.

Jelen establishes such a hierarchy most clearly. He prefers, more so than Barreau and Todd, endogamous families who have relatively recently emigrated from China and South Vietnam. However, these families had not yet formed enough unions with French partners to appear in 1992 mixed marriage statistics. Although Jelen hates (not too strong a term) what he calls *le terrorisme ultra-minoritaire* (terrorism by tiny minorities) (Jelen, 1993: 225) advocated by SOS Racisme and the English-speaking world, he celebrates the community spirit of the Vietnamese and Chinese living in the thirteenth *arrondissement* of Paris with their dedication to educational values, their strong kinship network and their entrepreneurial skills. The evidence of their 'successful integration' is not their mixed marriage rate which is conveniently dropped as an index of integration but the family values which prevent them from relying on state welfare. This neo-liberal position allows Jelen to compare such families most favourably with 'the welfare dependent Arab–Muslim families'. But since the endogamous Arab–Muslim families are being weakened through intermarriage, they are to be preferred to the 'African family' (*sic!*) whose pathology, created by immigration, includes illiteracy, scorn for schools and family violence.

Jelen's reasoning with regard to desirable/undesirable families is most perplexing. Let us take, as one example of his confusion, some teleological reasoning which he applies to the statistics. Jelen compares values and/or occupational achievements of families of North African origins with those from Asiatic migrations but none of the variables is measured independently from others. The good sides of the latter migrations are inferred from their partial success and then posited as the very cause of that success. To avoid such circular reasoning, one should compare only like with like: for instance, the occupational distribution of the second generations from, say, literate urban small shopkeepers who have settled at the same time in the same location. The relative importance of low mixed marriage rates with regard to integration could then be properly assessed for each group.

For Todd, the truly problematic immigration is Turkish. In 1990, only 4 per cent of children with a Turkish father had a French mother.[8] In spite of Tribalat's caution about inferring future trends from currently low numbers of intermarriage, Todd asserts that Turkish endogamy will remain resilient and notes that Franco-Turkish figures are close to German-Turkish figures. Why is Turkish immigration so endogamous in France? According to Todd's theories, Turks should behave differently in France than in Germany, given the greater compatibility between French and Turkish cultures, both universalist. They also share anti-clerical traditions. The solution to this lies in the fact that Turkish migration has diffused from Germany to Alsace and Greater Paris:

> Ce mouvement de diffusion partant du Rhin signifie que le groupe turc de France ne provient pas, sur le plan idéologique et anthropologique, de Turquie mais d'Allemagne, et qu'il véhicule inconsciemment les valeurs différentialistes du monde germanique, qui continuent de s'imposer à lui dans un environnement français.[9]
>
> (Todd, 1994: 332)

The threat to the French mix of particularism and universalism comes, once again, from Northern Germanic Europe as was the case with Ashkenazi Jewish migrations prior to 1791. Thus, somersaulting through *la longue durée* (a long time-span), Todd can deploy Franco-Turkish intermarriages to reinforce his anti-Maastricht position.

Demographic convergence

The 1991–95 INED publications on the changing structures of families of foreign origin situate rates of mixed marriage within an ethnocentric interpretation of the demography of migratory groups. The basis for all comparisons is 'the family model ... at play in the host country' (Tribalat, 1991:170). Such comparisons are premised on the notion of 'assimilation', considered the most apt term to represent this process. The 1995 study claims to deploy the same conceptualization as the Haut Conseil à l'intégration (see below) for whom assimilation means:

> la réduction des spécificités par les mélanges de populations et par la convergence des comportements.[10]
>
> (Tribalat, 1995: 13)

Such a definition justifies mixed marriage as one of the privileged phenomena under study. The use of the term 'norm' and the deliberately overstretched opposition between 'assimilation' and 'integration' betray some defensiveness towards the thick layers of euphemism which this terminology evokes in immigrationist discourses (see, for instance, Gaspard's (1992) critique). The 1991 text proceeds with a proclamation of its neutrality:

> Toute indication de rapprochement des comportements est interprétée comme un signe de progression. Ce concept n'implique aucun jugement de valeur ... Il s'agit simplement du phénomène de banalisation des comportements.[11]
>
> (Tribalat, 1991: 106)

Such self-conscious detachment towards what are nothing but 'simple' behavioural changes went hand in hand with a soundly scientific rationale for shifting from a binational model of mixed marriage to an ethnic-led one. The need to measure mixed marriage over time contributed to the exceptional procedures of the latest study which categorized 13,000 interviewees into three groups: those born in France but with parents from Algeria, Spain, Morocco, Portugal, Turkey, Black Africa and South East Asia;[12] those who came to live in France when under 16; and those who arrived as adults. In the book version of the study, *Faire France*, the stress is on identifying acculturation processes.

One strength of French demography is to test currently controversial policies: for instance, the immigration laws which police the right of foreigners to become French upon marriage. Overall, both INED and INSEE analyses, while urging caution, seek to refute the claim that naturalization upon marrying a French woman leads to marriages of convenience. The studies also point out the consistently low fertility rates to be found among mixed couples, thus taking on board French ambivalence towards the fertility of foreigners in general and children of mixed parentage in particular.

French demographers tackle another key debate when they document an increase in Franco-North African unions (marriages and cohabitation) and in single motherhood especially among younger Algerian women (with the attendant rise in illegitimate births). Do all these trends mean, as the neo-assimilationists have argued, the disappearance of families which are statistically associated with Islam? The answer is not so simple. For French demographers, the increase in such mixed unions and in convergent demographic patterns (fertility, age of marriage and so on) signals a major break from family traditions for some groups but much less so for others. This is why demographers repeatedly reject reductionist views of the weakening of endogamy among Turkish and Algerian migrants. Unlike Todd,[13] they have consistently advocated caution in the interpretation of Turkish trends as a long-term refusal of intermarriage. The 1995 study confirms that very few Turks who came to France as children married out (6 per cent for males; 2 per cent for females) (Tribalat, 1991: 171; Tribalat and Munoz-Perez, 1991: 131–2; Tribalat, 1995: 88). For Tribalat, matrimonial markets in France and Turkey may be warped by restrictive immigration controls which enhance the value of women of Turkish origin living in France for immigrants-to-be living back in Turkey. This factor, not unique to Turkish migration, could work congruently with frequent contacts with Turkey and the customary dowry paid to the bride's parents. Situating Turkish rates of mixed marriage in the context of ongoing exchanges between kinship networks across borders and French immigration policies departs sharply from the essentialism of Todd and Jelen. At the same time, it reflects their concern with Turkish 'segregationist traits'.

The 1995 study offers a similar analysis in relation to the transnational matrimonial markets of Algerian migration which are also affected by state controls. Furthermore, the three cohorts under study intermarry at different rates and with different groups. The place of birth and time of settlement in France interact with gender to create different rates of mixed unions (see Table 8.4).

A greater exogamy for males than for females is also found in figures related to the origin of boy/girlfriends. For Tribalat, young men and women have to negotiate endogamous values in various ways, for example, by choosing their own partners, delaying their age of marriage, cohabiting. But there are still vital kinship pressures between Algeria and France which resist exogamy, especially for women.[14] Similar trends apply to Franco-Moroccan unions. For instance, for women born in Algeria and Morocco, marrying a Frenchman means entering the middle classes and the job market. Such results suggest that Jelen's and Todd's vision of the destruction of North African endogamy through its daughters is, for the time being, at least inflated. By contrast, the assimilationism of demographers is non-essentialist, as it acknowledges diversity in the acculturation processes under study by constituting ethnic mixing into generational and transnational phenomena which are related to the rich history of each migratory movement. This raises questions as to the dialectic of modernity and tradition, for instance, in relation to divorce. Thus, among unions which include a partner brought up in Algeria and a partner also of Algerian origin but brought up in France, more than half lead to divorce within 10 years compared to the French national divorce rate of 12 to 15 per cent for a similar period (Tribalat, 1995: 85). Why is this so? Is there a 'false cultural proximity' between these two ethnic groups as Tribalat implies? Does this apply to other migrations? Also, does this mean that the split between modernity and tradition is less ossified than implied by neo-assimilationists? If mixed marriage signifies entry to waged labour for immigrant Algerian women and

Table 8.4 Origin of partner of Algerian immigrants and of those with Algerian parents in either first cohabitation or first marriage (all figures are percentages)

	French national	Immigrant	Born in France of immigrant parent(s)
Men			
First marriages			
arrived after age 16	15	78	7
arrived before age 16	17	60	23
born in France with both parents born in Algeria	n/a	n/a	n/a
First cohabitation			
arrived after age 16	20	73	7
arrived before age 16	25	54	21
born in France with both parents born in Algeria	50	17	33
Women			
First marriages			
arrived after age 16	9	87	4
arrived before age 16	9	89	2
born in France with both parents born in Algeria	15	54	31
First cohabitation			
arrived after age 16	10	85	5
arrived before age 16	14	77	9
born in France with both parents born in Algeria	24	47	29

Source: M. Tribalat, *Faire France* (1995: 77)
n/a = not available

their daughters, should one deduce that those who do not live with a Frenchman by birth refuse change? Studies of families living in France or Algeria indicate various ways in which family-oriented cultural innovations keep occurring with Muslim women at their centre (Rude-Antoine, 1990; Lacoste-Dujardin, 1994).

Franco-Algerian/Moroccan relationships have become an index of demographic procedures which select and unify disparate phenomena into complex evolutionary models. But such marriages become prescriptive for all Franco-non-European unions. This is why, at a time of near silence about immigration by the main contenders to the presidency from March to May 1995, the resort to 'ethnicity' as a statistical measure was publicized by the press as salutary, anti-xenophobic and anti-segregationist (Perotti, 1995). The new policy tool was welcomed as a means of keeping the spectre of differentialism at bay.

The genius of French families

Demography as an instrument of knowledge reflects national sensibilities towards minorities. French demography is not alone in this orientation but as in the past (Le Bras, 1994) it is extraordinarily unashamed about the links between its ideological concerns and its procedures. For instance, a 1991 INED publication concludes by stressing that demographic interest in foreigners' families has been closely tied up to the failure of immigration control. Such a regime of knowledge is likely to reinforce rather than undermine the slippage between 'statistical procedure' and 'norm' which situates 'demographic convergence' in both 'scientific' and 'political' orthodoxies. Although the focus is on disparity of norms, the emphasis is consensual. After mapping out different trends towards mixed unions, the *Faire France* study nevertheless concludes, like Jelen, that a mixed ethnic identity is unlikely to be reproduced as a separate identity through a second generation. Little is said, for instance, of the 13 per cent of children of Franco-Algerian couples who do acknowledge a religious practice. Nothing is said either about the French partner as a negotiator of convergence; the onus of deculturation and acculturation is placed on the other partner solely. Up to 1995, French demography remained indifferent to the production of ethnic identities and the wider social structures which, according to the pluralists, impinge on mixed couples in specific ways, given disparities in status, income and gendered cultural orientation (Merton, 1941: 361). If future studies remain within a positivist conception of ethnicity as a birthmark, unmediated by agency, their explanatory powers will be limited.

Conclusion

The essentialist and non-essentialist manifestations of neo-assimiliationism are to be primarily understood as antidotes to differentialism. For both, rates of mixed marriage serve to redefine the category of 'the assimilated' as they seek to incorporate individual families who manifest demographically defined convergences. Mixed marriage statistics have become a 'scientific' index of 'French genius'. This is no small achievement. It is, therefore, not surprising if the Haut Conseil à l'intégration, an agency regulating families of foreign origin, found it appropriate in its first report to select rates of mixed marriage along with fertility rates with a view to ranking predisposition to family integration *en raison des automaticités de francisation* which mixed marriage brings in its wake.[15] The Haut Conseil dismissed the rise of foreign–foreign mixed marriages enacted in France as a 'sign of integration'. No explanation was offered. Yet one can reasonably argue that, for two foreigners, firstly getting married and secondly choosing the French registrar, and thus French law, constitute an acquiescence to the dominant culture. This rejection of a form of intermarriage which is not uncommon illustrates the selective use of mixed marriage as an administrative instrument to police families of foreign origin which, with fertility rates, leads to the valuing of a few mixed unions (particularly those including Algerian women and their daughters) and, in parallel, the demonization of others (currently Africans and Turks). This process is achieved to the exclusion of other potential measurements.[16] Whatever the categories used, mixed marriage is now being constructed as one significant form of the private organization of migratory movements whose chief merit, for immigration policy, is that the gallicization it produces seems to happen irrespective of state intervention. This view, which is strongly supported by Jelen, dissociates mixed marriage from the dialectic of private and public institutionalization of the family and of discrimination. But, as implied by Philippe's definition of mixed marriage, mixed couples in irregular situations cannot opt out of such processes. Should the future of descendants of non-European immigrants be determined by evolving family structures, there would indeed be a virtue in advocating non-interventionism: waiting for people to fall in love with the other. But this Panglossian standpoint runs the risk of overlooking the complexities, at times nightmares, of the contemporary experience of mixed families who are all, willy-nilly, embedded in the mutation of both family structures and republican models of immigration.

Let us conclude by stressing two points. Firstly, in spite of some major exceptions, and in contrast to the 1950s, a message of hope is inherent in currently dominant representations of mixed relationships. As always, optimism is the *raison d'être* of French assimilationism. Positive symbols attached to immigration are in dire need of renewal. Neo-assimilationism takes a step towards this by creating the mixed union as a suitably vague but potent metaphor of the French family as a melting pot. Secondly, neo-assimilationism is also constructing the mixed union, in orientalist style, as an instrument of knowledge for discourses which are constantly in need of new categories for regulating the Other.

Notes

1. In 1982 the biographical data of 23,000 women born outside France was analysed out of 300,000 interviews (Tribalat, INED, 1991: 78). The last survey of this type, *Enquête familles*, took place in 1990.
2. In 1982, about 40 per cent of female and male immigrants (foreign or naturalized) lived with a French partner in unions formed between 1934 and 1949. The proportion dropped to 20 per cent (female) and 27 per cent (male) among marriages contracted between 1960 and 1964. After the official curbing of foreign labour in 1974, such unions rose again to earlier levels (Tribalat, 1991: 112–13).
3. Children from such marriages will be unable to define a singular and separate origin.
4. [The] change is faster in France because the French anthropological system requires a reduction in cultural differences to a lesser extent than the American system.
5. The strategic problem of French Jews was the geographical proximity of Germany and not the specific activity of French anti-Semitism.
6. Todd (1994: 296) begs a number of questions about colonization, citizenship and racism in relation to the absence of Muslim–European marriages between 1880 and 1955 in Algeria.
7. The strength of collective hostility does not imply a high level of hostility to individuals.
8. 27 per cent of children with Algerian fathers, and just under 15 per cent of children with Moroccan or Tunisian fathers, had a French mother: estimate from Todd's tables (1994: 302 and 304). In 1990, 197,712 Turks had settled in France, most being immigrants from 1968–75.
9. This movement spreading from the Rhine signifies that the Turks in France do not come, in terms of ideology and anthropology, from Turkey, but from Germany, and unconsciously carry differentialist values from the Germanic world which continue to surface and influence them within the French milieu.

10. The reduction of differences through the mixing of populations and the convergence of behaviour patterns.
11. Any sign of any convergence in behaviour is conceived as a sign of progression. This concept in no way implies any value judgement ... It signals no more than a simple movement towards the standardization of behaviour.
12. Immigrant families from these areas represent about 60 per cent of all such families. South Asia means Laos, Cambodia and Vietnam. *Afrique noire* includes such countries as those in western and central Africa as well as Cape Verde, Madagascar, Mauritania and so on (Tribalat, 1995: 21–2).
13. See Todd's arguments concerning the disintegration of the North African anthropological system (1994: 280).
14. See Table 8.4. Thus, only 10 per cent of those women who emigrated when single adults married out compared with 14 per cent for those who left Algeria as children and 24 per cent for those born in France.
15. In France, racial mixing in marriage moves, on the whole, towards integration not only as a result of the racial mixing itself ... but also as a result of those automatic processes of gallicization which it brings in its wake' (Haut Conseil à l'intégration, 1991: 177).
16. Why not identify, say, immigrant women's rates of employment as a measure of family integration? Such rates would also underline a convergence across both minority groups and generations, notwithstanding major discrepancies (*INSEE Première*, March 1995: 3).

References

Barreau, J.-C. (1991) *De l'Islam en général et du monde moderne en particulier*. Paris: Le Pré aux Clercs.

Barreau, J.-C. (1992) *De l'immigration en général et de la nation en particulier*. Paris: Le Pré aux Clercs.

Collet, B. (1991) Couples mixtes en France et en Allemagne; statut juridique et caractéristiques des couples, *Migrations-Société*, **3**(14), 19–38.

Collet, B. (1993) Couples mixtes en France, couples bi-nationaux en Allemagne, *Hommes et Migrations*, **1167**, 15–19.

Cordeiro, A. (1995) De quelles familles parle-t-on? *Hommes et Migrations*, **1185**, March, 40–4.

Gaspard, F. (1992) La société française confrontée à la polygamie, *Revue Française des Affaires Sociales*, 181–97.

Gaspard, F. (1992) Assimilation, insertion, integration: les mots pour 'devenir' français, *Hommes et Migrations*, **1154**, 14–23.

Groupe d'information et de soutien des travailleurs immigrés: a. (August 1994) *Le Mariage des étrangers*; b. (December 1994) *Entrée et séjour des étrangers: la nouvelle loi Pasqua* (3rd edn).

Guillaumin, C. (1992) *Sexe, race et pratique du pouvoir*. Paris: Editions Côté-femmes.

Guyaux, A. and Delcroix, C. (1992) *Double mixte: la rencontre de deux cultures dans le mariage*. Coédition Contradictions/L'Harmattan, **68**, March.

Haut Conseil à l'intégration (1991) *Pour un modèle français d'intégration*. Premier rapport annuel. Paris: La Documentation Française.

INSEE (1993) *Etat civil.* Paris.

INSEE (1994) *Les Etrangers en France.* Paris: Edition Contours et Caractères.

INSEE (1995) *INSEE Première*, **368**, March.

Jelen, C. (1991) *Ils feront de bons Français: enquête sur l'assimilation des Maghrébins*. Paris: Robert Laffont.

Jelen, C. (1993) *La Famille, secret de l'intégration*. Paris: Robert Laffont.

Lacoste-Dujardin, C. (1994) *Des mères contre les femmes*. Paris: La Découverte.

Le Bras, H. (1994) *Le Sol et le sang*. Paris: Editions de l'Aube.

Le Monde, Le casse-tête des couples mixtes, 6–7 February 1994.

Levy, M. (1994) La population de la France de 1990 à 1993, *Population et Société*, **288**, 1–5 March.

Marchand, H. (1954) *Les Mariages franco-musulmans*. Algiers: Vollot-Debacq Frères.

Merton, R. (1941) Intermarriage and the social structure: fact and theory, *Psychiatry*, 361–74.

Perotti, A. (1995) L'étude de l'INED sur l'intégration des immigrés et de leurs enfants: les commentaires de presse, *Migrations-Société*, **7**(39), May–June, 102–10.

Philippe, C. (1983) *Le Couple domino et bigarré*. Mémoire de DEA. Paris: EHSS.

Quiminal, C. (1995) La famille Soninké en France, *Hommes et Migrations*, **1185**, March, 26–31.

Rude-Antoine, E. (1990) *Le Mariage maghrébin en France*. Paris: Karthala.

Said, E. (1978) *Orientalism: Western Conceptions of the Orient*. Harmondsworth: Penguin.

Silverman, M. (1992) *Deconstructing the Nation*. London: RKP.

Streiff-Fenart, J. (1989) *Les Couples franco-maghrébins en France*. Paris: L'Harmattan.

Streiff-Fenart, J. (1993) The making of families' identities among the Franco-Algerian couples. In A. Hargreaves and M. Hefferman (eds), *French and Algerian Identities from Colonial Times to the Present*. Lampeter: Mellen Press.

Tillion, G. (1966) *Le Harem et les cousins* (4th edn). Paris: Seuil.

Todd, E. (1994) *Le Destin des immigrés.* Paris: Seuil.

Tribalat, M. (1991) *Cent Ans d'immigration, étrangers d'hier, Français d'aujourd'hui.* Paris: INED/Presses Universitaires de France.

Tribalat, M. (1995) *Faire France: une enquête sur les immigrés et leurs enfants.* Paris: La Découverte.

Tribalat, M. and Munoz-Perez, F. (1991) Les mariages d'émigrés avec des Français. Leur évolution depuis quelques décennies. In T. Hibert and L. Roussel (eds), *La Nuptialité: évolution récente en France et dans les pays développés.* Paris: INED/Presses Universitaires de France (congrès et colloques, no. 7).

Part Two

Work, Health and Education

9.

French companies faced with an ageing workforce

CATHERINE MOREL

The debate over the division of wealth between the working and retired population has recently brought to the forefront the problem of France's ageing population which, whilst not a new problem, has been overlooked during recent years. A longer life expectancy and a drop in the birth-rate go a long way towards explaining a phenomenon which should speed up from the year 2005. While there are only 11 million people in their sixties today, there will be 17 million of them in 2020 (that is, more than a quarter of the population) and almost 22 million in 2050. The number of the very old is also going to double between now and the year 2025 to reach 7 million. Likewise, the number of young people under the age of 20 will continue to dwindle: from 28 per cent at the present to 25 per cent in 2050 and even to 17 per cent according to the most pessimistic hypothesis. It is therefore safe to predict that from the year 2020 there will be more elderly people in France than people under the age of 20 (Herzlich, 1994).

The consequences of France's ageing population on the job front are quite easy to predict: we will witness over the coming years not only a shrinking but also a much older working population (Guillemot and Marchand, 1993). This trend, which began a few years ago, will also increase from 2005 onwards.

The aim of this chapter is to show a reluctance on the part of employers to retain older employees, even though this would seem to be one of the first solutions to the problem of the imbalance in companies' age pyramid.

The problem of the shortage of labour will be the subject of the first part of this chapter. The figures provided by INSEE are the starting-point for the analysis and will enable us to determine the variations that the working population should undergo in the years to come. The presentation of solutions to this problem are followed by an evaluation of their success at company level. The second part of this chapter looks at the problem of an ageing workforce. After having measured the extent of the phenomenon and mentioned its repercussions on the working world, it will be seen that for most companies the management of human resources does not take this variable into consideration and that awareness of the problem is extremely low. The third and final part of the chapter deals with keeping older employees in employment as a solution to a labour shortage. A brief historical reminder will explain how the general implementation of early retirement to fight against unemployment has permanently affected the mentality and attitude of employers towards their older employees. The reform of the gradual retirement scheme PRP (*préretraite progressive*), which should be viewed as a way of rejuvenating the age pyramid in companies, rather than a means of disposing of surplus labour, shows the government's awareness of this problem. A short case-study reveals, however, that this is not an immediate priority, as far as companies are concerned.

Shortage of labour

The possibility of a shortage of labour may appear surprising in a country such as France where unemployment is relatively high. However, all the demographic projections confirm that sooner or later a halt in the growth of the working population, indeed a reversal of this growth, can be expected.

In March 1990, the date of the last census in France, the working population rose to 25,287,000 (Guillemot and Marchand, 1993). This figure corresponded to an increase of 1.5 million in relation to 1982, that is, an annual average increase of 185,000 in the working population. Whilst satisfactory, this growth rate was already lower than that of 225,000 per year recorded between 1968 and 1982. This tendency should be confirmed in the years to come. Thus, INSEE's demographic projections show that the French working population should continue to increase until the year 2005 to reach 26 million and to decrease after that (Blanchet and Marchand, 1991).

Four birth-rate hypotheses allow for different scenarios and help measure the extent of the phenomenon. In the most pessimistic hypothesis, that is, a birth-rate of 1.5 children per woman, the number of people eligible to work would reach 1985's level by the year 2020 (that is, 24 million). The current birth-rate – 1.8 children per woman – would extend this deadline to 2025. If the birth-rate returns to the level of population regeneration (2.1 children per woman), the working population would only decrease slightly beyond 2005 to stabilize at about 26 million. Finally, a high birth-rate hypothesis (2.4 children per woman) would not prevent a transitional decrease in the workforce towards 2010, but this would then be followed by an increase towards 2012.

There are three possible solutions to the shortage of labour (Blanchet and Marchand, 1991).

The first solution consists of increasing the working population by means of immigration. The highest estimates suggest that 100,000 immigrants per year are needed to compensate for the current shortfall in the number of births in order to reach the number required for population regeneration. According to INSEE forecasts (Herzlich, 1994: 21), the 'migratory figures' should stabilize at 50,000 per year on average, which is still a long way short of the mark.

Besides the problem of integration, which is outside the remit of this chapter, the main problem with this solution concerns the quality of labour. How can employers be sure that the qualifications offered by immigrants are those that they are looking for? It is equally likely that other countries with similar population profiles will be reluctant to part with their qualified labour force.

The second solution would be to increase productivity, by investing either in new technology or in education and training. It should be pointed out here that, since 1960, France has made more than average progress compared with other OECD countries in terms of labour productivity and that its productivity levels are already amongst the highest in Europe (Frémeaux, 1995). Thus, the increase in labour productivity between 1979 and 1992 increased by 2.3 per cent in France whilst the OECD average for the same period was 1.6 per cent. In fact, according to Coudert (1993), it would seem that this increase already relied heavily on using technology for productivity gains.

The third possible solution would be to increase the number of women and older people in employment. Whilst the working population is ageing, it also includes more women than previously. In the last 30 years women have taken over the working world (Desplanques, 1993): 6.6 million women were either looking for or had a job in 1962 compared to more than 11 million in 1990, that is, an increase of more than 60 per cent in 30 years. In 1990, 44 per cent of the working population was female. Is it possible to imagine an even bigger mobilization of potential resources in female labour? The figures given at the beginning of this chapter include a continued increase in the number of female workers (with the rate tending towards a little more than 80 per cent, that is, 10 to 15 per cent lower than the male rate). We have seen that these rates will not prevent a reversal of the trend towards 2005. The authors of these projections (Blanchet and Marchand, 1991) have, however, speculated even further: they have aligned the rate of female workers with those of male workers and come up with the hypothesis of a birth-rate of 1.8 children per woman. This simulation shows that the working population will level out at 29 million people by the beginning of the year 2000 but that it will fall below 25 million in 2035, which is 15 years later than the original scenario. The increased activity of women will therefore only give a brief respite. In addition, it is difficult to ignore a possible correlation between women working and the evolution of the birth-rate. Encouraging them to work without offering better childcare facilities would, without doubt, have implications.

Favouring older workers at first seems an attractive solution: increasing the retirement age by about 2.5 years would be sufficient to keep the working population of the year 2040 at its 1985 level. In addition, it would mean reducing the number of retired people and therefore take the pressure off the pension system.

However, maintaining and recruiting older workers is an idea which still meets with a lot of resistance. Firstly on the part of employees, who are attached to the idea of retirement at the age of 60, and secondly on the part of companies, who prefer to employ a younger workforce which, theoretically, adapts far more easily to an increasingly complex technological environment.

An enquiry carried out for the Ministère du travail, de l'emploi et de la formation professionnelle in 1992 (Guillemard, 1994) evaluates the appeal of each of these solutions to companies.

Recruiting foreign labour in times of labour shortage arouses little support from companies since 60 per cent of the 8533 establishments questioned said that they would not use this option in the future (only 15 per cent of them use it today).

The increase in productivity was a popular present and future choice. The Ministry enquiry shows that the development of training programmes is one of the strategies already put into practice by companies (35 per cent of those questioned) as well as replacing the workforce with machines (19 per cent of those companies questioned have already started investing in technology as a way of cutting back on staff and 32 per cent see this as a future option). It is interesting to note that the strategy of technology investment, already widely used by big companies, is becoming increasingly popular with medium-sized and small businesses.

If companies already use female labour (27 per cent), they do not really see this as a future solution (44 per cent rejected this possibility).

Recruiting, keeping and retraining older employees are strategies little used by companies (1 per cent, 1 per cent and 5 per cent respectively). Only gradual retirement seemed to find favour amongst employers: 36 per cent of the companies questioned said they were in favour of gradual retirement as a means of partially keeping older employees in a job.

Ageing workforce

Alongside this phenomenon of a labour shortage, the tendency of the working population to age is expected to become more pronounced.

First of all, we need to look at activity at the bottom of the age pyramid: there is a rapid decrease in the proportion of workers under the age of 25. There are proportionally fewer and fewer young people for demographic reasons (a drop in the birth-rate since 1974) and also there are fewer and fewer of them in the working world. If they made up 17 per cent of the working population in 1975, they made up no more than 10.5 per cent in 1990 (Le Minez, 1994).

People staying on at school out of fear of unemployment helps explain the drop in juvenile activity. It is interesting to state that France, together with Japan, has the highest number of students. Likewise it also has the lowest rate of youth employment (34.4 per cent compared to 76.4 per cent in the UK in 1991) and this has dropped more in France than in any other country since 1979 (it was then 48.6 per cent) (Servin, 1995). The falling number of young people in employment unbalances companies' age pyramid. As an example one could cite the banking and insurance sector where, from 1982 to 1990, youth employment dropped by 42 per cent. Likewise in the transport and telecommunications sectors it dropped by 36 per cent over the same period (Lebaube, 1994). Some researchers go further in explaining this phenomenon (Elbaum and Marchand, 1993), and do not hesitate to talk about a protected job market and the mechanism of 'selective exclusion' of young people, who would be deliberately excluded from the working world until the age of 25. Adults would therefore monopolize the stable, full-time, permanent, well-paid jobs (Gaullier, 1990).

Activity at the top of the age pyramid is closely linked to the ageing baby-boom generation. At present, the working population is concentrated towards the middle of the pyramid. The 25- to 49-year-olds hold three-quarters of the jobs, as opposed to a little more than half in 1970 (Servin, 1995). If demographic evolution explains this concentration around the middle age-groups, it is important to point out that the drop in employment over the last few years, at each end of the age-groups, has reinforced this tendency. In fact, the average age of the workforce is steadily increasing; it was 37 in 1990 and it will be 40 in 2010, on the hypothesis of a birth-rate of 1.8 children per woman (Blanchet and Marchand, 1991: 66). From 2005, the baby-boom generation will be in its sixties and will thus inflate the top end of the age pyramid.

The implementation by companies of a concrete policy of 'age management' – helping to attract and ease the integration of new staff, developing the future of those over 40, and keeping on those who are older – could be the solution to an ageing workforce. It could also alleviate an imbalance in both the retirement systems and the age pyramid (Normand, 1994: 3).

At the same time, these challenges seem extremely difficult to meet because they are diametrically opposed to the current attitude of excluding young people and those over the age of 55, as well as to age discrimination policies which are currently practised in the majority of French companies. It is imperative to answer certain questions. How should one motivate young graduates whose promotion prospects are limited by the overwhelming presence of their elders ? Furthermore, a reform of the promotion system based on seniority, which together with the ageing working population takes up an increasing part of the wage bill, is called for.

The 30 to 50 age-group is also in danger of being disappointed with career developments. Effectively, organizational changes in the manufacturing and service sectors have led to a decline in the number of hierarchical levels. The chances of gaining promotion are reduced as those in the middle age-groups become more numerous.

In addition, working conditions for those over 40 could deteriorate, especially for those employees in a physically demanding job (Molinié and Volkoff, 1993). Statistical and ergonomic studies have revealed the existence of age limits above which it is difficult to perform certain tasks (Volkoff *et al.*, 1992). What will happen when, through a lack of younger employees, it is impossible for companies to provide easier working conditions for those over 40, as is the current practice?

Likewise, within the framework of an age management policy, companies should organize training at all stages of professional life so as to keep qualified staff for as long as possible. Currently, employees over 45 are excluded from training, with employers favouring younger staff who, it is thought, are more likely to be able to cope with technological changes than their elders (Aventur, 1994).

Finally, the current management of older employees consists entirely of organizing their retirement, instead of concentrating on how to use them to their maximum potential towards the end of what could become an even longer working career.

How can one explain that the management of human resources in the majority of French companies is today in complete contradiction with measures which would enable them to put the problem of their ageing workforce into perspective?

The lack of any means of long-term planning and also the very weak realization of the problem provide an initial explanation.

An enquiry by the Délégation à l'emploi carried out in 1990 revealed that only 14 per cent of company bosses believed that they would find themselves faced with an imbalance in their age pyramid in the medium term (Huet, 1994). The DARES-Démoscopie enquiry mentioned previously confirmed these results and highlighted the fact that the drop in the number of young employees was perceived as even less of a problem than ageing at the top end of the age pyramid (Guillemard, 1994).

It also established a certain ignorance amongst companies as to data concerning their workforce. Thus, according to those establishments questioned, the proportion of young people would increase (43 per cent) or would remain stable (39 per cent) which is in complete contradiction to the available global data which shows a drop in the number of young people in employment.

An analysis of the answers given shows a clear difference between the large companies and the medium and smaller ones and suggests that the level of concern about ageing increases with the size of the company. This result is certainly linked to the existence of diagnostic tools used by the large companies but which are desperately lacking in other cases (less than 10 per cent of companies have such facilities).

The other notable fact is that most companies, having diagnosed an age problem, are unable to provide any solutions. When they do, they favour external measures (early retirement, redundancy schemes) to internal measures (internal redeployment). Their intentions therefore differ from those of the government which, for some years, has been trying to reduce the number of older employees leaving. Keeping on such workers in the company would allow a partial response to the problems of an ageing workforce and a labour shortage. It is with this solution that the third part of this study is concerned and especially with the measures of the PRP (*préretraite progressive*) which could provide a conciliatory link between companies and the government.

The different measures for early retirement put into place in the 1960s are largely responsible for companies' lack of enthusiasm for keeping on and recruiting older workers. At that time, some sectors of the French economy, notably the steel industry, were in trouble and their survival depended on restructuring (Temam, 1994). In order to soften the effects of this modernization, it was decided that those close to retirement age would bear the brunt of the reductions in the workforce. From 1963 the FNE (Fonds national pour l'emploi), a fund for early retirement, was created. The economic crisis of the 1970s marked the beginning of 'the early retirement decade' (Gaullier, 1990). In order to manage a surplus in labour the government chose to encourage early retirement. The objective, however, was to avoid redundancies of middle-aged workers and to make room for the younger unemployed. This idea was reinforced elsewhere with the creation of *solidarité préretraite* contracts in the 1980s. Early retirement as a means of managing excess staff met with notable success in companies. It effectively allowed them to get rid of the most expensive and less adaptable employees without leading to disputes, since there was a consensus between all the different parties involved (De Block, 1994). Little by little there was an in-depth transformation in mentalities; the end of one's professional life was brought forward by 5 to 10 years and became less and less associated with retirement (Kerschen, 1994). From then on France became one of the countries with the lowest rate of employment of men over the age of 55 (57.9 per cent) (Normand, 1994: 3). These measures have helped to weaken the status of employees over the age of 50 and explain to a large extent the discrimination with which they are faced. However, the ill effects and the cost of early retirement as well as the question of the ageing population have meant a reappraisal of the system. The new proposals now favour gradual retirement.

Gradual retirement: a viable solution?

Gradual early retirement is a relatively recent development of the early retirement package as it has only existed for about 10 years. Originally, there were two measures whose objectives of encouraging workers over 55 to leave their company were barely concealed.

The *contrats de solidarité de préretraite progressive* were introduced in January 1982 and modified in 1984. The signatory company agreed to maintain its staff and to take on new employees by transforming the full-time jobs of workers over 55 into part-time jobs. In return, the state financed 30 per cent of the part-time salary. The contracts have remained undervalued and the total number of agreements remained very modest (Salzberg and Baktavatsalou, 1994): 30,700 signatories took part from 1982 to 1992. An enquiry carried out in 1990 by the Délégation à l'emploi highlighted three factors explaining the poor success of this measure: firstly, the lack of interest on the part of employees who preferred complete early retirement which allowed them to keep up to 65 per cent of their previous salary; secondly, the difficulty in setting up part-time work in some sectors and especially in industry; finally, the undertaking to maintain staff levels imposed on companies.

The ASFNE agreements (*conventions d'allocations spéciales du fonds national pour l'emploi à mi-temps*), set up by decree on the 15 April 1987, were an integral part of a scheme facilitating job cuts aimed at workers aged 56 years and 2 months who, on signing it, agreed that their job would become part-time rather than full-time. A special allocation of 30 per cent of the original salary made up the part-time wage paid to the signatory. A part of the salary was therefore paid by the company, a second by UNEDIC (Union nationale pour l'emploi dans l'industrie et le commerce), and finally a third paid by the state. Le Fonds national pour l'emploi is managed by la Délégation à l'emploi and financed by the government's budget. The UNEDIC is managed by all the social partners and is financed by social contributions.

The law of 31 December 1992 (law 92–1446) merged and replaced these two systems to give rise to the PRP conventions whose terms were again relaxed by the law of 20 December 1993 relating to work, employment and professional training (*loi quinquennale de décembre 1993*, no. 93–1313). Reform of the system tried to resolve those difficulties mentioned previously. According to a circular of 26 March 1993, the PRP convention had three objectives: to participate in the development of part-time work and new forms of work organization; to contribute to the integration of marginalized workers; and to provide for better age management within companies.

The new version of the PRP deals with employees who are at least 55 years old and under 65 and who agree to have their job converted from full-time to part-time status (in fact, 40 or 50 per cent of their previous total number of hours). In exchange they receive a salary corresponding to their part-time job plus 30 per cent of their previous remuneration which is paid to them by Assedic. A special benefit (*l'allocation de préretraite progressive*) is also paid to them by the FNE.

In exchange, the signatory companies agree either to appoint new staff, a large proportion of which must come from the long-term unemployed, or to make a financial contribution to compensate for the lack of recruitment. The company is therefore no longer obliged to maintain its original staffing levels.

On the face of it, the PRP offers only advantages for each of the partners involved, starting with the employees who can choose whether to sign or not and who benefit from a smooth transition from full-time employment to retirement. They also have the right to freely manage the end of their career which was not the case with previous systems. The financial package is equally very attractive. As to the organization of working hours, the employee and the company can decide how to modulate them from one year to the next (pluriannualization). Therefore for a five-year agreement, the employee can work 80 per cent the first year, 60 per cent the second, 50 per cent the third, 40 per cent the fourth and 20 per cent the final year (L'essor des préretraites progressives, 1995: 11).

As for the state, the PRP has the advantage of costing less than complete early retirement which costs it 300,000 francs per employee per year (Briec, 1994). This system also provides a life-saver for financing pensions as it allows for a decrease in the number of retired people and an increase in contribution years.

The PRP is equally attractive for companies on several fronts. Firstly on a financial level: a 30 per cent reduction in social contributions for part-time workers applies to employees on the PRP and to those taken on on a part-time basis within the framework of the convention. Secondly, the constraint of maintaining staffing levels has been abolished. The PRP could enable the passing on of expertise and company spirit, which used to leave the company with the older employees. The development of 'mentoring' also serves a dual purpose; the PRP employees use their remaining time in the company usefully and advantageously by training a young employee who will perhaps one day replace them. Finally, the company is able to rejuvenate its age pyramid at less cost as, without increasing labour overheads , it can acquire 'new blood'.

It would appear that the 'new formula' PRP is all the more attractive to companies because any possible recourse to complete early retirement has been made more difficult; 8900 people took up the PRP in 1993, twice as many as in 1992 (Baktavatsalou *et al.*, 1994). It is a rising trend with the number of beneficiaries almost doubling between 1993 and September 1994, reaching 26,000 by the end of September 1994.

If the reform of the PRP enabled it to take a leap forward in 1993, it is also true to say that the system still remains quite marginal (it accounts for a little more than 10 per cent of the total number of early retirements) (Briec, 1994). In addition, the PRP is still a long way off being seen as a means of age management as can be seen in the following example. (The author wishes to express thanks to Mrs Andrée Bourrel, Manager in the personnel department of Française de Mécanique, who kindly contributed answers.)

In October 1993, Française de Mécanique, a subsidiary of both Peugeot and Renault based in Douvrin in the Nord-Pas-de-Calais region, signed its first PRP agreement. This agreement was signed for one year. It was open to employees aged at least 55. The agreement was aimed at a potential number of 75 people, spread over the whole site (which at that time numbered 4700 people). Management was deliberately excluded from the agreement. It was a mixed agreement and in compensation the company was to take on 50 new employees and pay compensation for the 25 lost jobs. If the first objective was to manage overstaffing, the company also wanted to organize the working week by developing part-time work. The problem of an ageing workforce had only been partially identified and the rejuvenation of the age pyramid was not a priority objective of Française de Mécanique.

Compared with the company's objectives, the take-up rate was disappointing, as only 32 employees opted for the PRP (that is, 42 per cent). The newness of the system and the financial implications for moving to part-time work could explain this low percentage. The fear of a loss of revenue, accentuated for those a long way off retirement age, explains to a large extent the lack of interest. As a consequence the job offers were lowered: the 32 PRP cases were replaced by 16 new employees. A codicil to the agreement allowed the redeployment to Française de Mécanique of employees who had lost their job on another site in the region. Contrary to what is provided for by the law, the long-term unemployed were not offered jobs, but this is exceptional. A mentoring system was not necessary as the 'new employees' already knew the job and were of an average age of 42.

Regarding the working week, Française de Mécanique preferred to opt for part-time hours whether they were organized by one day out of two, one week out of two or two weeks out of four, the limit being fixed at a month. If the administrative follow-up of the PRP did not seem to have posed any problems (the personnel department dealing with all administrative requirements), the reorganization of the part-time jobs seems to have been much more difficult to manage, especially the administrative jobs. The dilemma was the following: how to limit the impact of the PRP on the company's organization whilst maintaining a continuity of work, motivation and satisfactory productivity. Only the first part of the equation seems to have been resolved. It is probably in order to avoid this pitfall that at the time of the next PRP agreement, Française de Mécanique will increase the minimum age to 57; 'it is easier to manage over 3 years than over 5'.

Conclusion

The Française de Mécanique example and the results of a study carried out by two GIP researchers within a large industrial group allow a number of conclusions to be drawn regarding the use of PRP (Burdillat and Charpentier, 1995).

Firstly, it would appear that companies see the PRP not as a means of age management but as a means of getting rid of surplus staff based on a logic of pushing aside older employees. There is therefore a discrepancy between the official objectives and the way in which they are put into practice by companies. But how could it be otherwise after years of encouraging early retirement?

Secondly, it would appear that putting the system into practice is not always easy, especially when it comes to organizing the working week and defining job content. This is all the more true where the starting age is lower. Companies are not always disposed to implement far-reaching organizational changes on the signature of a PRP agreement.

Thirdly, the status of early retirement, in addition to its hybrid nature (the person taking early retirement is both an employee and seen as practically retired) is not very fulfilling (Gaullier, 1993: 151). It appears to marginalize older workers. The mentoring system, which is an interesting feature, has been little developed. In addition, the idea that moving into PRP carries with it demotivation and underproductivity is firmly established in people's minds and does not encourage companies to give particularly interesting tasks to the employees concerned. They, in their turn, already feel as if they have one foot outside the company. This goes a long way to explaining the lack of interest in the PRP with management staff.

In conclusion, one can therefore say that a long-term view is one of the *sine qua non* conditions for the PRP to become an efficient tool in the struggle against both an ageing workforce and a labour shortage. Otherwise, the system will continue to be used by companies as a 'godsend'. Besides the necessary reglementary and legislative measures to guide companies' actions, raising consciousness and providing more information is all the more essential as the issue depends on changing people's attitudes.

References

Activité professionnelle et emploi, permanences et inflexions depuis 10 ans, *Economie et Statistiques*, INSEE, **261**: whole issue.

Aventur, F. (1994) La formation continue des salariés à partir de 45 ans, *Emploi et Vieillissement, Cahier Travail et Emploi*, La Documentation Française, April, 89–95.

Baktavatsalou, R., Cosnefroy, R.-F. and Pérès, N. (1994) Les préretraites progressives en 1993, *Premières Synthèses*, Direction de l'animation de la recherche, des études et des statistiques (DARES), **66**, 18 August, 1–8.

Blanchet, D. and Marchand, O. (1991) Au-delà de l'an 2000, s'adapter à une pénurie de main d'oeuvre, *Economie et Statistiques*, **243**, May, 61–7.

Briec, N. (1994) Préretraites progressives: le bond en avant, *Partenaires*, Ministère du Travail, de l'Emploi et de la Formation Professionnelle, **50**, 1–15 March, 4–5.

Burdillat, N. and Charpentier, P. (1995) Les préretraites progressives: entre gestion des sureffectifs et partage du travail, *Les Cahiers de Recherche*, **67**: whole issue (January), GIP Mutations industrielles.

Coudert, V. (1993) Les effets du vieillissement sur la croissance à long terme dans les pays industrialisés, *Problèmes Economiques*, La Documentation Française, **2330**, 24–31.

De Block, C. (1994) *Travail, emploi et vieillissement*. Paris: La Documentation Française, 180–5.

Desplanques, G. (1993) Activité féminine et vie familiale, *Economie et Statistiques*, INSEE, **261**, 23–44.

Elbaum, M. and Marchand, O. (1993) Emploi et chômage des jeunes dans les pays industrialisés; la spécificité française, *Premières synthèses*, Ministère du Travail, de l'Emploi et de la Formation Professionnelle/DARES, **34**: whole issue, October.

L'Essor des préretraites progressives (1995) *Partenaires*, Ministère du Travail, de l'Emploi et de la Formation Professionelle, **7**, 9 January.

Frémeaux, P. (1995) Productivité et emploi, *Alternatives Economiques*, **123**, January, 33–6.

Gaullier, X. (1990) La mutation des âges, *Le Débat*, September, 116–37.

Gaullier, X. (1994) La transition emploi activité retraite, *Travail, emploi et vieillissement, bilans et rapports*, La Documentation Française (Colloque européen du 22/23 November 1993), 151.

Guillemard, A.-M. (1994) Attitudes et opinions des entreprises à l'égard des salariés âgés et du vieillissement de la main d'oeuvre, *Emploi et Vieillissement, Cahier Travail et Emploi*, La Documentation Française, April, 57–77.

Guillemot, D. and Marchand, O. (1993) 1982–1990: la population active continue à croître, *Economie et Statistiques*, **261**, 7–21.

Herzlich, G. (1994) Une France plus peuplée et plus vieille au XXIème siècle, *Le Monde*, 30 November, p. 21.

Huet, M. (1994) Les attitudes des entreprises vis-à-vis des travailleurs vieillissants, *Emploi et Vieillissement, Cahier Travail et Emploi*, La Documentation Française, April, 71–7.

Kerschen, N. (1994) La préretraite comme statut et comme instrument, *Revue Française des Affaires Sociales*, January, 45–50.

Lebaube, A. (1994) Les jeunes défavorisés, *Le Monde Dossiers et Documents*, Dernier état de la France, **221** (May), 3.

Le Minez, S. (1994) Evolution des structures par âge de l'emploi, *Emploi et Vieillissement, Cahier Travail et Emploi*, La Documentation Française, April, 27–8.

Molinié, A.-F. and Volkoff, S. (1993) Conditions de travail: des difficultés à prévoir pour les plus de 40 ans, *Données Sociales*, INSEE, 195–201.

Normand, J.-M. (1994) Le monde du travail pris en étau, *Le Monde Dossiers et Documents*, La population française, **224**, September, 3.

Projections démographiques. Population de la France à l'horizon 2050 (1994), *Economie et Statistiques*, INSEE, **274**, December: whole issue.

Salzberg, L. and Baktavatsalou, R. (1994) Le temps partiel après 50 ans, *Emploi et Vieillissement, Cahier Travail et Emploi*, La Documentation Française, April, 79–88.

Servin, M.-J. (1995) La part des 25–49 ans, *Partenaires*, Ministère du Travail, de l'Emploi et de la Formation Professionnelle, **7**, 9 January, 4–5.

Temam, D. (1994) Les limites du système des préretraites, *Problèmes Economiques*, La Documentation Française, **2381**, 22 June, 14–16.

Volkoff, S., Laville, A. and Maillard, M.-C. (1992) Ages et travail: contraintes, sélection et difficultés chez les 40–50 ans, *Travail et Emploi*, **54**, April, 20–3.

10.

Strands of militancy in the history of the CGT

MICHEL DREYFUS

TRANSLATED BY ANABEL TAYLOR

Throughout this book the consequences of demographic evolution are being examined. One further aspect, which is the subject of this chapter and which has implications for current social policy, is the historical nature of union defence of social rights in France. September 1995 marked the centenary of the CGT (Confédération générale du travail, General Confederation of Labour): it was then, between 23 and 28 September 1895, that 75 delegates from a wide variety of trade union groups laid the foundations for this organization at a congress held in Limoges (Dreyfus, 1995; Groux and Mouriaux, 1992; Labbé, 1994). Today however there is little occasion for happy celebration of the first century of French trade unionism. Like all trade union organizations in France, the CGT has been in crisis for over a decade, as shown by that harsh but indisputable barometer, the number of its members. Since 1975, membership has declined from 2,370,000 to 630,000, which is one of the lowest figures recorded in the history of the organization, even lower than the combined memberships of the CGT and the CGTU (Confédération générale du travail unitaire) immediately after they split in 1921.

One hundred years of militancy

There is therefore no room for rejoicing, as Louis Viannet, the leader of the CGT since 1992, admitted when he became the first General Secretary of the CGT to attend a Congress of the CFDT (Confédération française démocratique du travail) at Montpellier in March 1995. By claiming 650,000 members at that time, the CFDT established itself as the leading group of affiliated trade unions in France. Whether or not this is true is not the issue: the CGT, like all trade union groups, faces

Table 10.1 Membership of the CGT from 1920 to 1995

Year	Membership
1920	2,000,000
1921	700,000
1937 (March)	3,900,000
1940 (April)	500,000
1945	3,700,000
1948	2,000,000
1975	2,377,000
1995	630,000

Source: Dreyfus, 1995

serious problems. Nevertheless, however critical the situation may be, it should be seen in the wider context, in that it merely emphasizes the problem constantly underlying the trade union movement in France: lack of members. This can be eloquently shown with a few statistics. With some 400,000 members in 1913, the CGT mustered only 7 to 8 per cent of the potentially organizable workforce, whereas German and British trade unions attracted three times this figure (Louis, 1913). The CGT has witnessed extraordinary swings in its membership, with sharp rises followed by equally strong declines; this is shown in Table 10.1.

In spite of these shifts, which characterize the history of the CGT, the inescapable fact remains that the oldest and most powerful trade union organization in France, outside some brief and exceptional periods, has never recruited more than 20 per cent of the workforce. This reflects a general trend in French trade unionism, the deep-rooted causes of which go back to the French Revolution and the upheavals of the early years of the CGT.

The difficult early years

The story begins with the French Revolution, and the infamous Le Chapelier law of June 1791 as Jaurès described it (Gibaud, 1989) against organized labour, which abolished the ancient structures that the working population had struggled to establish (brotherhoods, corporations and companionships). From that date, the only option for organization available to the workers were the Sociétés de secours mutuels (mutual aid or 'friendly' societies) which, until the Second Republic, were still tolerated by the authorities. While these societies could be dangerous – they often provoked popular uprisings – they served none the less to relieve the worst excesses of poverty in that era of primitive capitalism, when there were no labour laws and social welfare was almost completely non-existent. Often with paltry funds, mutual aid societies fulfilled the dual role of pre-syndicalist labour organization and the provision of financial assistance.

This rough equilibrium was upset by Napoleon III, who, from the first years of the Empire, made a radical distinction between protest movements and administrative organizations. He could not have imagined the impact of his reforms on the social history of France. With the creation, from March 1852, of an 'approved' network of mutual aid societies, sometimes known as 'Imperial' mutual aid societies, Napoleon laid the foundations for an organization which was soon able to exercise effective social control over the popular masses. These 'Imperial' societies had several advantages over their competitors, but the cost of these was the loss of all independence; the presidents of these societies were appointed by the local government representative, the Prefect, to whom they were obliged to give guarantees of good behaviour. From this time, moralization and apolitical attitudes combined to turn these societies into pillars of the Establishment. In addition, the societies were now tied to the geographical boundaries of each Commune, whereas a large number had previously been organized on the basis of a profession, providing a pre-syndical blueprint for labour organization. These groups were effectively controlled by 'honorary members', local dignitaries who were loyal to the authorities, and who were placed in charge of administration. Conversely, the members who actually received the insurance benefits were not allowed to be involved with management. The societies, which crossed class barriers and represented the essence of the mutual aid system, became perfect guarantors of the established order (Hatzfeld, 1989; Gibaud, 1986; Saint-Jours *et al.*, 1990).

The Napoleonic reforms were a complete success. By the end of the Empire, the 'approved' societies represented three-fifths of all mutual aid society membership. 670,000 members organized in 4,400 societies were strictly controlled by 110,000 honorary members (Gueslin, 1987). It should be noted that these figures were much higher than those of the CGT, which in 1914 only had some 400,000 members.

For the next half century and more, the rift between the syndicalists and the 'mutualists' widened considerably. The latter were almost absent from the Commune fighting of 1871, except perhaps in Marseilles and Lyons. This split explains the very strong influence of revolutionary syndicalism in the CGT during its early years. Anything reformist or administrative in nature was more likely to be taken over by the syndicalists. Conversely, and in contrast to their German and British counterparts, the vast majority of French syndicalists favoured protest and developed a culture of dispute, ruining opportunities for assimilation. Thus, the revolutionary spirit of syndicalism burnt fiercely up until the eve of the First World War, which accounts for the trade union organizations' lack of interest in providing 'services' (Pigenet, 1993) (such as educational or cultural activities), or in any issue related to health (Rebérioux, 1989) and social welfare, which they considered contemptible, and left to the despised mutualists.

In April and May 1906, the CGT faced a test of fire in the form of widespread strikes, and passed with flying colours, winning the right to be considered a national organization. However, this success was followed by a 'calm' period, during which the Confederation discovered the difficulty of maintaining its membership levels. This was particularly evident when the *Retraites ouvrières et paysannes* (Workers' and Peasants' Pensions) were introduced in 1910; it was the first attempt to establish a universal, obligatory pension scheme for the poorest categories of wage earners. Introduced after a mere 30 years of debate, it was a modest scheme which in 1913 covered at best only 3.5 million people. Its supporters were not to know that they were opening the path to the social security system of 1945. The CGT was strongly opposed to this first measure, predominantly because it feared that it would encourage a process of integration with the state. The CGT therefore refused to uphold this law any more than any of the legislation drafted by the state it sought to overthrow, and denounced the new pensions as 'pensions of the dead'. It is true that they were paid to workers aged 65 and over at a time when the average life expectancy of the population was little more than 50 years (Guillaume, 1993). The issue reveals the culture of protest which dominated the CGT.

All of these reasons combined explain the Confederation's low membership levels up to 1914. It was not until much later, after the Popular Front and, more significantly, after the Liberation, that this state of affairs began to change, and the CGT began to gain experience in social welfare administration.

The CGT and social welfare administration after the Liberation

It is not possible in this chapter to cover the entire history of the CGT from 1914 to 1945. Let us focus on the fact that this history, marked by numerous splits and fusions (1921, 1936, 1939, 1943 and 1947–8, with the creation of the CGT–FO (Force ouvrière),[1] is woven around two important strands of left-wing history.

The first of these is the rise in power of the former Unitarians, the Communists, who, having held the majority in the CGTU from 1924–5, were once again in the minority when the CGT and the CGTU reunited in March 1936 at the Congress of Toulouse. During the Popular Front, the Communist Party experienced a great surge in membership, and by 1937–38, the ex-Unitarians had gained a majority in the CGT, although they still did not run it. The Second World War was an extraordinarily difficult period for the CGT: one of the first acts of the Vichy Government was to dissolve it in July 1940. In its aftermath, the Communist syndicalists were able to benefit from their activities in the Resistance. Like the Communist Party (Buton, 1993), the CGT experienced a new surge after the Liberation, with the ex-Unitarians gaining a substantial majority (80 per cent) at the twentieth National Congress in April 1946, the first time since 1938. From that time, the CGT became the right arm of the Communist Party and, although the relationship between the two organizations was often far more complicated than it appeared, this state of affairs has continued until the present.

The second strand began with the CGT's increased skill at management and negotiation. For the faction which supported Léon Jouhaux, General Secretary of the CGT from 1909 to 1947, these skills were first learnt during the First World War, when the CGT joined the coalition government, known as the Union sacrée (Sacred Union) (Robert, 1989; Horne, 1991). This faction practised a policy of taking a seat at the negotiating table at every opportunity in order to defend workers' rights. During the 1920s, the Communist syndicalists denounced this tendency, which they saw as treason. However, they themselves began to take up these issues during the Popular Front, encouraged by the social benefits which were achieved, particularly paid holidays. For a long time, these were the symbol of the Popular Front: workers must have holidays, and the means to achieve this goal must be secured. The rapid rise in membership, and therefore in contributions, enabled a number of leisure centres to be built which were run by the Communist syndicalists. However, very soon this experiment was brought to a sudden end by the Second World War.

The Liberation gave a great boost to this new appreciation of the value of administrative responsibility. Three important reforms were introduced during the period of national reconstruction which primarily affected the delegates of the CGT: the policy of nationalization; the creation of Enterprise Committees; and the introduction of the social security system. The Communist syndicalists, who had first learnt the value of such activity alongside the mutualists during the Popular Front, revived the trend with even greater enthusiasm after 1945. The Communists, therefore, had good reasons for wishing to see more activity in the area of social welfare administration. This development did not follow a straightforward chronological pattern: the impact of the Cold War after 1947 to 1948 caused the Communist Party and the CGT to break away from the policies pursued between 1944 and 1947, known as the 'bataille de la production' (Lacroix-Riz, 1983).

However, the CGT continued to steer a course towards increased social administration activity throughout the 1950s and the 1960s, in spite of the political storms which ensued (Leterrier and Trempé, 1994). Certainly, economic circumstances during the *trente glorieuses* (1945–75) had favoured the general improvement of living and working conditions, and encouraged continuing interest in better welfare provision.

The Conseil central des oeuvres sociales (Central Council for Public Works, known today as the Caisse centrale d'activités sociales, CCAS) was established as a sort of umbrella Comité d'entreprise (Enterprise committees set up to provide a works forum for employers and employees), accommodating the Comités d'entreprise of Electricité de France–Gaz de France (nationalized in 1946), Renault (nationalized in 1945) and RATP (the Paris passenger transport system), as well as various metal processing and aviation factories. The number of these committees rose steadily until there were some 4000 by 1958. When the first elections for the Comités d'entreprise were held in 1946, the CGT gained almost 80 per cent of the vote (Labbé, 1994), leaving only a small share for the other trade union group, the CFTC (Confédération française des travailleurs chrétiens), which had been founded in 1919, but the membership of which, by 1937, was still only one-tenth the size of that of the CGT.

The trend carried on during the 1960s, with the trade unionists continuing to dominate the Comités d'entreprise: in 1966, the combined trade union groups (CGT, CFDT, CFTC, CGC and FO) gained almost 82 per cent of the vote. But the economic crisis which erupted in France in 1973, and which intensified after the second oil crisis of 1979, undermined the strength of the trade unions, even in the Comités d'entreprise. In 1993 the CGT was still the leading trade union organization in France, but it had lost one-fifth of its electorate.

It was not therefore until half-way through its current lifetime that the CGT showed an interest in social welfare. It took the political and social upheavals of the Popular Front and the Liberation to lead the way. Until then, the CGT had paid dearly for its lack of such interest with low membership levels and insufficient funding. After the Liberation, by contrast, awareness of the importance of social welfare administration increased, as shown by the example of the Fédération de l'énergie, which protects the employees of the EDF–GDF. The influence of the CGT, and the level of union membership, have been particularly strong in the energy sector since nationalization, although the Federation, like the CGT, has declined in strength recently. Like all trade union movements, it was badly affected by the crisis.

Four reasons combine to explain the current crisis in the CGT which, to repeat, is affecting all trade union groups in France, not to mention the rest of Europe.

Firstly, there are the effects of the economic crisis in industry. Between 1982 and 1990, in France, over 800,000 jobs were lost in industry, particularly the traditional bastions of the CGT: mining in the north of France, iron and steel manufacturing in Lorraine, shipbuilding in the Marseilles region and so on. The strength of the secondary sector declined steadily over the same period, while white-collar tertiary activities, the most resistant to trade union organization, increased. These economic changes were accompanied by an unprecedented growth in unemployment, from 1 million in 1975 rising to 1.5 million in 1980 and more than 3 million at the time of writing. Over the last decade there has been considerable growth in temporary employment: currently there are possibly as many as 3.5 million part-time workers (*Alternatives Economiques*, 1995: 7).

The second reason is the decline, since the Liberation, of the French Communist Party, the most powerful in Europe alongside the ancient Italian Communist Party. Just as the growth of the Communist Party and the CGT went hand in hand during the Popular Front and after the Liberation, so their respective problems today are closely linked. In the presidential election of 1969, the Communist Party candidate, J. Duclos, gained 21 per cent of the vote. In the presidential election of May 1995, R. Hue managed to get 8.4 per cent of the vote, which was an improvement, albeit small, on the result obtained by A. Lajoinie seven years previously. The question which arises today is whether the crisis in the Communist Party has caused the crisis in the CGT or vice versa.

The changes which have taken place throughout Eastern Europe since the break-up of the Soviet Union in 1989–91 have deepened the crisis of French Communism, although it is still difficult to assess the exact extent of the damage: several militants had already distanced themselves to some extent from the influence of the Socialist states, which seemed to have become a less and less satisfactory role model. Nevertheless, as we shall see, these changes have had a direct effect on the international ties maintained by the CGT.

Lastly, the policy of denationalization and privatization pursued in France since 1986 has sapped the strength of the public sector, where the CGT, like other trade union organizations, was well established. There is now a new general attitude in French society, a wind of change which is quite different from the feeling which existed from the time of the Popular Front until the first three years of the Mitterrand era. Until then, the notion of nationalization had continued to gain support, whereas now feelings have turned against this. To take just one example: the Renault car factory is soon to be privatized, a fact which has provoked scarcely a ripple of protest. We should recall the controversy between the Socialist and Communist parties during the discussions on the updating of the Common Programme, where one of the pretexts put forward to justify the split was disagreement over the number of nationalizations.

The reasons for the trade union crisis come from changes at the heart of French society. In spite of their efforts to confront the crisis, it is uncertain whether the trade union organizations have considered all of the consequences.

Conclusion

Confining ourselves to the CGT, let us conclude by pointing out some of the limited changes in direction which could point to an awareness of these difficulties. At the 1995 presidential election, the CGT gave no voting recommendation, unlike previous elections, when it has supported the Communist Party candidates in the preliminary round. At its forty-fifth congress in December 1995, the CGT was officially to leave the World Federation of Trade Unions, to which it had been linked since the 1940s. This is a direct consequence of the break-up of the Soviet Union, since the Federation is now only a shadow of its former self. Will this step lead to closer links with the European Confederation of Trade Unions, which has been the CGT's unfulfilled goal for several years?

In addition, by being prepared to meet Jean Gandois, the new head of the Conseil national du patronat français (the National Council of French Employers) officially in January 1995, Louis Viannet has broken a taboo: the last meeting between these two organizations took place in

1978. The CGT, with other trade union organizations, has accepted the need to enter into negotiations, particularly regarding the reduction of working hours. It is too early to know whether these negotiations will achieve anything, but the simple fact of the CGT agreeing to participate is a significant event for social issues in France.

Finally, the presence of L. Viannet at the last national congress of the CFDT (Montpellier, March 1995), already mentioned above, is perhaps evidence of a stronger desire for unity amongst trade unions. At his return speech held, on the occasion of the centenary, on 12 September 1995 at Limoges, the General Secretary of the CGT reported the overwhelmingly awful state of health of French trade unionism, under-mined by its divisions (Costemalle, 1995: 21). Surely, these have been around throughout its entire history. All through 1995, the CGT celebrated its centenary with numerous initiatives. These have allowed it to reflect on the different strands of militancy which are woven into its history, and still mark it today.

Notes

1. The CGT–FO (Confédération générale du travail–Force ouvrière), usually known by its shortened title FO, was created after a split within the CGT at the end of 1947. Its relations with the CGT have since been fundamentally marked by its anti-Communism.

References

Alternatives Économiques (1995), **130**, September–October: whole issue.

Buton, P. (1993) *Les Lendemains qui déchantent. Le PCF à la Libération.* Paris: FNSP.

Costemalle O. (1995) Rentrée d'attaque pour Viannet, *Libération*, 13 September.

Dreyfus M. (1995) *Histoire de la CGT. Cent Ans de syndicalisme en France.* Bruxelles: Edition Complexe.

Gibaud, B. (1986) *De la mutualité à la sécurité sociale.* Paris: Editions Ouvrières.

Gibaud, B. (1989) *Révolution et droit d'association.* Paris: Mutualité française.

Groux, G. and Mouriaux, R. (1992) *La CGT. Crises et alternatives.* Paris: Economica.

Gueslin, A. (1987) *L'Invention de l'économie sociale.* Paris: Economica.

Guillaume, P. (1993) *Histoire sociale de la France au XXème siècle.* Paris: Masson.

Hatzfeld, H. (1971) *Du paupérisme à la sécurité sociale, 1850–1940*. Paris: A. Colin, republished by Presses Universitaires de Nancy, 1989.

Horne, J.H. (1991) *Labour at War. France and Britain, 1914–1918*. Oxford: Clarendon Press.

Labbé, D. (1994) Les travaux sur la CGT, 1945–1993, *Communisme*, special edition (Les Communistes et la CGT), **35–7**, 191–237.

Labbé, D. (1995) *Les Elections aux comités d'entreprises (1945–1993)*. Grenoble: CERAT.

Lacroix-Riz, A. (1983) *La CGT de la Libération à la scission, de 1944 à 1947*. Paris: Editions Sociales.

Leterrier, J.M. and Trempé, R. (1994) *Construire. Protection sociale et activités culturelles*. Montreuil: Editions CCAS.

Louis, P. (1913) L'état présent du syndicalisme mondial, *Mémoires et Documents du Musée Social, Paris*, 165–84.

Ouvrage Collectif (1995) *CGT, 1895–1995. Le premier siècle*. Paris: VO Editions.

Pigenet, M. (1993) Prestations et services dans le mouvement syndical français (1860–1914), *Cahiers d'Histoire de l'Institut de Recherches Marxistes*, **51**, 7–28.

Rebérioux, M. (1989) Mouvement syndical et santé. France, 1880–1914, *Prévenir*, special issue, **18–19**, Mouvement ouvrier et santé: une comparaison internationale, 15–30.

Robert, J.L. (1989) Mouvements ouvriers parisiens pendant la Grande Guerre et l'immédiat après-guerre. Histoire et anthropologie. Unpublished thesis, Université de Paris I.

Saint-Jours, Y., Dreyfus, M. and Durand, D. (1990) *La Mutualité. Histoire, droit, sociologie*. Paris: LGDJ.

11.

An ecologist's critique of work in France

FRANÇOISE GOLLAIN

Chapter 9 examined the likelihood of employers altering working practices to cater for a potential labour shortage in the future. Chapter 10 introduced the essential characteristics of organized labour in France and its traditional response to changing employment patterns. As with the demographic hot potato issue of population replacement examined in earlier chapters, there is not always a consensus about whether or not there is likely to be a shortage of labour. A novel approach to the question of who should be in work and for how long is the French ecologist interpretation outlined in this chapter.

Unemployment, currently prevalent in France and other European countries and affecting an ever-increasing percentage of the population, is not the temporary phenomenon of a crisis to be solved upon the resumption of economic growth. Behind the unemployment problem there is in fact a formidable revolution of work as a social value, practice and source of citizenship, which is shaking the very foundations of modernity. According to the leading figures of the French political ecology movement, Marxist philosopher André Gorz and sociologist Guy Aznar, 'la société de travail est caduque' (the society of work is obsolete) (Gorz, 1988: 70) or more humorously, 'le travail c'est fini' (work is finished) (Aznar, 1990). This means not simply that we are living through an economic crisis, but that our civilization has entered a period of profound transformation, of which the crisis of work is a blatant symptom.

Confronting a change of era

Let us examine this transformation in more detail. For the first time in the history of humanity, the driving force of economic growth has shifted away from the mastery of energy to the mastery of information systems. In order to illustrate the importance of this phenomenon, ecology-motivated thinkers compare this major shift with the advent of the neolithic era which saw the invention of agriculture (Robin, 1989).

After the higher labour demands of the energy-based order, which reached its peak with the Industrial Revolution, the revolution of information technology now entails a net saving of labour. In every industrialized country human labour was the major productive force, but now the irrepressible and accelerated trend towards a global reduction of the labour time needed to produce consumer goods and services has drastically reduced the number of full-time jobs.

In other words, our economic system produces an increasing amount of wealth with a decreasing quantity of labour. Studies indeed show that the total number of working hours offered by French companies is increasing systematically more slowly than the potential working population. Between 1896 and 1991 employment expanded with the creation of fewer than 1.6 million jobs while the active population increased by 3.6 million. The microchip revolution has thus merely served to exacerbate this trend (Rigaudiat, 1993: 80). The INSEE data indicate that this population will increase by 0.5 per cent in France by the year 2000. The number of French people of working age will represent 26.7 per cent of the total population by 2005, compared with 24.2 per cent at the time of writing; equivalent, if all the other factors are constant, to 2.5 per cent more unemployed (Aznar, 1993: 37).[1] The forecast of the intellectuals among the Greens (as well as other commentators on the French Left) is that this shortage is expected to worsen thanks to predictable technological improvements, and if the present norm of full-time employment remains the need for labour will continue to decline rapidly.

This phenomenon has radical and permanent implications for the structure of employment. Having begun with agriculture, followed by industry, with the current revolution of information technology, the service sector, including qualified posts, is affected too, despite having provided the majority of new jobs over recent decades.

> Avec l'automation informatisée qui s'étendra bientôt à la quasi-totalité des secteurs, la quantité de travail fournie n'a plus qu'un lointain rapport avec la quantité de richesses produites; ... Il faut donc désormais faire toute sa place au paradoxe d'une création de richesses avec perte et non création d'emplois.[2]
>
> (Robin, 1989: 33)

To be precise, it is worth adding that the savings in labour are not just the product of the computerization and automation process but also of a more accurate, flexible, hence efficient use of human resources, which has become of vital importance in the present context of harsh international competition. This is what is meant by the generic term 'flexibility' which takes very different forms. What is probably most relevant to this issue is that, in many companies, the core of workers on a permanent contract is declining. The United States and Britain in particular exemplify future trends: in these two countries both job seekers and casual or part-time workers account for more than 45 per cent of the total working population. As Gorz pointed out in 1991, 90 per cent of the jobs created in the previous five years in Britain have been temporary and/or part-time posts (Gorz, 1991: 55–6; 1994: 46).

According to the supporters of political ecology, the implications of this trend clearly indicate the type of employment policies which need implementing. This unprecedented situation makes unworkable any adjustments using traditional methods, whether Keynesian or neo-liberal. The erosion of the link between wealth creation and job creation in particular is destroying the credibility of the traditional argument that a return to economic growth will solve our employment ills. The (fragile) return of growth regularly publicized by the media will, on the contrary, increase the numbers of people disenfranchised.

The Green thinker Jacques Robin claims that, beyond the economic domain itself, it is vital to give serious thought to the deep changes in the social and cultural order occurring as a result of information technology. The issue of work is too global and fundamental to be left to the economists alone; rather a multidisciplinary approach is the appropriate way to meet the psychological and socio-cultural transformation we are facing. Along these lines, in 1983, Robin founded GRIT (Groupe de réflexion inter et transdisciplinaire) which produces the biannual newsletter *Transversales science/culture* and acts as a forum where different approaches can meet.

What makes the thinkers of political ecology interesting, in the opinion of the author, is that they have been the first in France to draw attention to facts which have since become universally accepted, and to express the urgent need for a radical rethink about work in its many dimensions. They have contributed greatly to the widely debated issue. It is worth noting here the originality of both the French and the German contributions in Europe. Thus, through the impetus of the German Greens (*die Grünen*), the crisis of work and of our work-based civilization has been lying at the centre of an intellectual debate for the last ten years in Germany.

Alongside their radical critique of the employment policies implemented in France, the aim of this chapter is to introduce the founding principle of the alternative, as supported by André Gorz and Guy Aznar (and other Green thinkers). Because of the constraints of the chapter, it is impossible to go into the fine detail of the current debates – however productive and exciting they may be – about the methods of implementation of this alternative put forward by the various strands of French political ecology. Furthermore, rather than reviewing the Green Parties' political programmes which are relatively better known through election campaigns, a brief account of these intellectual analyses is considered, which the author believes to be of interest and still little known on this side of the English Channel.

The critique of employment policies

For the theorists in the field of political ecology, it is beyond doubt that the numerous measures which are part of an economic and/or social 'treatment' of unemployment are now reaching their limits. Instead of a far-reaching political intervention in order to develop a policy appropriate to the gravity of the structural decline in the need for human labour, successive governments are confined to contain social damage: unemployment benefit, RMI (*revenu minimum d'insertion*),[3] early retirement, subsidies to various training schemes and 'back to work' contracts and so on. The result of this has merely been an alarming rise in social costs, leading to an explosion of the social security budgets feeding the crisis of the welfare state. Thus, the funds allocated to the employment budget for 1996 (138.2 billion francs) show a 6.7 per cent increase over 1995 (*Le Monde*, 10 August 1995: 7).

Against a dual society

At the root of the problem are the general directions of the policies being implemented, in particular, the increase of the various forms of work flexibility, which is proving to be of benefit to employers but seldom to employees. In this respect, the five-year plan on employment, adopted in parliament in autumn 1993, clearly reinforces the trend observed over the last ten years in that it grants businesses greater flexibility on matters such as employment contracts and working hours (*droit social*, 1994). This flexibility goes alongside a tendency towards lowering the cost of labour, qualified as well as unqualified, and the undermining of certain employment and social rights.

The aborted plan of the CIP (*contrat d'insertion professionnelle des jeunes*), named SMIC-jeunes by its opponents, or the lower social security contributions on the part of employers allowed in the case of low-paid jobs are an example. This drop comes after the numerous and attractive cuts in contributions already granted to businesses in order to boost job creation. While the creation of wealth by the economy continues, these policies, according to the Greens, do nothing but reinforce the process currently known as *dualisation de la société* (creation of a dual society). Coined during the presidency of V. Giscard d'Estaing (1974–81), the term *socio-économie duale* conceptualizes the split of French society into two sectors resulting from the fragmentation of the employment market: on the one hand, a very efficient sector open to international competition, employing a stable, well-motivated, qualified and highly paid workforce: on the other hand, a protected sector of essentially craft and tertiary activities, such as the tourist industry, private security firms, contract cleaning, sales and, increasingly, personal and home services, which are often thankless, seasonal or temporary, and badly paid.

Against the new service sector jobs and part-time work

The jobs newly created in the service sector have recently been considered (and still are) as employment gold mines by the various governments. This type of work has been subjected to caustic attacks from Green intellectuals – especially those jobs traditionally belonging to the domestic sphere – because they represent the quintessence of the dual society. Childminding, basic nursing, home cleaners, home delivery of pizzas and so on, are mainly low-skilled jobs with low wages, often of a casual nature and part-time. According to Gorz, they only exist:

> parce que ceux et celles qui assument une heure de tâches domestiques à votre place gagnent beaucoup moins que vous-même pouvez gagner en une heure de votre travail. Les services personnels se développent grâce à la paupérisation d'une masse croissante de gens, paupérisation constatée tant en Amérique du Nord qu'en Europe occidentale.[4]
>
> (Gorz, 1991: 62)

In other words, their development:

n'est possible que dans un contexte d'inégalité sociale croissante où une partie de la population accapare les activités bien rémunérées et contraint une autre partie au rôle de serviteur.[5]

(Gorz, 1988: 195)

If, as it is often claimed, 'the future lies in the service industry', Gorz invites us to question the model of society which we are being promised, pointing out similarities with the Victorian era, during which thousands of jobless offered their labour as servants as a result of the concentration of agricultural land and mechanization in the textile industry. This group represented 14 per cent of the working British population between 1851 and 1911 (Gorz, 1988: 273; 1989: 226).

In this context, the policy encouraging the development of part-time work (with a proportional drop in pay) is viewed by ecologists as the laissez-faire, and positively unacceptable, version of the 'sharing of work'. Full-time jobs with full wages tend to become a privilege, whilst the substantial reduction of work hours with commensurate reduction in wage levels – in other words, partial, unpaid redundancy – is a practice which is spreading, even in the public sector. Statistics clearly show that part-time work, wrongly named *temps choisi*, literally 'chosen time', concerns posts which have an 80 per cent female workforce and are, once again, low skilled and offer little job security.

The diagnosis made by Green intellectuals is therefore irrefutable. Unemployment, underemployment, impoverishment and, also, marginalization of an increasing portion of French society: all of this perfectly illustrates the fact that today, our culture proves incapable of producing effective regulatory mechanisms, suited to the progress of productivity. The employment policies implemented by the Right and the Left alike under various labels over the last 10 to 15 years have failed and have been detrimental to employees. The only viable alternative is to campaign against a dual society by carrying out an active policy of reduction of work hours.

For a real sharing of work

To try and slow down productivity would be suicidal in the present climate of intense international competition. It would also be unrealistic to hope to alter the mechanisms of the job market. Therefore, not only the militants of the Green and alternative circles, but also a fraction of the Left and a few free-market thinkers, are convinced that a real policy of work-sharing will eventually be viewed as essential in solving the devastating effects of social exclusion. The historic theme of the reduction of work hours, revived by Alain Lipietz, candidate of Les Verts (the French Greens), and recycled by the Socialists during the electoral campaign in March 1993, has returned to the public arena.

Equally, although it has not always translated into law, work-sharing has now acquired a new legitimacy: since 1992, the number of such agreements signed jointly by trade unions and management in order to save jobs has soared. However, this is merely sharing of unemployment, and should not be mistaken for genuine sharing of work. Against a background of high unemployment, this 'choice' is often actually experienced by the workers as an ultimatum, and to accept it is an ultimate solidarity gesture and, of course, survival strategy.

The questions are now clear: a reduction in working hours is presently taking place and will continue to do so, but what form will it take? Will it mean social regression or, on the contrary, social progress? According to the Green theorists, what is essentially (and implicitly) at stake in the debate on shorter working hours is: must the waged society we have known since the *Trente Glorieuses* (1945–75) be saved or not?

The ecologists' answer is that we have to transcend waged society by going beyond *ad hoc* measures of limited efficiency. We have to differentiate between measures of an essentially temporary nature which aim at reducing existing unemployment from a policy of progressive, long-term redistribution of work, of collectively produced wealth and of time freed thanks to increased productivity. This distinction is essential in Gorz's works:

> La réduction de la durée du travail sans perte de revenu doit être comprise non comme une mesure mais comme une politique d'ensemble suivie. Il ne s'agit pas de redistribuer les emplois et les ressources qui existent mais de gouverner en s'inscrivant dans sa dynamique, un processus qui exige de moins en moins de travail mais crée de plus en plus de richesses.[6]
>
> (Gorz, 1988: 246)

The reduction in working hours is part of a wider vision of social transformation and represents the leading principle of social and political action:

> Elle doit être le but que la société se donne, donc la variable indépendante à laquelle toutes les autres variables vont être appelées à s'ajuster en un laps de temps déterminé.[7]
>
> (Gorz, 1988: 246)

This society will be the society of 'extra leisure' time.

Once the necessity of a law requiring all businesses to comply with the obligation to negotiate in a given time is accepted, the detail of such law would remain to be determined, and it is precisely on this point that the scenarios differ. This debate – even controversy – within the field of political ecology fairly clearly reflects the vitality of the national debate and the wide range of points of view involved: a general reduction to a 35-hour and even a 32-hour working week, for example, or an encouragement to adopt the principle of *temps choisi*? The part to be played respectively by legislative initiative and decentralized negotiations? The pace of this process of shortening work hours? A total compensation for loss of pay or not? For all or for low wage earners only? (But what is a low wage?) Or a more radical type of redistribution (see below)?

As should have become clear, the variables, and therefore the scope for choice, are numerous and complex, and for this reason, we will simply limit ourselves to defining the essence of the critique of work by political ecologists in France.

Sharing income too ...

Although a number of disagreements remain concerning the strategies to adopt, the general philosophy is the same everywhere: a redistribution of work must necessarily be accompanied by a redistribution of income. No argument in support of a reorganization of working hours is valid unless it includes a rethink of sources of income. What is raised again here is the whole issue of the future of a fair distribution of income: since work is no longer the measure of wealth, the size of the income should no longer depend on the actual quantity of labour supplied.

Here again the constraints of an international economic context are accepted: no plan for a redistribution of work is credible if it supposes that companies' overheads will suddenly be increased by imposing extra labour costs likely to impact on their competitivity, or that a further burden will be placed on public finances when the latter are already in a dire state: a double constraint which may well be expected to give rise to harsh debate about a new, balanced formula for redistributing income. The basic argument however is that we must stop considering wages as a unique source of income – they are no longer so, if we take into account the increasing share of social benefits in the total household budget (family allowances for example). The concept of a 'wage' is linked inextricably to a particular industrial society. Today:

la nouvelle civilisation informationnelle nécessite que l'on invente un
concept nouveau pour assurer la redistribution des richesses produites
collectivement avec moins d'hommes et beaucoup de robots.[8]

(Aznar, 1993: 103)

Different versions of this new concept exist. Some authors, who
develop fully the logic of a lack of quantifiable relationship between
work and pay, are part of a wider movement in favour of a *revenu
minimum d'existence* (basic income for living), or an *allocation universelle*
(universal allowance), also a *revenu de citoyenneté* (citizenship income),
which is at present the subject of an abundant literature in several
European countries. These labels refer in fact to quite different proposals. Let us say, however, that the common objective is to grant every
citizen the right to an income which gives her/him a decent living
standard with no implied obligation to work. No longer must 'worker'
and 'citizen' be indistinguishable concepts: the work ethic must become the ideology of the past (*Futuribles*, 1994).

On the other hand, Aznar and Gorz do warn against an overhasty
severing of the link between work and citizenship: waged work provides
a sense of belonging and of social worth. A lifelong allowance does not.
A leftist alternative proposal to a fragmented society is a society where
each citizen must and can work, but in fact works very little.

Aznar has therefore put forward his concept of a *deuxième chèque*
(second cheque), taken up subsequently by Gorz. Its principle is as
follows: every time the working hours are reduced, wages are lowered
proportionately, but employees are compensated for the resulting loss
of income from a guaranteed public fund. This is the second cheque,
which will pay for the hours freed up from work on the same basis as for
the hours actually worked. In an increasingly mechanized society in
which the role of human labour is systematically decreasing, the cheque
will tend to become by far the largest source of income. This second
cheque will be financed thanks to retargeting of the unemployment
budget and to a reorganization of the tax system (both direct and
indirect taxes): setting up eco-taxes for instance (Aznar, 1993: 101).
The choice of criteria for financing and targeting the fund will obviously be crucial.

Apart from the various problems concerning the implementation of
one formula or another, it will also be clear that the present debate
comes up against a number of philosophical and political issues, such as
the connection between solidarity and citizenship, the principles underlying social cohesion or the possible recasting of the social contract,

demanded by the present changes in work patterns. Such questions, which appear abstract, certainly difficult, will become more and more unavoidable in the coming years. Evaluation of, and comparison between, the different scenarios and economic models of the reduction of working hours currently taking place in France are necessary but do not go far enough because the problems raised by the multiform crisis of work are not essentially of a technical nature.

For a policy of (free) time

As well as the recognition of the need to combine the sharing of work and the sharing of income, the argument defended by the Green thinkers is essentially concerned with the best way to deploy time saved on work. The time savings at work must be equally distributed in the form of free time, for the current:

> incapacité de nos sociétés à fonder une civilisation du temps libéré a pour conséquence une distribution complètement absurde et scandaleusement injuste du travail, du temps disponible et des richesses.[9]
>
> (Gorz, 1991: 53)

Economic rationalization is the freeing up of time and will continue to be so and, therefore:

> la précarité de l'emploi, la dualisation de la société sont les formes perverties que prend la libération du temps que ce système social refuse d'avouer et d'assumer.[10]
>
> (Gorz, 1991: 66)

We must then conclude that the individual and collective appropriation of time is crucial to the ecological project of a post-industrial or information-based society.

At this point, the critique of work by French political ecologists converges with the contemporary works of the *sociologie des temps sociaux* (sociology of social time), the most advanced theses of which have been developed by Roger Sue in his latest book *Temps et ordre social* (Sue, 1994). He insists that a fundamental connection exists between work and modernity and reminds us that after 'the religious time' characterizing the Middle Ages, the 'time of work' has steadily become the major factor governing the social order throughout industrialized countries.

The principles underlying the organization of work, created and developed during the eighteenth and nineteenth centuries within companies, shaped attitudes and behaviour. In other words, work imposed itself as the structuring element of society and its time was the *temps pivot* (pivotal time), the *grand ordonnateur des temps sociaux* (the great regulator of social time) of industrialized civilization. The current crisis of work is therefore serious because it is related to this underlying principle of social regulation, to the dominant social time of modernity (Sue, 1994: 183). It follows that, for the sociologists of the sociology of time as well as for the thinkers of French political ecology, the revolution of work time must be considered in the context of a global project of social change.

For the preceding three centuries, work had been the fundamental factor of socialization for the individual. Now work time is rapidly disappearing from everyday life. The average working time represented 18 per cent of waking time in 1980 and 14 per cent in 1990 (Robin, 1994: 23). A quantitative transformation but, equally, a transformation of values: in the surveys of the sociology of leisure the instrumental value of work (work to make a living) is regularly at the top of people's motivations. For the individual in search of self-fulfilment, work is no longer at the centre of her/his life; fulfilment through freely chosen activities has, in just a few decades, overtaken fulfilment through paid work activities, imposed by the dominant social order.

Consequently, the challenge now is to allow free time which is dominant in practice to become so officially. The argument which places the emphasis on the value of work as the sole source of personal identity and social integration is anachronistic and conservative in the sense that it aspires to maintain a time structure which is obsolete. However, the end of work as the only basis of the social bond is still difficult to conceive. Jacques Robin (1994) has, in this respect, expressed his particular disappointment with a few prominent figures in the Socialist Party, such as Martine Aubry, Laurent Fabius and especially Michel Rocard, who had, at one time, appeared to be ready to make the length of time spent at work a key element of their plans to transform society.

Towards a society of full activity

To venture in a new direction would mean facilitating a reversal of the present relationship between the time devoted to work for economic reasons, and time devoted to leisure activities which do not belong to the sphere of the market. The principle is simple: in addition to work required to ensure the continued operation of the greater social machinery, one has to redistribute the time freed from work so that everyone can work less and less, and also better, and develop the abilities and human skills that work leaves fallow.

Over ten years ago, Aznar was already declaring: 'travailler à mi-temps, c'est vivre à double temps' (to work part-time is to live double-time) (Aznar, 1980: 136). To a dual society, he opposes the project of bipolar society where each individual belongs to the sphere of income-generating activities and to the sphere of autonomous activities. The only solution lies in the organization of a social space including two distinct spheres and a life punctuated by the movement from one to the other. This dual role represents, along with the redistribution of work and income, the third principle of an 'alternative' philosophy of work.

In Gorz's thought this division is linked to the conceptual opposition between the sphere of 'heteronomy' and the sphere of 'autonomy'.

Paid work belongs to the first sphere that Gorz defines as the totality of specialized activities that individuals have to accomplish as functions co-ordinated from the exterior by a pre-existing organization. The nature and content of these activities and the work relationships are 'heterodetermined' in order to get individuals and collectives to function as the wheels of a huge industrial, administrative or military machine. Postal and railway networks are a good example of this. Whatever the degree of self-determination granted in the tasks to be accomplished, their fundamental heteronomy does not disappear.

This type of work (waged, 'heteronomous') has not always been the dominant human activity. It has progressively become dominant throughout society only when the free-market exchanges which characterize capitalism became generalized. This generalization of waged work has progressed jointly with, on the one hand, specialization and a highly developed division of labour and, on the other hand, a terminal decline of the other forms of social exchange (including the traditional solidarity within neighbourhoods and other social groups).

However, it is out of the question, for Gorz, to be retrogressive and abolish waged work completely. Hence his opposition to the idea of a universal allowance. Moreover, he attacks the illusory and dangerous dream of a return to a pre-industrial self-sufficiency.

His purpose is not to liberate citizens from economically necessary work but to regain spheres of autonomy. The polarizing effect of work on the individual's lifestyle must be reduced by widening the field of non-professional activities, whose aims are chosen freely, and through which everyone will be able to cultivate the part of humanity which cannot be expressed through specialized and very often technicized work. This concept is the sphere of autonomy.

According to Gorz we have to strive to develop a new form of culture. By extending the range of available time slots, non-work time can stop being the reverse of time at work, that is to say, a complementary time to recuperate, devoted to subordinate activities, a time alienated by a booming leisure industry. As the time available increases, the possibility and need to structure it with different activities and relationships grow. Thanks to this inversion between the time at work and the time available, a new social sphere is opening. It consists of self-determined activities, new co-operative relationships, quality communication and exchange. These activities are, in effect, a factor of integration for they generate authentic social links, and the domain outside work can then stop being one of privacy and consumption. In brief:

> chacun doit pouvoir accéder à la fois à la citoyenneté économique par un travail dont le système a besoin, un revenu que ce travail légitime, et à la production de société au sein de communautés organisées, de réseaux d'échange, de coopération et d'autoproduction.[11]
>
> (Gorz, 1993: 17)

Conclusion

It is apparent that an ecologist critique of work as interpreted by these Green authors rebels against an invasion of everyday life by capitalist economic logic and attempts to devise a model of sustainable development for a new society (for Gorz, a Socialist society) which would not be forever increasing the production of goods but would convert part of the savings in productivity into a qualitative gain: free time. Their texts advocate the transformation of our ways of living. The development of autonomous activities is an essential tool in this process.

The Utopian nature of the proposals of political ecology which have been outlined here should be obvious. However, that Utopia is not devoid of theoretical relevance. Let André Gorz defend himself on this point by concluding:

> Peut-être me reprochera-t-on de privilégier l'utopie au dépens du court terme. Mais l'utopie . . . consiste seulement à penser jusqu'au bout de ses

conséquences le *sens possible* qui pointe à l'horizon des mutations en cours. C'est à la lumière de ce sens seulement qu'une société peut prendre sur elle-même le recul critique lui permettant de juger ce qu'elle fait ou omet de faire.[12]

(Gorz, 1993: 17)

Notes

1. *Travailler moins pour travailler tous: 20 propositions* was the 1993 legislative election manifesto of the Génération ecologie party of which Aznar is the general secretary.

2. With computer-controlled automation, which is soon to extend to most economic sectors, the amount of human work accomplished will bear only a distant relationship to the amount of wealth produced; ... Full consideration will in future have to be given to the paradox of wealth creation with loss and not creation of jobs.

3. *Revenu minimum d'insertion* is an income-support allowance introduced by the Socialist government, 1988–93, in an attempt to rescue the increasing numbers of welfare outcasts who were no longer eligible for any existing welfare benefits system.

4. Because in most cases those who perform an hour of domestic labour in your stead earn much less than you can earn in an hour of your work. Personal services are developing as a result of the pauperization of a growing mass of people, a pauperization found both in Western Europe and in North America (Gorz, 1994: 50).

5. Is only possible in a context of growing social inequality, in which one part of the population monopolizes the well-paid activities and forces the other part into the role of servants (Gorz, 1989: 156).

6. The reduction in working time without loss of income has to be understood not as a measure but as a coherent general policy. The point is not to redistribute existing jobs and resources but to manage an ongoing dynamic process which demands less work but creates more and more wealth (Gorz, 1989: 200).

7. It must be the goal society sets itself and therefore the independent variable to which the other variables will be called to adjust themselves over a determinate period of time (Gorz, 1989: 201).

8. The new information-based society requires the invention of a new concept to ensure a fair redistribution of wealth collectively produced by fewer men and far more robots.

9. Inability of our societies to establish a civilization based on free time leads to a completely absurd and scandalously unjust distribution of work, disposable time and wealth (Gorz, 1994: 45).

10. The casualization of employment and the dualization of society are the perverse forms assumed by the liberation of time which this social system refuses to acknowledge or take into account (Gorz, 1994: 52).

11. Everyone must be able to get access to economic citizenship through a job which the system needs, an income legitimized by this work, and to the production of society from within self-organizing communities, exchange networks, co-operation and self-production of goods for home consumption.

12. I might be reproached for prioritizing Utopia at the expense of short-term planning. But Utopia ... simply means taking through its logical development the *sens possible* (potential guiding principle) which is appearing on the horizon of the current transformations in society. It is only in the light of this meaning that a society can look at itself from a critical perspective, enabling it to evaluate what it is doing and what it is omitting to do.

References

Aznar, G. (1980) *Tous à mi-temps!* Paris: Seuil.

Aznar, G. (1990) *Le Travail c'est fini (à plein temps, pour toute la vie, pour tout le monde) et c'est une bonne nouvelle.* Paris: Belfond.

Aznar, G. (1993) *Travailler moins pour travailler tous: 20 propositions.* Paris: Syros.

Droit Social (1994) La loi quinquennale relative au travail, à l'emploi et à la formation professionnelle, 2 February: whole issue.

Futuribles (1994) Pour ou contre le revenu minimum, l'allocation universelle, le revenu d'existence?, special issue, **184** (February), 3–94.

Gorz, A. (1988) *Métamorphoses du travail: quête du sens.* Paris: Gallilée.

Gorz, A. (1989) *Critique of the Economic Reason.* London and New York: Verso.

Gorz, A. (1991) *Capitalisme, socialisme, écologie.* Paris: Gallilée.

Gorz, A. (1993) Sortir de la société salariale, *Transversales Science/ Culture*, **25**, 13–17.

Gorz, A. (1994) *Capitalism, Socialism, Ecology.* London and New York: Verso.

Rigaudiat, J. (1993) *Réduire le temps de travail.* Paris: Syros.

Robin, J. (1989) *Changer d'ère.* Paris: Seuil.

Robin, J. (1994) *Quand le travail quitte la société industrielle.* Paris: GRIT.

Sue, R. (1994) *Temps et ordre social.* Paris: Presses Universitaires de France.

12.

The social security headache: the necessary but elusive reform

JACQUES RELAND

Even though Jacques Chirac had denied during his campaign for the presidential election of 1995 that the Sécurité sociale (National Insurance) system was in need of an overhaul, his first Prime Minister, Alain Juppé, found himself obliged to announce in the middle of August an 'ambitious salvage plan' for the main institution of the French welfare system.

Although a great majority of the population realizes some serious measures need to be taken, they tend to react badly at the mere whiff of reform proposals to combat the deficit of the social security accounts. These plans usually follow the annual July publication of the final accounts of the previous year and of their estimates of the current and following year's financial positions. Since the mid-1970s, they have made for grim reading, confirming that the system was in the red and would worsen, unless steps were taken soon. As a result, governments would take a set of measures involving a rise in contributions and/or a cut in benefits which would often limit the shortfall and sometimes even lead miraculously to a surplus, as in the 1983–85 period. The deficit had become part of the French socio-economic landscape, a regrettable side effect which did not prevent patients from being treated, or pensions and family benefits from being paid. So, what pushed Juppé to act so quickly at the risk of dragging down his already low popularity rating even further? The rapidity of his reaction might have been prompted by the short-term economic drawbacks of the social security financial burden, but the wide-ranging scope of the reform he initially proposed showed that the medium- to long-term threat of France's demographic evolution to the survival of the French welfare system could no longer be ignored.

The economic challenge

Juppé's reforming zeal was prompted by the publication, a week earlier, of the definitive 1994 accounts of the Régime général de la sécurité sociale showing that the deficit which had widened from 17.7 billion francs in 1992 to 56.7 billion francs in 1993 had only dipped to 55.9 billion francs in 1994 in spite of the 1993 *Plan Veil*. Moreover, the shortfall was forecast to exceed 60 billion francs in 1995 and 1996. The 'trou de la Sécu' had become a 'gouffre' (the hole had become a chasm) as *Libération* put it. This is, however, rather an exaggeration when measured against its budget of over 1800 billion francs and compares favourably with the 322 billion franc deficit of the much lower state budget which weighed in at a mere 1436 billion francs in that same year of 1994. But, although the financial imbalance of the system is proportionally fairly modest, the huge social security budget shows how costly French welfare is. Health, old-age and family benefits accounted in 1993 for 25.8 per cent of the GDP, an ever-growing share of the wealth created by the country (13.8 per cent in 1960, 14.7 per cent in 1970, 22 per cent in 1980, 23.9 per cent in 1990). It is a cost which the economy finds increasingly difficult to bear (figures from the *Comptes de la protection sociale*, June 1994, cited in Minc, 1994: 250).

The cost of welfare has brought the total level of taxation, what is known in France as *les prélèvements obligatoires*, that is, taxes, duties and social contributions, to 44.8 per cent of the GDP in 1995, one of the highest levels in the EU, with social contributions accounting for 19.6 per cent of the GDP. This is perceived as an obstacle to the economic competitiveness of the country in an increasingly open and free-trading international market environment. Majnoni stresses the European dimension of the problem and points out that in more 'dynamic' countries, such as Japan and the USA, the total tax bill hovers around 30 per cent, as against 43 per cent in the EU (1993: 56).

The Juppé plan was motivated by the need for France to meet the Maastricht criteria. Chirac's conversion to the merits of EMU has committed the French government to its calendar which would oblige France to bring its public deficits (state, social security, local authorities and public companies) down by one percentage point each year to 3 per cent in 1997 from 6 per cent in 1994. The projected 1995 64.5 billion franc social security deficit amounts to nearly 1 per cent of the GDP; eliminating it would make the 3 per cent objective more easily attainable. Besides, Maastricht or not, the government has no other option but to try and reduce France's public deficits in an effort to reassure the financial markets so as to implement the much needed cut in interest rates on which their immediate economic strategy is based.

Economically, however, the main charge made against the French system relates to the vicious circle created by its method of financing. Although social security benefits have been extended over the years to 99.5 per cent of the population, the French system has retained its socio-professional basis for funding. Contributions from employers, wage earners and the self-employed accounted for 86.2 per cent of the system's revenue in 1994, the rest being made up from state subsidies, special duties and taxes. The financial stability of all welfare systems is dependent upon the level of economic activity, but it is even more so in France where the method of financing makes the system more highly sensitive to the level of activity and employment but also to the level of wage settlements. Even though the population available for work has been increasing since the early 1970s, unemployment has soared to remain at around 12 per cent in the last few years. As only people actually in work contribute, it has seriously limited the growth of revenue, as has the exceptional French wage restraint of the last ten years.

The demographic challenge

The social security system is a victim of its own success. It has enabled the whole population to have access to a wide range of medical services and goods which has led life expectancy to rise spectacularly to 81.8 for French women and 73.6 for men (INSEE, 1996). In 1990, 50 per cent of men born in 1920 were still alive, in 2040, 75 per cent of men born in 1970 will still be alive. The number of over-60s is expected to increase from 11.3 million in 1993 to 17 million by 2020. It will have a dramatic impact on health care: in 1987, the over-60s represented 18.5 per cent of the population but 42 per cent of health spending. They now account for 20 per cent, a proportion which will rise to 25 per cent in 2015 and 30 per cent in 2030. Even though the over-60s are in much better health than they used to be, the problem will be made acute by the subsequent steep rise in the numbers of very old people.

The main worry arising from the ageing of the population centres obviously on pensions as the French system is based, in the name of intergenerational solidarity, on the *répartition* principle. Current employers and employees pay for today's pensioners. As the working population is still growing and the people of retirement age were born in the 1930s, when the French peacetime birth-rate was at its lowest,

French pensioners are now living through a golden age. Thanks to a 75 per cent average replacement rate, the average pension is now higher than the average wage. The generosity of the French pensions system stems from a deliberate government-inspired upgrading of pension benefits from the early 1970s to the mid-1980s:

> De 1970 à 1984, les pensions versées aux plus de 65 ans ont été multi-pliées par 1,8 en francs constants alors que dans le même temps le salaire ouvrier moyen n'a bénéficié que d'un coefficient de 1,4.[1]
>
> (*Le Monde*, 23 August 1995)

This process was partly motivated by a genuine desire to improve the pensioners' lot, but also by the growing awareness that the old tend to vote 'en masse', and was facilitated by favourable demographic factors. In 1970 there were 3.8 members of the working population for each state (*régime général*) pensioner, a ratio which fell to 3 in 1976, 2.5 in 1982 (when the retirement age was lowered to 60). It now stands at 1.75, leading to a 12.7 billion franc deficit in 1994, and is expected to drop to 1.2 by 2015.

It is therefore obvious that the French system which was based on economic and demographic dynamism is no longer suited to a new context involving modest economic growth and an ageing population. Current and projected growth rates do not allow the maintenance of benefits at current levels without raising contributions to unacceptable levels. The time has come for a serious long-term reform of the system which must address these two issues: firstly, to shift some of the burden of financing the system away from the payroll and secondly, to ensure that the Sécurité sociale system's share of the GDP does not rise much higher which means containing health care expenditure and reducing the level of pension benefits.

The issues: a political minefield

It is easy to understand previous governments' inability to implement a serious reform of the system which must necessarily involve a deterioration of the services provided by an institution to which the French are strongly attached. This is indisputably linked to its generous old-age pension and family benefits and to the user-friendly character of its easily accessible health care system, qualities which override the low 73 per cent level of reimbursement of medical care. The importance of the *Sécu* goes beyond these purely material considerations:

L'Etat-providence est au coeur de l'idée de nation ... il est le pendant de
la citoyenneté. Il incombe des principes de solidarité.[2]

(Rosanvallon in *Le Monde*, 5 November 1995)

It is in a way the embodiment of the French post-war social contract
whereby some of the fruits of economic expansion resulting from the
hard work of the whole population would be redistributed through the
Sécu in the name of the national solidarity principle.

There might be an overall unity of positive feelings towards the *Sécu*,
but this cherished institution is far from being monolithic. Often
described as a mosaic, it is a patchwork of different regimes (19
different schemes for health and 150 for basic pensions as well as 387
complementary pension schemes) leading to inequalities in terms of
contributions and benefits between various socio-professional categories (Hantrais, 1982; Ashford, 1982; Chatagner, 1993; Majnoni, 1993;
Huteau and Le Bon, 1993).

Financing a hybrid system

In spite of these inequalities and in spite of the fact that the Sécurité
sociale never became the unified system Pierre Laroque, its founder
and father, intended it to be, it has nevertheless become general,
covering since 1978 some 99.5 per cent of the population as against 56
per cent in 1946. While family benefits have been available to all since
1945 as a result of 'the nation's preoccupation with demographic
issues' (Hantrais, 1982: 79), the extension of health and pension
benefits to the whole population took place in the 1970s. The French
system then covered the quasi-totality of the population, but, as mentioned above, has retained its socio-professional basis for funding. Since
the 1970s the onset of recession and the successive governments'
willingness to extend and improve benefits financed by social security
contributions put unbearable strains on the system's financial balance.
Unions point out that were it not for the estimated 60 billion francs
extra burden arising from expenditure not linked to contributions
(cover for the unemployed, the handicapped, housing benefits paid for
by the family allowances budget) and from the cost of government
exemption of employers' contributions in job creation schemes, the
Sécu would balance its books (Huteau and Le Bon, 1993: 93–4, 100). It
would therefore seem logical to introduce a clearer separation between
the expenditure linked to the insurance principle and financed by
contributions and that linked to the solidarity principle which should
be financed by taxation (a process known as *fiscalisation*).

Even though there is no miracle tax, as every tax penalizes consumption and therefore growth and employment, many solutions have been mooted to make financing less inhibiting for employers and also more equitable in redistribution. Basing employers' contributions more on the added value produced by companies than on their labour costs would be a step in the right direction. Raising the VAT rates and allocating its yield to social spending (Social VAT) is no longer a possibility now that Juppé has increased it to 20.6 per cent and would not be equitable in redistribution anyway.

The taxation process started in January 1991 with Rocard's introduction of the CSG (*contribution sociale généralisée*), a 1.1 per cent levy on all incomes, raised to 2.4 per cent by the Balladur government in 1993, which helps to finance the cost of the FSV (Fonds de solidarité vieillesse), the organization in charge of basic state pensions for people who have not contributed enough and with the gradual taxation of the financing of the family allowances budget since 1 July 1994. Even though the CSG is levied on most sources of income, from capital gains to pensions, it met with hostility from the unions. This is not so surprising since any union is bound to oppose a new tax imposed on its members, notwithstanding the fact that a rise in payroll contributions to raise a similar amount of money (one CSG point was worth 38.2 billion francs in 1994) would have hit workers even harder. They can however point out that the CSG is, in the words of CGT leader Louis Viannet, 'un pâté d'alouette' ('a lark pâté', a misleading name for a pâté containing a token amount of the eponymous bird) (*Le Monde*, 1 September 1995), as labour-related revenue accounts for 75 per cent of its yield whilst only 7 per cent comes from capital gains. Unions were however more concerned by what they perceived as the start of a process which would undermine the role they play in the running of the *Sécu*.

As a result of the French mutualist tradition (see Chapter 10) presiding over the previous incarnations of the then far from comprehensive French welfare system and in an effort to promote the concept of social democracy, the management of the Caisses de sécurité sociale, which were divided into three national branches after 1967 (Health, Pensions and Family) themselves subdivided in regional and departmental *caisses* (offices), was entrusted to the representatives of the employers and employees whose contributions finance 80 per cent of the whole system. This is known as *paritarisme* (parity in partnership), a principle which was dear to Pierre Laroque, who saw it as a way to make beneficiaries feel responsible thus preventing the advent of a dependency culture. This never became the case, as Laroque admitted in an interview in *Le Monde* (29–30 September 1985): 'Les salariés n'ont jamais eu conscience que la Sécu était leur chose' (employees have never felt a sense of ownership of the social security system). Moreover, even though the system is run by employers' and employees' representatives, governments could not ignore the political and macro-economic implications of social welfare and the system is therefore under the tutelage of the state:

> The management of social welfare is based on what all authors call '*un mythe*' [a fiction]: the autonomy of '*Caisses*' [funds] run by elected or appointed union and employers representatives. It is the state which has the final word on the main issues: the level of contributions and that of benefits.
>
> (Murard, 1993: 87)

Thus the state sets the rules while the offices administer, pay and control *a posteriori* their application by interested parties, especially health service providers. In spite of these reservations, the *paritarisme* is crucially important for the unions, especially FO which controls the most important CNAM (health branch) and the CFDT which controls the CNAV (Pension) whilst the CFTC runs the CNAF (family branch). It compensates for the low membership of French trade unions, the lowest in the OECD with around 10 per cent of workers, bringing them jobs for militants, income and many fringe benefits as well as a political and economic representation and influence without common measure with their numbers (see Chapters 10 and 14). It also benefits French governments as the unions' involvement in running a system with an overall budget higher than the state's is widely considered to be an important factor contributing to industrial relations, promoting dialogue and economic responsibility.

This is why the FO especially reacted so virulently to the proposal to give parliament the power to control the budget of the *Sécu*. It required a constitutional reform, duly voted through by the parliament on 19 February 1996, which allows MPs to examine the revenue of the system and to set the expenditure targets for the coming year. Although FO and the CGT were quick to denounce the reform as a process of the state take-over of welfare, the government's argument that the *Sécu* budget has become too big and economically significant to be left in the hands of mutually dependent controllers and actors (FO and doctors principally) won the day over FO warnings that it would lead to the dismantling or privatization of some of the *Sécu* services.

Pensions

The unions' privatization fears centre mostly on pension schemes. As demographic evolution can only lead to a deterioration of their financial position, they rightly believe that the government will introduce an element of capitalization into the funding of retirement benefits. This is inevitable, as is the slow but sure depreciation of the relative value of the current system's pensions, a process already undertaken with the *loi Veil* of August 1993 which consisted of three measures. Firstly, a person retiring will need to have worked for 40 years, instead of 37.5, to qualify for a full pension. This extension is taking place progressively at the rate of a quarter-year per year from 1994. It actually puts paid to the retirement age of 60 for the growing number of workers who will have studied well into their twenties. Secondly, the level of pension benefits will eventually be calculated on the 25 best-paid years as against the best ten. This target will be achieved by 2010 as the raising of the reference period is taking place at the rate of one year per year. Thirdly, annual increases in pensions are now based on the rate of inflation rather than wage increases. Even though this measure only ratifies what had become the norm since 1988, it is the most significant measure in the short to medium term. Linking pensions to inflation had brought down the statutory 50 per cent replacement rate of the basic pensions to 47 per cent in 1993. According to Stéphane Hamayon (*Nouvel Economiste*, 18 June 1993) the rate will now slump to 42 per cent in the year 2000 and 37 per cent in 2010.

Although these measures only affect 42 per cent of pension benefits, as they do not yet apply to special regimes, a step which Juppé proposed but was forced to postpone following the December 1995 unrest (see Chapter 14), nor to complementary schemes, they will lead to considerable savings. A CNAV study has concluded that as a result, the volume of benefits will increase by only 50 per cent by 2010 instead of doubling. This will not however be enough to balance the books, according to a pensions expert quoted in the *Financial Times* (14 November 1994):

> The deficit under the existing system seemed set to reach 300 billion francs by the year 2020. It now seems more likely to be in the region of 100 billion by that date.

This explains why governments have long been toying with the idea of introducing an element of capitalization through the creation of pension funds. This idea had even been mooted in 1990 by Socialist Finance Minister Bérégovoy, who saw it as a way of compensating for the shortcomings of the *répartition* (distribution) system but also as a way to provide French companies and financial markets with much-needed liquidity:

> Pension funds could provide the answers to the perennial problem of capitalism without capital.
>
> (*Financial Times*, 14 November 1994)

The deflationary process and the prospect of a strong single European currency make capitalization a safer bet than it was in the 1970s, but it still remains a sensitive issue which has since led to much debate on how the funds should be organized, who would run them and which safeguards would have to be introduced to prevent disasters of Maxwell proportions. Unions are either hostile (CGT and FO): 'Les fonds de pension c'est du vol' (Pension funds are a rip-off) (Blondel, *Le Monde*, 2 March 1995), or cautious, as they fear they could be of less benefit to their members than to whoever runs them, employers, insurance companies or financial institutions. This is why Jacques Chirac, who had promised to create pension funds in the opening speech of his official campaign, felt the need to stress later that they should be run by unions and employers:

> J'entends que soient mis en place des fonds de pension non seulement pour assurer le complément indispensable de la réforme des retraites, mais aussi pour collecter une épargne nouvelle qui pourra s'investir dans les entreprises en faveur de l'emploi.[3]
>
> (*Le Monde*, 17 February 1995)

If serious measures affecting pension benefits were adopted with little popular backlash, it would not be the same for health care because, as *Le Monde* (8 December 1994) pointed out, 'the narrow set of measures which was adopted will only be painful in another ten years whilst health reforms will require more varied solutions with a more immediate financial impact.'

Health care

The health insurance scheme (CNAM) deficit continues to widen from 6.3 billion francs in 1992 to 27.3 billion in 1993, 31.6 billion in 1994 and 36.6 billion francs in 1995 (Commission des comptes de la sécurité sociale, 1995), making it the largest and most immediately worrying issue. The main obstacle to wide-ranging reform lies in the strength of the medical and pharmaceutical lobby, which has successfully opposed all serious attempts at curbing the relentless growth of health spending, which rose by 4.8 per cent a year between 1985 and 1994, against 2.2 per cent in the European Union. The medical profession has always had close links with the RPR and the UDF, as shown by the presence of 70 of its members in the current parliamentary majority. Its strength was shown when 200,000 representatives of the medical professions, accompanied by leading right-wing politicians such as Alain Juppé, marched through Paris in November 1991 to protest against health spending reforms proposed by Bruno Durieux, the Socialist health minister. Due to the lack of an absolute majority in parliament and to the popular support for doctors, he was forced to abandon his plan to set a growth-rate target on doctors' prescribing, a measure which ironically Prime Minister Juppé would now like to impose. The French love their health system which has indeed many qualities, mainly easy equal access to the abundant services it provides. Patients and doctors seem to have the best of both worlds in a system which combines 'universal insurance with a pluralist system of provision and fee for service payments for a large proportion of health services' (OECD, 1994: 66).[4]

The whole medical profession wants to preserve the 1.6 million jobs provided by this highly successful economic sector, which represents 7.4 per cent of the working population against 4.6 per cent in the UK.[5] This system however is inflationary and costly (Rodwin, 1981). Although France has only 272 doctors per 100,000 inhabitants (Germany 323, Italy 334 but UK 142) they tend to concentrate in certain geographical areas (the Paris region and the south) where it is estimated that many thousands are surplus to requirements. This medical overpopulation in some towns and regions creates competition leading to overprescribing. As a result, a French person spent on average 1898 francs on medicines in 1992 against 1843 francs in Germany and 959 francs in the UK (*Echos de la Santé*, November 1994: 4).

Most cost containment measures have until now focused on increasing revenue through higher contributions (of employees rather than employers) or on reducing demand through 'the responsabilization' of consumers/patients. The latter has invariably taken the form of a reduction of the reimbursement rate, through an increase of what is known as the *ticket modérateur*, that is, the share of the cost of visits or prescriptions to be borne by the patient, or of the non-reimbursable amount charged to hospital patients for their residential costs. The Juppé plan, for example, has raised the daily hospital charge from 55 to 80 francs. As a result of these cost-cutting measures, the French 73 per cent basic average health care reimbursement level is one of the lowest in Europe. Hence the need for complementary cover, which explains why 87 per cent of patients subscribe to a socio-professional mutual fund or to private insurance against 74 per cent in 1980 (*Echos de la Santé,* June 1994: 23). Acting on demand has, however, proved to be, not only socially unfair, as it penalizes patients without complementary cover or with a low level of complementary cover (the unemployed and those with the least-secure and worst-paid jobs), but also fairly ineffective:

> Il n'est pas d'exemple de pays dans lequel, comme en France, la régulation du système soit principalement recherchée à travers la responsabilisation financière des assurés.[6]
>
> (Commissariat général du plan, 1994: 130)

This is because most health insurance expenditure (70 per cent) is concentrated on a small section of the population (9 per cent) who are excused from paying any charges because they suffer from a long-term serious illness, or because they are disabled or pregnant or have been the victim of an accident at work. This compounds the detrimental effect of the ageing of the population as nearly 32 per cent of the over-64s are thus totally covered (Bocognano *et al.*, 1994: 10).

However, in order to contain the cost of health care, the state has another weapon which it has used to full effect: the setting of prices for medical services and goods which it has managed to keep artificially low:

> Compared to other EC countries, price levels are lower for most goods and services, and government controls have had considerable success in containing inflation in the health sector. France is the only country where health-care prices have risen less than overall inflation.
>
> (OECD, 1994: 71)

To compensate for low prices, doctors and the pharmaceutical industry have therefore gone for volume. Pharmaceutical companies have also neglected research and development to the benefit of promotional expenditure directed at doctors, a factor which explains why only 3 per cent of prescribed drugs are generic against 25 to 35 per cent in the rest of the EU.

The combination of demographic factors, new technologies and new diseases such as AIDS makes cost containment and better allocation of resources a priority. But this is not the only reason as the *Livre blanc*

(White Paper), along with many other analysts, concludes. France spends more than any other European country on health care, but there are growing doubts about whether it gets good value for money. France's health performance is not significantly better than that of its neighbours (OECD, 1994: 69) in terms of life expectancy, perinatal and infant mortality. It must be said, however, that France's excellent record on cardiovascular disease, where it ranks second to Japan, is due not just to the amount of red wine and duck fat consumed in the country, as many would like to believe, but also to the huge volume of tests and *antihypertenseurs, vasodilateurs* and other drugs prescribed. The down side of this prescribing largesse is the world record held by France for the consumption of sleeping pills and tranquillizers (see Table 12.1).

Any serious reform of health care must therefore act on supply to make it more cost effective:

> Les pays qui réussissent le mieux à maîtriser leurs dépenses (de santé) sont ceux qui exercent une pression renouvelée sur les acteurs, notamment les producteurs de soins, par des mesures successives.[7]
>
> (Commissariat général du plan, 1994: 129)

This is, however, easier said than done, given the doctors' militancy in the defence of their 'liberal tradition' (Hantrais, 1982: 90). Every time reforms were proposed aiming to curb their prescribing or at least to control it, they objected on ethical and professional grounds, sheltering behind their Medical Charter, *le secret médical* and their expertise: doctor knows best. All attempts at setting a limit on doctors' turnover failed until 1993 when Simone Veil got them to agree to three measures in exchange for a 5-franc increase in their consultation fee: a 3.4 per cent limit on the growth of ambulatory care expenditure; the creation of medical references for 24 main illnesses or medical conditions which doctors will have to respect, for example, no more than three ultra-sound scans per pregnancy (this would have the dual advantage of

Table 12.1 Daily drug dose per 1000 inhabitants (1992)

Drug	France	UK	Germany
Antihypertensives	166.1	118.9	–
Vasodilators	56.4	2.9	–
Hypolipidaemic drugs	31.8	2.1	–
Antibiotics	26.2	13.3	–
Psychotropic drugs	161.1	52.6	52.6

Source: *Echos de la Santé*, November 1994

eliminating waste but also of providing a framework for good practice); a more precise record-keeping of what a doctor is treating a patient for. At the moment the record only gives an indication of the cost. This will allow for a better supervision by the Caisses d'assurance maladie (CAMs) of doctors' prescribing.

To avoid superfluous visits and tests, plans were drawn up to introduce (in March 1995) medical files for patients over 70 suffering from at least two diseases who required medical supervision for at least six months (*sic*). The measure was postponed due to the presidential election, and when doctors, 80 per cent of whom voted for Chirac in the second round, realized their favourite candidate looked likely to win, they threw caution to the wind. Ambulatory care expenditure, which had risen by 3.2 per cent in 1994, suddenly picked up from the second quarter of 1995 to rise by 6 per cent over the year, twice the 1995 target.

The Juppé plan reinstated a 1996 2.1 per cent growth target, the forecast inflation rate, and initially contained punitive measures which have since been watered down or postponed pending further negotiations. Pharmaceutical companies will however have to pay 2.5 billion francs to the *Sécu* as compensation for the 12 per cent 1995 rise in their sales. The exact content of measures affecting doctors will be known in the spring of 1996 but it will certainly involve a continuation of the process initiated by Simone Veil. It will require the computerization of all practices so as to implement better the more detailed controls required for checking their activity. The nature and content of sanctions also remain to be determined, as do the details surrounding the creation of a medical card aimed at preventing medical nomadism among patients.

Better record-keeping and improved computerization are also required for a better control of hospital expenditure, which accounts for around 50 per cent of medical consumption. The Veil plan had launched that process to measure and assess the activity of a hospital more precisely so as to eliminate waste and allow for a fairer allocation of funds and resources through a better-informed comparison of the activity of various establishments. The completion of this process will, however, take a long time, but it is necessary since the method used until now to curb the growth of hospital spending is highly unsatisfactory. It involves setting a growth target on the volume of a hospital's activity. Although this measure, introduced in 1984, has had a certain degree of success, resulting in a slowdown of expenditure in public hospitals from a 3.1 per cent average yearly growth in 1980–85 to 2 per cent in the following five years, it is unfair. The global budget constraint penalizes large efficient hospitals to the benefit of small unproductive institutions. Furthermore, it does not help to correct the unfair and uneven level of hospital provision between regions.

The Juppé plan set a 2.1 per cent volume growth target for 1996 and will continue with the dual process of computerization and of region-alization of hospital provision planning to improve France's medical geography. Of all major countries, France has the highest number of hospital beds per person, with over 12 per 1000 inhabitants against just above 6 in the UK and the Netherlands. This high figure is partly related to the low population density of the country, but it is never-theless estimated that 50,000 to 60,000 of France's 546,000 public beds are surplus to requirements. They are mostly located in small to medium-sized towns in small, underused local hospitals which are often the main local employer. To diminish the political fall-out from the cuts or closures which will soon affect these hospitals, the Juppé plan stipulates that mayors are no longer entitled automatically to preside over their boards of directors.

Health is priceless, but it has a cost which can no longer rise uncontrollably, especially as 'le système de santé français ne nous permet pas de dire que chaque franc dépensé . . . apporte une améliora-tion de notre système de soins' (Commissariat général du plan, 1994: 27).[8] Health care provision should therefore be rationalized not just for economic reasons but also for quality of care and public health reasons. If something is not done seriously, and soon, to control the growth in health spending, rationing measures could be needed, thus under-mining further the French principles of national solidarity and equal access to care:

> Plus on tarde à réformer notre système de santé, plus les mesures devront être brutales et risqueront de mettre à mal les principes auxquels les Français sont attachés.[9]
>
> (Commissariat général du plan, 1994: 12)

Conclusion

In a society where an increasing number of people are excluded or marginalized, the 'Touche pas à ma Sécu' slogan can appear somehow selfish as the system benefits the middle classes more than the poor and some categories of workers more than others. It does not redistribute wealth very effectively, does not cover some urgent needs sufficiently, whilst the high level of social security spending has an 'opportunity

cost' (Majnoni, 1993: 57) which contributes to reducing the money
available for other worthwhile investments such as social housing,
education and training. Its benefits, however, compare well with other
European countries and help to preserve its role as a key instrument of
social cohesion, thus making the *Sécu* a highly sensitive issue. This
explains why none of the presidential candidates had felt compelled to
outline detailed reform proposals, as these would inevitably alienate
one section or another of the electorate.

Although the Juppé plan appeared ambitious, it was unfocused. In
wanting to show Bonn and the financial markets his determination to
curb deficits, Juppé tried to tackle too many problems at once. Instead
of concentrating on the two most pressing issues, clearly thought-out
reforms of the financing and of the health care system, he adopted a
half-hearted but wide-ranging repressive stance in aiming firstly to clear
the 250 billion francs debt backlog accumulated between 1992 and
1995 through the introduction of the RDS (*remboursement de la dette
sociale*), a 0.5 per cent levy on all incomes; in aiming secondly to
improve the financial position of the health scheme through higher
charges and financial penalties for permissive doctors; thirdly, in con-
fronting public sector workers over the not immediately crucial issue of
their pension schemes; fourthly, giving parliament some degree of
control over the *Sécu* budget at the expense of employers and unions.

In a domain requiring consultation and sensitive handling, the
hurried, rash and multifaceted measures advocated by Juppé upset too
many vested interests. As a result of the December strikes and of the
intense lobbying of the medical profession, the Juppé plan has been
seriously scaled down. The proposal to align the civil servants and
public sector employees' special pension schemes on to the general
regime has been postponed pending further consultations, as has been
the decision to tax family benefits. Much more importantly, concessions
have been made to doctors over the threat of financial penalties for
overstepping their spending limits, the removal of some of their special
tax benefits and the planned closures of hospitals. It remains to be seen
whether the eventual measures relating to the crucial issue of health
care, to be adopted in the spring, will be as courageous as they need to
be in order to have a marked impact on supply. As it stands now, the
health care reform merely consists of an increased contribution to the
system's running costs in the form of higher hospital charges and
higher health insurance contributions from pensioners and unemployed.

Granting parliament increased control over the finances of the system may prove to be the crucial element of the reform in so far as it might give a more politically secure future government the impetus actually to implement the necessary in-depth reform of the system. The Sécurité sociale system could be described as a luxury the French economy can no longer sustain. It fuelled and was fuelled by the demographic and economic dynamism, but, even though the demographic and economic trends undermine its financial stability, its main features have to be preserved. Its survival will have to involve a curb on doctors' and patients' freedom and a depreciation of state and occupational pension benefits and will require the development of pension funds and a taxation reform to shift some of the burden of financing the welfare system away from payrolls. A cure for the social security headache remains as elusive as ever.

Notes

1. From 1970 to 1984 old-age pensions went up by a factor of 1.8 in real terms while the average wage only increased by 1.4 in the same period.
2. The welfare state is at the heart of the ideal of the nation . . . it is the counterpart of citizenship. It embodies the principles of solidarity.
3. By this I mean that there should be pension funds established which would not only be an indispensable complement to the reform of the pension scheme but would also start a new savings fund which could invest in companies which create jobs.
4. Patients are keen on the freedom of choice which they have in selecting their doctor, whether a GP or a specialist, on the personal relationship between patient and doctor and the mutual confidence a fee for service payment entails. They enjoy the opportunity to see as many doctors as they wish and the quality of service these generally provide as a result of the competition between them. Patients also appreciate the absence of waiting lists resulting from the great number of hospital beds, both public and private, which allow for quick treatment in generally comfortable and well-equipped establishments. Doctors are viscerally attached to their liberal tradition which allows them to set up a practice wherever they wish and to prescribe however much they see fit in the knowledge that little or none of the cost will be borne by the patient. Private specialists appreciate the ability which they have to run their surgeries and also to work in private or public clinics and hospitals.
5. The April 1995 CREDES survey reveals also that the 280,000 jobs created in the health sector between 1982 and 1992 accounted for 20 per cent of all the jobs created in the tertiary sector over that period.
6. France is the only country which seeks to run its system on the financial contribution of those contributing.
7. The countries which are the most successful at controlling their spending (on health) are those which pass a series of measures to pressurize the actors, especially those in health care.
8. It cannot be said that every extra franc spent on our health care system will help to improve it.

9. The longer we postpone a reform of our health care system, the harsher the measures will have to be, and the greater the risk of undermining the principles to which the French are attached.

References

Ashford, D. (1982) *Policy and Politics in France*. Philadelphia: Temple University Press.

Bocognano, A. *et al.* (1994) *Santé, soins et protection sociale en 1993*. Paris: CREDES.

Chatagner, F. (1993) *La Protection sociale*. Paris: Le Monde-Marabout.

Commissariat général du plan (1991) *Livre blanc sur les retraites*. La Documentation Française.

Commissariat général du plan (1993) *Santé 2010*. La Documentation Française.

Commissariat général du plan (1994) *Livre blanc sur le système de santé et d'assurance-maladie*. La Documentation Française.

CREDES (1994) *Echos de la Santé*, Special issue (June) and no. 14 (November).

Dumont, J.-P. (1993) *Les Systèmes de protection sociale en Europe*. Paris: Economica.

Hantrais, L. (1982) *Contemporary French Society*. London: Macmillan.

Haut Comité de la santé publique (HCSP) (1994) *La Santé en France*. Rapport général, La Documentation Française.

Huteau, G. and Le Bon, E. (1993) *Sécurité sociale et politiques sociales*. Paris: Masson.

INSEE (1993) *Données sociales*.

INSEE (1996) *Données sociales*.

Les dépenses de santé des Français 1993–5 (1995) *Economie et Statistique*, **265**: whole issue, INSEE.

Majnoni d'Intignano (1993) *La Protection sociale*. Paris: Poche.

Minc, A. (1994) *La France de l'an 2000*. Paris: Odile Jacob.

Murard, N. (1993) *La Protection sociale*. Paris: Repères–La Découverte.

OECD Economic Surveys (1994) *France 1994*. Paris: OECD.

Palier, B. (ed.) (1995) *Comparing Social Welfare Systems in Europe*. Vol. 1. Oxford Conference (MIRE) Ministère des affaires sociales.

Rodwin, V.G. (1981) The marriage of National Health Insurance and *la médecine libérale*: a costly union, *Milbank Memorial Fund Quarterly*, **59**(1).

Rosanvallon, P. (1981) *La Crise de l'état-providence*. Paris: Seuil.

SESI. Rapport annuel de la commission des comptes nationaux de la santé.

13.

Government policy and higher education: the numbers game

ROB TURNER

Political slogans can take on a life of their own and, although its author has long since left office, former Education Minister (19 July 1984 to 20 March 1986) Jean-Pierre Chevènement's call for 80 per cent of a generation to gain the *baccalauréat*, with its knock-on effect on student numbers, is still shaping French higher education policy. Similarly Lionel Jospin's concept of the *Universités 2000* set the time-span for the adaptation of the system to the vast increase in numbers and the present decade has rightly come to be perceived as a defining moment in the development of French higher education.

Relentless growth in student numbers

The trend of increasing numbers entering higher education which these slogans encapsulate is common to other industrialized nations, being the result of factors such as the increased public demand for higher education and the need for a competitive highly trained work-force, factors which do not need further elaboration here. What is unique to France, however, is the scale and the rapidity of the increase in numbers. Official figures are outdated and probably wildly in-accurate (Bédarida, 1994a: 29–44), but in France today at least one in four young people receives a university education and this proportion will rise to one in three by the end of the century. The number of university students has risen from 800,000 in 1980 to an estimated 1,285,000 in 1994 (Bédarida, 1994) and will rise further to one and a half million by the end of the century ('L'explosion scolaire et uni-versitaire', *Le Monde*, Dossiers et documents, **142**, 1 October 1991).[1]

French higher education in total already takes in more than two million students and numbers will rise to two and a half million by the year 2000 (Goedegebuure, 1994: 121). Any slowing or reversal of this trend is extremely unlikely since it is driven by the equally rapidly increasing numbers of *bacheliers* which, as stated, are intended to reach 80 per cent of an age-group by the year 2000. Pressure of numbers is intensified further by a growing tendency for students to prolong their studies. In 1993 the 9 per cent increase in the number of *deuxième cycle* students in the third-year *licence* and the fourth-year *maîtrise* courses was for the first time greater than the 4.8 per cent increase in the *premier cycle* constituted by first- and second-year students preparing the DEUG (*Diplôme d'études universitaires générales*) (*Le Monde Campus*, 1 December 1994: 16).

Even those students undertaking short vocational courses are affected by this trend, with a quarter of BTS (*Brevet de technologie supérieure*) students continuing their studies and half of IUT (Institut universitaire de technologie) graduates going on to other courses (Bédarida, 1994a: 18).

In addition to absorbing the increased numbers into the system, French policy-makers have been concerned with a second major policy imperative of engineering a shift within the state system to vocational education. This shift is dictated by the already mentioned need to train a competitive workforce but more immediately by the recognition that the traditional careers for university graduates in teaching and the civil service can no longer absorb the rapidly increasing numbers of graduates and by the fact that the bulk of the increasing numbers will be made up by holders of the *baccalauréat technologique* who are unsuited to the range of traditional open-access university courses.

The numbers-driven policy which results from these imperatives is not based on any desire to undertake radical reform and is not a scenario for change, being essentially reactive:

> Dans la brève histoire de la planification de l'éducation à la française il ne manque pas d'exemples où la fuite en avant s'est avérée un chemin plus facile à suivre que la promotion de véritable changements.[2]
>
> (Jallade, 1991: 115)

If this interpretation can be viewed as somewhat cynical in terms of the motivation of policy-makers it is accurate enough in terms of results.

Unique constraints on French policy-makers

Coping with the 'breaking wave' of increasing student numbers and the training of an internationally competitive workforce left little room for manoeuvre but it should be added that higher education policy-makers in France also have to cope with rigidities in the system which greatly constrain their freedom of action. The hyper-selective and highly prestigious *grandes écoles* have attained an almost sacrosanct position within the education system. Their determination to remain élite institutions led them to refuse to bow to government pressure to increase numbers of entrants significantly and as a result they had shrunk as a proportion of the overall system from 25 per cent to only 4 per cent by 1991 (Flory, 1993: 104). This Malthusianism has meant that the *grandes écoles* have had to be left out of the equation in government plans to increase vocational education. At the same time they ferociously resist the initiatives which threaten them with competition from the university sector. Finally, along with *classes préparatoires* which prepare students for the entrance exams for the *grandes écoles*, they swallow up a massive 30 per cent of the higher education budget to train a mere 4 per cent of students, a figure which, apart from making their success appear rather less meritorious, considerably reduces the funding available to other sectors of higher education.

In his role as *Monsieur Université* of the Rocard government, Claude Allègre (1993) experienced not only the élitism of the *grandes écoles* but also what he terms the 'viscosity' or resistance to change of the university system, rooted in the vested interests and corporatist attitudes of an independent and combative teaching body, the *République des professeurs* (name given to the Third Republic because of the high number of political representatives from that profession) which, clinging to discipline-based research interests, refused to entertain innovations, particularly those which have a vocational purpose and which cut across traditional boundaries.

If university staff are resistant to the dictates of policy-makers, the aspirations of individual students, which often outstrip what the system is designed to offer them, can subvert state attempts to engineer student flows through the system. The diverse structures of the higher education system as a whole are also rigidly stratified as experienced by student entrants. Job opportunities and social status are, in what is an extremely hierarchical system, determined not so much by student performance in their higher education studies as by their route choice in the higher education system or indeed at an even earlier stage by their route choice and performance in the *baccalauréat*. As Frédéric Gaussen comments:

L'université s'efforce de mettre en place des formations de tout niveau et de toute nature tandis que se multiplient les filières sélectives et spécialisées. Cette harmonie plus ou moins voulue est satisfaisante pour l'esprit. Si toutefois on examine non l'architecture académique mais la réalité vécue par les étudiants, ses effets nocifs sautent aux yeux. Tout se passe, en effet, comme s'il n'existait qu'une seule voie désirable : la plus haute, celle des grandes écoles. Toutes les autres ne sont perçues que comme des pis-aller.[3]

(Gaussen, 1993: 3)

It is not surprising in this context that significant numbers of students determinedly attempt to break out of this straitjacket and to enhance their career prospects by moving from one route to another and indeed from one establishment to another and by prolonging their studies in patterns which policy-makers often fail to anticipate.

The most visible and most potent factor constraining government action in the field of higher education, however, resides not in the movement of students as individuals but in the potential for collective action of the student body and its defence of certain basic characteristics of the French university system, including open access for all *bacheliers*, a free choice of courses regardless of the type of *baccalauréat* taken, the maintaining of tuition fees at their current low level, the freedom to transfer between different university courses and institutions and the defence of the system of national diplomas. The underlying motivation for these attitudes, which clearly pose major obstacles to change, lies perhaps partly in a belief in universities as a bastion of equality of opportunity and partly in a recognition that for many students who have suffered rejection by selective sectors of higher education the universities represent the last chance (44 per cent of university students have unsuccessfully applied for a place in another sector of higher education) (Bédarida, 1994a: 50). Be that as it may, after the failure of the Devaquet bill, any direct attempt by government to impose selection across the university system is off the political agenda for the foreseeable future. Policy-makers are trapped in a dilemma as a result, since the only solution left to many of the problems besetting the university sector appears to be an increase in funding ('Fillon, du pognon!' and 'Bayrou, des sous!',[4] as the student slogans succinctly put it) which, given the increase in student numbers, would reach massive and politically unrealistic proportions.

Resourcing problems in the university sector

As France entered the 1990s the most pressing problems its higher education system faced were in the university sector, particularly in the *premier cycle* where the relentless increase in numbers inevitably put the system under massive strain. The problems of underresourcing and underfinancing were compounded by the lack of forward planning. The open-access system and freedom of route choice meant that individual universities and courses had no control over their intake and very little idea of the size of their intake from one year to the next. In these conditions, making adequate arrangements for first-year students becomes a near impossibility. Not surprisingly, failure rates in *premier cycle* reached dramatic levels, with only 29 per cent *Diplôme d'études universitaires générales* in the standard two years and with pass rates of students gaining the DEUG remaining under 50 per cent even after 3 years (Jallade, 1991: 91). If the definitive pass rate of around 80 per cent, which is arrived at after resitting examinations and changing courses, was achieved within the two years from entry intended, then many of the pressures on the university *premier cycle* would vanish. However, those university systems elsewhere which achieve such pass rates do so by selection and efficient student route guidance. As many observers have pointed out, the French system amounts to a kind of post-entry selection, 'la sélection en cours d'études' (Jallade, 1991: 75), or what Flory terms, 'la sélection à rebours', and qualifies as: 'la forme la plus détestable, la sélection par l'échec' (the most despicable kind of selection, selection by failure) (Flory, 1993: 102).

The need for student guidance

Not only is selection a political taboo in France at present but there often appears to be a disastrous lack of student guidance and a consequent mismatch between student choice of course and qualifications and ability. Large numbers of *baccalauréat* candidates from the technological F and G streams, who might be expected to follow short vocational courses, find themselves excluded from such courses by selection on entry and turn to university courses as second choice – with predictable results, since their *baccalauréat* studies provide little foundation for the open-access university courses in disciplines such as law and economics for which many opt in the last resort (Fauconnier and Fohr, 1995: 16). What has been termed the 'brutal anarchy' of the DEUG (Lapeyronnie and Marie, 1992: 30) offers them little opportunity to adapt. F and G stream candidates averaged respectively success rates of 21 per cent and

20.6 per cent in 1988 as against 54.5 per cent for *bacheliers généraux* in the DEUG (Bédarida, 1994b: 66). In contrast those F and G stream students who are accepted by the IUTs, where support systems are stronger, tend to do well (Lapeyronnie and Marie, 1992: 113). As both Flory and Jallade point out, the situation in France is the opposite to that in other comparable countries, where the weakest students follow short vocational courses and the most academically able follow long university courses. Furthermore, a survey jointly commissioned by *Le Monde Campus* and the Ministry of Education (*Le Monde Campus*, 20 June 1990) revealed that 65 per cent of students considered themselves to be inadequately informed or not informed at all about career opportunities at the end of their studies and indeed chose their course at the moment of enrolment rather than in the context of any career plan. The result is that the supply of graduates in subjects such as law and economics, which are mistakenly perceived to be vocational subjects by students, massively exceeds demand. All these problems are further compounded by what is termed the *illisibilité* of the system, the complex and fragmented nature of which all too often baffles students seeking a course appropriate to their abilities, interests and career plans. This is particularly the case for university vocational courses where a flurry of new courses and establishments have been created in recent years, leaving even the Minister for Higher Education admitting to being lost in the maze of acronyms that constitutes this sector (*Le Monde*, 25 July 1995: 8).

Appropriate guidance systems must be based on adequate information systems, and a further basic problem lay in the absence of any reliable indication of market demand for graduates in different disciplines. Allègre relates his astonishment (1993: 170–1) at discovering that there was no system in existence for gathering and collating information on employers' needs when he took up his advisory post to Lionel Jospin in 1988. He was not proposing to inaugurate a French 'Gosplan', as he put it, and the national Conference on the *Universités 2000* project in June 1990 (Ministère de l'éducation nationale, 1991) recognized the impossibility of the state accurately matching supply to demand (there are many examples of the state's response to the market being too little or too late and ironically, in the midst of the drive towards 'vocationalization', the healthiest job prospects for university graduates are currently for those in traditional arts subjects, where there is a shortage of teachers due to demographic trends (*Le Monde de l'Education*, February 1994: 34). In this type of context, however, a market-driven system required much more effective careers guidance and information being provided to student consumers than responses to surveys indicated (*Le Monde*, 8 July 1995: 10).

Even when a clear demand for increased numbers of graduates was forthcoming from employers, events seemed to conspire against a satisfactory outcome. There had been constant calls for an increase in the number of engineering graduates, particularly in the field of production engineering but whilst the *grandes écoles* limited their output – who largely went into management posts anyway – they also resisted any attempts to open up training in the university sector of engineers with equal status.

A second major problem lay in the IUT (Institut universitaire de technologie) sector which, whilst undoubtedly successful in producing graduates who were sought after by industry and commerce for middle management and specialist technician posts, had not expanded at the rate initially envisaged to take 25 per cent of the student population, partly because of their anomalous status as semi-autonomous establishments within the university system (technically they were classed as faculties with exemption from standard regulations on issues such as recruitment of staff and selection of students) and partly because of the prohibitive cost to the state of their intensive courses compared with traditional open-access courses. Furthermore, even the limited number of graduates emerging from the IUTs did not enter immediately into working life, as the policy-makers had intended. Because of their favourable success rates of over 70 per cent as compared with the less than 50 per cent of open-access courses, and thanks to better conditions of study as compared with university open-access courses, the IUTs began to attract increasing proportions of candidates from *baccalauréat général* streams rather than *baccalauréat technique* streams. As these candidates often had academically superior records they began to push out the candidates with a vocational background in the *baccalauréat* for whom the IUTs had been designed. On completing their studies in the IUTs they then moved across into a *grande école* or into the *deuxième cycle* of the university, calculating that their career prospects would be further enhanced by the acquisition of a *maîtrise* or even a DESS (*Diplôme d'études supérieures spécialisées*). In reality, however, these further studies moved them beyond the middle management career slot that the IUT graduates were intended to fill. Furthermore, job opportunities at the higher level of *bac* + 5 were far fewer than at the *bac* + 2 level of IUT graduates (Garagnon, 1995: 6). None the less, by 1988 42 per cent of IUT graduates were continuing their studies and this proportion was rising.

Government policy under the Socialists 1988–93: universities for the year 2000

When Lionel Jospin moved into the Ministry of Education in 1988, his immediate priority, as we have noted, could only be coping with the increase in numbers of *premier cycle* university students whose numbers were swelled not only by the increase in *bacheliers* but by a demographic upturn in the number of 18-year-olds. With education the chosen priority of François Mitterrand's second presidential term, Jospin and his adviser Allègre were in a strong position to press for a substantial increase in funding, and this was achieved with it rising by 90.5 per cent from 1984 to 1992. The *Universités 2000* reform allocated 16,000 million francs to the universities over a period of five years with the intention that this amount should be matched by the regions (Goedegebuure, 1994: 123). Increased funding was devoted largely to increases in staffing and to new building to meet the needs of rising student numbers. The participation of the regions was a necessary part of the government's strategy since it judged that central government alone could not bear the burden of the financial outlay required. Although the regions gained no formal involvement in the running of the universities, there has inevitably been closer co-operation since they have become major paymasters, with new courses being launched to meet the needs of local employers and chairs being created to promote disciplines of local relevance. The major quid pro quo for regional funding was to be the creation of a university presence in medium-sized and smaller provincial towns. It had initially been envisaged that this would take the form of the implantation of university *antennes*, or satellite campuses, offering *premier cycle* courses but concerns over the quality of teaching and resources in such outposts led to a switch to the creation, in a heavily politicized round of negotiation between central government and local *notables*, of a second wave of autonomous IUTs and STS (*Section de techniciens supérieurs*), the *lycée*-based, post-*baccalauréat* courses. This proposal met with a more favourable reception and held several advantages. The number of students in IUTs and STS was intended to double to match that of the university *premier cycle* and to relieve pressure on that problem area. Furthermore it would make appropriate provision for the increasing numbers of *bac technique* students, giving them a far better chance of academic success and employment prospects than *premier cycle* courses.

Allègre also moved to provide a focus for vocational education within the universities through the creation of Instituts universitaires professionnalisés (IUPs). These are selective institutions recruiting at one year post-*baccalauréat* level and leading through the conventional university structure of DEUG and *licence* to *maîtrise* with the concurrent award of *ingénieur-maître*. (It should be noted that the concept of 'engineer' is remarkably wide in scope in France. Dijon IUP, for example, trains engineers in the management of culture and education.) The creation of IUPs went ahead at a very rapid rate, often on the base of existing selective vocational courses, and over 80 were in place by 1992. Allègre pinned high hopes on the IUPs, intending them eventually to absorb over half of the *premier cycle* students and to relieve the pressure of numbers on open-access courses, but numbers initially were held at a low level.

As well as a source of new funding, Jospin and Allègre also looked to the local level to rationalize forward planning in the universities, which were henceforth required to draw up long-term contracts with government and regions covering staffing and other resource needs for their full range of courses. To enable at least rudimentary projections of student numbers to be made, *recteurs* of local *académies* were brought into the planning process to forecast numbers moving into higher education on the basis of those sitting the *baccalauréat* in local secondary schools. The contractualization process also served to give university presidents and their teams a rather more managerial role as they drew up their forward plans.

The final facet of the *Universités 2000* reform, which was to be implemented by Jospin's successor Jack Lang, was the renovation of the structure and content of the DEUG, which suffered most from the pressure of numbers. In an attempt to make the *premier cycle* more user-friendly, the DEUG was in effect transformed into a foundation course covering a broader spread of subjects and offering students the opportunity to try out a range of subjects and change direction more easily, being able to opt for either major or minor modules in specific subject areas to reflect their developing interests. The introduction of a credit accumulation system was intended to reduce the number of students resitting a full year. Finally, teaching methodology was modified to palliate the alienating effects of mass education by delaying student exposure to the notorious *cours magistraux* in packed amphitheatres and holding down class numbers in the first months to a maximum of 40. (The influential law faculties have since persuaded the government to exempt them from these changes, although arguably their antiquated teaching methods and high failure rates indicate that they stand in most need of this reform.) A rudimentary tutorial system was created by bringing in advanced students to act as tutors to first-year students. An attempt to bring in *agrégés* from the secondary sector to take over *premier cycle* teaching was torpedoed by the teaching unions, but the scheme remains in favour in present government circles because of its cost-cutting implications.

All this amounted to an honest attempt to deal in a practical, albeit piecemeal fashion, with the major problems of the traditional open-access university courses, particularly at *premier cycle* level, with some observers going so far as to qualify it as a quiet revolution. Some modest success was achieved, with pass rates in DEUG rising from just below 50 per cent to 55 per cent, a rate comparable with the STS but still well below the 77 per cent achieved by the IUTs (Bédarida, 1994: 67). It was, however, very much dependent on funding keeping pace with the continuing increase in numbers if the improvements were to be sustained.

Government policy 1993–95: the Right in power – financial stringency

The incoming right-wing government of Edouard Balladur in 1993 soon made it clear that the financial effort required to sustain the Jospin reforms was beyond its means. By 1995 the press was headlining the imminent danger of the collapse of the system (Ces facs qui craquent, *Le Nouvel Observateur*, 22 March 1995: 9; Education: la poudrière financière, *L'Expansion*, 6–19 March 1995: 78–81).

To these renewed problems should be added the perennial problem of the absence of selection, which neither Jospin nor his successors had tackled. Allègre argued that selection is a false problem, that a selective system like that of the UK still places virtually all students and, conversely, that an open-access system like that of Germany can operate perfectly satisfactorily. The main issue, he claims, is allocating or guiding students to the right courses and establishments. This may well be the case for a wholly selective system or a wholly open-access system. The problem comes when, as in France, the two systems coexist. The selective system inevitably drains the most able students from the open-access system and distorts its functioning. This is even more the case when, as in France again, the two systems coexist within the same establishments and it is painfully apparent that neither the selective routes nor the open-access routes in French universities are attracting the students for whom they were designed and who are best fitted for them.

Radicalism rebuffed

In the first flush of its 1993 victory in the parliamentary elections, the new right-wing majority, which had always had visceral objections to the mass open-access system, pushed through parliamentary legislation amending key points of the *loi Savary*. Following the pattern of the newly created universities of the Paris region, all universities would be allowed, on a voluntary basis, to opt out of the provisions of the *loi Savary* relating to open-access and to set up selection systems for *premier cycle* courses. This approach had the advantage of avoiding a Devaquet style head-on confrontation between minister and students, although there was clearly government complicity with the private member's bill. The legislation was passed over the summer vacation when student reactions were muted and it was expected that individual university presidents, whose managerial powers were reinforced by the same bill, would then bear the brunt of local student protest if they chose the Scylla of selection rather than the Charybdis of ever-increasing student numbers. However, the legislation fell foul of the Conseil constitutionnel, which abrogated it in its entirety on account of technical faults in its drafting. It became apparent that radical changes of this nature would need to be incorporated in a major set piece of government legislation – something that François Fillon was not prepared to risk.

Any new reform was postponed until wide-ranging consultation and debate had taken place on the basis of two major reports which had been commissioned by the ministry. Fillon's caution was to be further reinforced by the reception accorded to the first of these, the *Rapport Laurent* officially entitled : *Universités : relever les défis du nombre* which was produced by a group chaired by Daniel Laurent, president of the University of Marne-la-Vallée, and published in January 1995. Laurent produced a radical set of proposals to tackle the problems of the university sector but inevitably came up against the vested interests of both students and staff – his proposals to extend teaching throughout the academic year and to introduce evaluation by students as a criterion for course approval inevitably drew the wrath of teaching unions, while the proposals to increase tuition fees, even though grants would be increased in compensation, brought students out on to the streets. The proposal to create Instituts universitaires régionaux for the *filières technologiques* was also seen as a threat to the principle of national diplomas which students hold dear as a guarantee of equality and as posing a threat to university autonomy from local government intervention in management. It also engendered hostility from students and staff who saw it as a devaluation of the *premier cycle*. There was, in short, something to alienate everybody. Fillon moved rapidly to distance himself from the report's findings, describing them as simply a preliminary contribution to a nation-wide debate with decisions being left to the next government following the presidential elections.

François Fillon did, however, move to boost the IUPs which, although they had increased in number to over 120 institutions, were not absorbing significant numbers of students. Fillon recognized that expansion of the IUPs would resolve three of the major problems which have been outlined, that is, it would simplify the fragmented structures of vocational education in the universities and thus facilitate student guidance, it would restore the IUTs to their vocation of producing *Bac technique* + 2 entrants to the labour market and finally it would hold down any potential growth in the open-access *premier cycle*. His first proposal was to bring all vocational education in the universities under the aegis of the IUPs which would encompass all the *filières technologiques*, including the DEUST (*Diplôme d'études universitaires des sciences et de la technologie*) and *DEUG technologiques* up to the selective vocational *maîtrises* such as the MST (*Maîtrise de sciences et techniques*) and MIAGE (*Maîtrise de méthodes informatiques appliquées à la gestion*). This attempt to produce a single, coherent vocational route in the universities which would also enjoy all the advantages of selective entry and cater for the academically strongest *baccalauréat général* candidates was, however, eventually undermined by the pro-*grandes écoles* lobby, who exercise considerable influence in right-wing circles and who feared the competition that the new heavyweight status of the IUPs might bring. Directors of the *maîtrises technologiques* also showed little enthusiasm for being absorbed into the IUPs and finally employers felt that expansion of the IUPs might undermine the increase in *bac* + 2 entrants into the labour market which they favoured. Faced with this coalition of vested interests Fillon retreated and the IUPs were consequently divested of the DEUST and all *2e cycle* (*maîtrise technologique*) courses (*Le Monde*, 7 May 1995: 11).

Fillon's attempt to restore the IUTs to their original vocation was also defeated when the *circulaire Bardet*, published by the Director General of Higher Education, which withdrew the automatic right of entry of IUT graduates into the second year of IUPs, sparked furious student protests and had to be withdrawn. This left Fillon with only the less effective and more costly measure of introducing an optional third year in the IUTs and STS which it was hoped would retain those students not wishing to enter the labour market. Once again vested interests had triumphed over the government's attempts to promote change in the system.

A return to gradualism

The second major report which concentrated on the *premier cycle* by Dmitri Lavroff, former president of Bordeaux University, arrived on Edouard Balladur's desk on the day that he left office, and it was left to the new Juppé government to consider its findings. Lavroff rejected any radical legislative solutions stating:

> Il serait absurde et dangereux de croire qu'une seule grande réforme prise par une autorité résoudrait les problèmes qui sont posés.

and favoured a softly, softly approach, continuing:

> Il convient donc de réformer progressivement, de mesurer les résultats obtenus par chacune des expériences et les bonnes solutions s'impo-seront.[5]

(Lavroff, 1995: 3–4)

Specifically rejecting any change to the open-access system, Lavroff pointed to the mismatch between the routes followed to the *baccalauréat* and subjects studied in DEUG as a fundamental problem, particularly in the case of *bacheliers techniques*, and proposed the creation of a student guidance system which would take in all sectors of higher education along with greater flexibility in relation to route changes at an early stage in students' academic careers. He also proposed the modification of *premier cycle* courses to cope with a wider range of student abilities through a more flexible academic year and the provision of extra teaching for weaker students. Finally, he suggested the introduction of new *premier cycle* courses more suited in content to *bacheliers professionnels* which would lead directly into the job market, and the addition of *DEUG de technologie tertiaire* alongside the existing *DEUG de technologie industrielle*. These proposals for adapting courses to meet the needs of an evolving student population were supported by a call for further involvement of local government in funding and planning new courses to meet the needs of the local economy, whilst at the same time exercising a strict quality control over the development of satellite university establishments.

These modest and relatively uncontroversial proposals, which essentially recommend continuing down the path taken by Claude Allègre, were largely endorsed by François Bayrou who continued in his post of Education Minister and by his new Minister for Higher Education, Jean de Boishue. Both ministers maintained a low profile in their first few months in office, contenting themselves with a reassuring statement that no form of selection would be imposed:

> Il n'était pas question d'organiser sous une forme quelconque la sélection du nombre d'étudiants. D'abord parce que la nation n'en veut pas et qu'un pays qui arrête de former est un pays qui appauvrit.[6]
>
> (de Boishue cited in *Le Monde*, 18–19 June 1995: 8)

and pointing to the need for route guidance and flexibility that Lavroff had emphasized:

> Il faut leur donner [aux étudiants] assez tôt les moyens d'une orientation réussie, leur proposer des voies nouvelles, et pour ceux qui cherchent vraiment une formation générale inventer des passerelles pédagogiques efficaces.[7]
>
> (Bayrou cited in *Le Monde*, 23 June 1995: 11)

This apparent commitment to continuity and gradualism in the reform of the *premier cycle* seems however at odds with the call for a *refonte des premiers cycles universitaires* which Jacques Chirac had made in the course of his election campaign and which he intends to incorporate in his forthcoming referendum on the education system. The policies currently being mooted by his education ministers would hardly seem to warrant recourse to a national debate and popular vote and one may speculate that the spectre of selection may arise once more, possibly in the form of devolution of decision-making powers on such issues to local level where universities and local authorities would share the onus of dealing with the numbers issue. Otherwise, if selection is excluded, it seems likely that some form of further financial involvement, along with a say in planning new developments, will be proposed for the regions, since it is at this level that the issues of numbers and vocationalization can be tackled most effectively.

Avoiding the apocalypse

When considering the record of government policy-making in the first half of the decade the immediate question that arises is not so much what remains to be done before the year 2000 but how it is to be done.

The creation of new institutions in the accretive tradition of the past would only increase the confusion stemming from the current proliferation of institutions and courses. Any major legislative reform risks being blocked by the formidable coalition of vested interests which defends the status quo. The kind of fine-tuning of the existing system which Allègre favoured and which seems to be currently in favour with the present government has had some limited success but requires a constant increase in funding to match increasing student numbers. This approach is based on the premise that the current system can be made to work through managing student flows through the system:

> L'avenir des enseignements supérieurs en France viendra de la maîtrise des flux. Flux par type d'établissement, flux par filières, flux de transfert entre les uns et les autres.[8]
>
> (Allègre, 1993: 171)

Even with proportional increases in funding this approach is likely to run into difficulties. As the shift towards vocational routes within the universities gathers pace, the disparities between the well-funded, well-resourced selective vocational courses and the open-access courses will become more glaring, as will the gulf between traditional universities and the new universities such as Dauphine and Compiègne, which have been exempted from the obligation of open-access and which are beginning to compete with the *grandes écoles*. The hope is that as open-access course numbers stabilize and decrease proportionally they will become more manageable, but given the volatile nature of the student body and its ideological commitment to equality in the system this seems overoptimistic. As Flory points out:

> Il convient de remarquer que le système ouvert parce qu'il est ingérable se rétrécit, certains secteurs universitaires se dotant plus ou moins régulièrement de la capacité de sélectionner. La charge de l'ouverture n'en pèse que plus lourdement sur les lettres, les sciences sociales, l'économie et le droit.[9]
>
> (Flory, 1993: 102)

Moreover, within these areas many basic problems remain. Bédarida emphasizes with regard to *premier cycle* students that:

> A ce public porteur d'aspirations déstabilisantes pour le système universitaire l'institution offre un enseignement globalement inchangé. Chacun de ses acteurs sait que les cours sont mal organisés, les filières mal conçues, les contenus et les programmes en partie désuets.[10]
>
> (Bédarida, 1994: 12)

and forecasts an apocalyptic scenario for the future: 'scénario 2005 l'école explose, l'état craque' (Bédarida, 1994: 200).

Conclusion

Setting aside the issue of the 'manageability' of the open-access sector, present policies raise other fundamental questions. Apart from the unsettling contrast it creates with the open-access sector, the appropriateness of the resource-intensive and expensive *grande école* model for the vocational sector is debatable. At a time when surveys of employers are emphasizing the need for adaptable and multi-talented graduates with the capacity to make career changes as the market evolves *(Les filières technologiques de l'enseignement supérieur*, 1994) the heavily specialized vocational model might be becoming less relevant to market needs. It also risks further weakening the link between the content of teaching programmes and staff research which could be one of the few advantages enjoyed by universities in relation to *grandes écoles.*

Even more fundamentally it might be argued that policy-makers' attempts to channel students through the system from *baccalauréat* via the corresponding higher education route into predetermined sectors of a labour market which is itself characterized by excessively rigid career structures run counter to the principles of equality of opportunity which they espouse and are likely to be a continuing source of student discontent. Such fundamental issues are, however, unlikely to be addressed in the context of the present relentless numbers-driven policy. France has tended towards reform by default rather than forwardly planned reform (Minc, 1994: 12). Rectifying this approach is the key to preparing France for the twenty-first century. This is true above all for French higher education.

Notes

1. For further reading on other recent development in French higher education see R. Turner, Higher education, in S. Perry (ed.), *Aspects of Contemporary France.* London: Routledge (forthcoming).
2. In the brief history of French educational planning there is no shortage of examples of rushing blindly onwards proving an easier option than promoting real change.
3. The university system is attempting to set up courses at every level and of every kind whilst selective specialized courses are increasing in number. This more or less intentional harmony is intellectually satisfying. If, however, you examine not the academic structures but the reality experienced by the students the harmful

effects are striking. Everything happens as if there was only one desirable route: the very highest level, the *grandes écoles*. All the others are seen as second best.

4. François Fillon, Minister for Higher Education, 29 March 1993 to 17 May 1995. François Bayrou, Minister of Education, 29 March 1993 to present. *Pognon* and *sous* are both slang words for money.

5. It would be ridiculous and dangerous to believe that a single great reform by the authorities would solve all the problems we face. . . . It is therefore appropriate to undertake reform progressively, to evaluate the results for each experiment and the right solutions will become apparent.

6. There was no question of applying selection in any form to determine the number of students. Especially because the nation does not want it and a country which stops offering training is an impoverished country.

7. You have to provide students at an early stage with the means necessary for successful guidance, suggest new routes and for those who are really seeking a general education open up effective access onto further courses.

8. The future of higher education in France lies in controlling student flows. Flows according to the type of institution, flows according to courses, flows from one to the other.

9. It is worth noting that the open-access system is shrinking because it is unmanageable, with certain university sectors equipping themselves with means of selection on a more or less regular basis. The burden of the open-access system only weighs all the more heavily on the literature courses, the social sciences, economics and law.

10. This public whose aspirations are destabilizing for the university system is offered an education which overall remains unchanged. All of the protagonists know that the courses are badly organized, the routes badly designed and contents and syllabuses partially out of date.

References

Allègre, C. (1993) *L'Age des savoirs*. Paris: Gallimard.

Bédarida, C. (1994a) *SOS université*. Paris: Seuil.

Bédarida, C. (1994b) Enquête: les universités craquent, *Le Monde de l'Education*, 29–44.

Fauconnier, F. and Fohr, A. (1995) Le palmarès des universités, *Le Nouvel Observateur*, 22 March, 4–17.

Flory, M. (1993) *Etudiants d'Europe*. Paris: La Documentation Française.

Garagnon, J. (1995) IUT: la colère ne doit pas bloquer la réforme, *Le Monde de l'Education*, March, 6.

Gaussen, F. (1993) Gloire et perversité des grandes écoles, *Le Monde de l'Education*, March, 3.

Goedegebuure, L. (1994) *Higher Education Policy*. London: Pergamon.

Jallade, J.-P. (1991) *L'Enseignement supérieur en Europe*, Paris: La Documentation Française.

Lapeyronnie, D. and Marie, J.-L. (1992) *Campus blues: les étudiants face à leurs études.* Paris: Seuil.

Lavroff, D. (1995) *Rapport remis à Monsieur le Ministre de l'enseignement supérieur et de la recherche par la commission sur l'évolution du premier cycle universitaire présidée par Monsieur le professeur Dmitri Lavroff.* Paris: Ministère de l'enseignement supérieur et de la recherche, March.

Les filières technologiques de l'enseignement supérieur (1994) Ministère de l'enseignement supérieur et de la recherche, May.

Minc, A. (1994) *La France de l'an 2000.* Paris: Editions Odile Jacob.

Ministère de l'Education Nationale (1991) *Universités 2000.* Paris: La Documentation Française.

14.

Epilogue: May in December?

MICHEL DREYFUS

TRANSLATED BY MÁIRE CROSS

A few weeks after the ASMCF conference on 'France, Population and Peoples', from which these chapters are taken, France experienced its biggest general strike since May 1968. From 23 November to 20 December 1995, the country came to an almost complete standstill. Trains, the Metro, all public transport stopped working completely in the capital, as well as in many provincial cities. Huge demonstrations took place which were even bigger than those of May 1968. This was not just a Paris phenomenon; on the contrary, the biggest gatherings ever seen on their streets took place in Bordeaux, Marseilles and Lille as well as in most other cities. Smaller towns were also affected – Amiens in Picardy, Le Puy in the Auvergne and Libourne in the Gironde, even the traditionally quiet places such as Versailles, the Sun King's town, where more than 10,000 people demonstrated.

In their way the strikes and demonstrations marked the centenary of the CGT and the fiftieth anniversary of the founding of the Sécurité sociale, in October 1945. This was no coincidence of association, quite the opposite. It was precisely because of problems related to social welfare that the 'December Movement' spread like wildfire. Yet, contrary to what has been the case for other large waves of strikes France has seen in the past, wage claims were practically absent. Five times in this century, France has been shaken by protest strikes of national importance; the latest outburst should be added to that number. In what were very different contexts, strikes crippled France in 1906, 1917, 1936, 1947–48 and 1968.

From this perspective, December 1995 is in perfect continuity with the history of industrial relations in France. In order to understand the significance of the 1995 strike action it is useful to recall the main developments of France's history of industrial relations. After describing the plan for the reorganization of the social security system, presented by the prime minister to the National Assembly (the Juppé plan), this final chapter will look at the main characteristics of the December Movement. It will then examine the similarities to and the differences from previous strikes since the beginning of the twentieth century. Earlier chapters have discussed the social security crisis (see Chapters 9, 11, 12). There are numerous causes: an ageing population, progress in medicine, soaring unemployment and the exemptions granted to firms to reduce their national insurance contributions, apparently a necessary condition for job creation. It is important, however, not to forget to put this crisis in proportion in that, in actual size, the total social security budget – 1800 billion francs – is higher than the whole state budget. Having said that, it is undeniably true that the social security deficit has been rising constantly: in 1995 it was more than 65 billion francs. Faced with this reality, it is not surprising that various reforms have been envisaged over a number of years to stop this trend. They are based essentially on the idea that the social security system should not be financed by contributions from salaries alone: initiated in 1991 by the Rocard government and expanded two years later by the Balladur government, what became known as the CSG (*la cotisation sociale généralisée*, a general social contribution) aimed to widen the base of contributions.

The Juppé plan

On 15 November 1995, the prime minister, Alain Juppé, revealed his plan to the National Assembly. Henceforth there was to be a strengthened state administration of social security, which hitherto was supposedly run mainly by employers and trade unions. That had, however, been decreasingly the case, since the election of administrators of the social security offices had not taken place for many years. Furthermore the state had been gradually increasing its control of the system. However, the changes were quite significant. In future, management of social security was to be determined by an annual vote in parliament which would set the changes in social spending in relation to sickness insurance. A mechanism for reducing the social security debt, the RDS (*le remboursement de la dette sociale*, the social debt refund), was to be introduced but, despite the prime minister's assertions to the contrary, it would not be equally distributed among the various social categories of the population. According to *Le Monde*:

Ce sont les chômeurs qui devront participer au remboursement de la dette sociale, les familles modestes ou nombreuses dont les prestations seront gelées en 1996 et les bénéficiaires de petites retraites soumises à deux hausses successives de 1,2% de leur cotisation d'assurance maladie en 1996 et 1997 qui seront les plus pénalisés.[1]

(Bezat, 1995)

A 'universal sickness insurance system' was to be introduced, which was supposed to align contributions and benefits at the highest level and which was to be funded entirely by social insurance contributions. In order to break away from the multiple socio-professional anomalies which have existed since the creation of the social security system, the special schemes for the pensions of railway workers, Paris transport workers, post office workers, electricity and gas workers, local authority and hospital employees have been altered to the detriment of all these staff: they must have worked for 40 years instead of 37.5 before being entitled to receive their pension. A similar change had already been imposed by the Balladur government two years previously to apply to private-sector workers. Finally, the Juppé plan intended also to introduce a Contract Plan to reduce the SNCF (French railways) deficit, the existence of which had only just been discovered by many, unlike the well-known social security budget deficit, and the main consequence of which could mean the closing of nearly six thousand kilometres of railway lines.

This was truly a revolutionary change in the French social security system. Fifty years after its creation in 1945 and 28 years after the 1967 edicts (see below) which had altered the way it functioned, the prime minister was introducing reforms that, according to him, his predecessors had not dared to undertake for 30 years (Bezat, 1995).

Does France still have a social policy?

These reforms, which are notable for their scope, were drawn up without any consultation with the interested parties and their representatives or their trade union organizations. To its consternation the CGT–FO, which runs the largest part of the Social Insurance Offices, found out about the details of this plan at the same time as the general public. Only the CFDT was kept informed about the preliminary plans of the reforms. In parliament, a vote of confidence in the prime minister was immediately passed by 463 votes to 87 with 10 abstentions. The PS was divided over the Juppé plan, which the CFDT had approved on the whole and the PCF, the CGT and the CGT–FO denounced instantly as the end of the social security system. At first these divisions worked in favour of the prime minister. The following day, while conscious that he should not be carried away by this welcome, he declared rather rashly in an interview for a provincial daily, *Sud Ouest*: 'If two million people take to the streets my government will not survive.' He was to be reminded of this declaration in the weeks that followed.

On 19 November the minister for finances proposed a possible tax reform, which in the way it was presented signified serious penalties for salaried workers. It was the last straw; from that moment everything was ready for the movement to start.

Meanwhile thousands of students had been demonstrating in Paris and the provinces for several days, calling on the government to grant extra funding to universities. On 23 November the railway workers and RATP (Paris transport) workers began striking. There was an almost complete stoppage the following day. Post office, gas and electricity workers came out shortly afterwards. On 24 November almost 500,000 workers marched in Paris against the Juppé plan and Nicole Notat, general secretary of the CFDT, was taken to task by members of her own organization, who forced her to leave the demonstration. One after the other, the railway federations – the sector which placed itself very quickly at the head of the movement – voted for a continuation of the strike. A further demonstration took place on 28 November during which Louis Viannet and Marc Blondel, general secretaries of the CGT and FO respectively, publicly shook hands. For the first time since the split of 1947, the general secretaries of these two organizations agreed to march under the same banner. Serious disruptions began to affect the mail. On the same day (28 November) Alain Juppé insisted he would not change course. Following the initiative of the journal *Esprit*, a certain number of intellectuals, most of whom claimed to be on the Left, rushed to support the prime minister, backing the main outlines of his plan and praising Nicole Notat's courage and independence of mind (*Le Monde*, 3–4 December 1995).

The first climbdown began the next day. The prime minister announced the setting up of a commission to examine pensions. A further demonstration took place on 30 November to which the government retorted by floating the idea of the creation of a users' committee against the strikers. This initiative proved to be a complete flop and soon there was no further talk of such a committee. At the same time the strike, which was obviously affecting the daily life of millions of people in France and not just in the Paris region, was gaining increasing support. Marc Blondel for FO and Louis Viannet for the CGT – which held its forty-fifth national congress from 2 to 5 December – continued to demand the withdrawal of the Juppé plan. The movement hardened further as most of the *deputés* witnessed – including those of the *majorité* (the government side) in their constituencies. There were 250 demonstrations in Paris and in the provinces and the minister of education made a show of giving in to the student demands. On Thursday 7 December almost a million people took part in protests throughout France (*Le Monde*, 9 December 1995). On the same day two hundred left-wing intellectuals, the best-known being Pierre Bourdieu, responded to the appeal launched by *Esprit* by calling for support of the strike movement, on the grounds it was not so much a defence of particular interest groups, even less privileges, but rather a defence of the most universal gains of the Republic: equality of rights for all men and women, public service, state education, political and social equality of women, defence of all citizens in a social and an ecological Europe (*Libération*, 7 December 1995).

However, Alain Juppé kept his plan for reform of the social security system intact, declaring that it had never been his intention to dismantle the special funds (see Chapter 12) or to bring them into line with the general system. This declaration was a further government retreat. On 8 December Helmut Kohl publicly praised the French effort to reduce the public deficit (*Le Monde*, 9 December 1995).

On 10 December Alain Juppé had no choice. If he wanted to salvage the main aspects of his plan for the restructuring of the social security system, he had to give in to other demands, special pension schemes and the contract plan for the SNCF. Even better, he proposed to have a 'social summit meeting on employment'. Discontent remained as strong as ever. On 12 December more demonstrations throughout France meant the fateful mark, cited by Alain Juppé, of two million people in the streets was passed. It was calculated that there were more than 100,000 demonstrators in Marseilles, an unprecedented number for that city. The *Juppéthon* phenomenon appeared in these processions, a caricature of the charity show *Téléthon* where the maximum number of television spectators are invited to participate. The *Juppéthon* idea emerged in the popular political satire programme *Les Guignols de l'info* (a puppet show) in response to Alain Juppé's rash statement made to *Sud Ouest* that his government would have to go if two million people took to the streets in protest. The aim of the *Juppéthon* was therefore to reach that figure of two million demonstrators and beyond. In this way it would be possible to take Alain Juppé at his word and force him to resign.

Other demonstrations took place in the whole country four days later on 16 December. They were just as big as those of 12 December. But the weariness of the strikers was beginning to lie heavily on them. Some had now been on strike for four weeks. That demonstration was the swan-song. The movement was beginning to wane and with Christmas approaching, most people had drifted back to work by 20 December. The summit meeting of government ministers and trade unions held some days later led to nothing.

Tradition of mass protest

The strikes of November and December 1995 were the largest that had taken place since 1968. Yet they were not on the same scale – in May 1968 seven to eight million were on strike. At the end of 1995 the strike did not claim to be a complete stoppage: even at its height the CGT and some militants of FO had called for a widening to other sectors, but few called for a complete general strike. Followed only partially in the public sector, the strike was practically non-existent in the private sector. Nevertheless, the movement was momentous enough to challenge the analyses repeated so many times these past few years that predict the end of the working class and of its trade unions. It is easier to understand its underlying characteristics by placing this movement in the historical perspective of the most extensive strikes in France and by comparing them to the latest action. For a long time anchored to the CGT, which celebrated its centenary as recently as September 1995, French trade unionism in fact has developed from five significant strike movements. Some of their characteristics reappeared during the December Movement but there were as many differences.

In May 1906 the CGT had called for an eight-hour day. Unsuccessful, although it had shown it was capable of initiating a rallying campaign at a national level, this still fragile organization had only just gained the legal right to exist. It had been created eleven years previously, and was still at a very early stage of development, taking into account the fact that it was only after 1902 that the various groups had really begun to unify. In 1906 the level of union membership in France was scarcely less weak than it is today, less than 10 per cent. However, trade unionism was in its infancy. After building up a much higher membership during the Popular Front, the Liberation and then the decade from 1965 to 1975,

French trade unionism has suffered such a serious membership crisis during the past two decades that its very future is in question. For two or three years this haemorrhaging seems to have been halted but not reversed. Will the December Movement enable the trade unions to take off again? Nothing is less certain. It would appear that while the CGT emerged the stronger in December 1995, it has not been able to turn this to good account as it has since encountered further hurdles (Beuve-Méry, 1995). This movement has also had serious implications for the CFDT and FO but it is still too early to assess all the long-term consequences.

The industrial conflict of 1917–20 by metal workers and then by railway workers was in response to suffering brought about by the war years. To that was added disagreements among the CGT about the direction of the leadership since 1914 in favour of a policy of collective bargaining (*une politique de présence*); according to this policy the leaders of the CGT declared they wanted to be present wherever there were negotiations concerning the working class. On the other hand, minority groups who had been part of revolutionary syndicalism before the First World War refused to support this policy, which they denounced as collaboration with the state. The other major point of disagreement between majority and minority groups was the position to be taken towards the Russian Revolution. The trade union movement emerged from this second cycle of demands more powerful than it had been in 1914 but equally divided. Ever since, division has been a permanent feature of the history of French trade unionism; it has been exacerbated further in recent years. Let us recall the dates of these divisions and fusions, the latter being less frequent: 1921–22 saw a split between the CGT and the CGTU. Then came reunification in March 1936 into one single CGT. A further split occurred in 1939 over the German–Soviet pact. Reunification took place within the clandestine CGT in 1943 in the context of the struggle against Vichy and the Nazi occupation. By the end of 1947 there was a new split in the CGT with the creation of Force Ouvrière against the background of the Cold War. To this must be added the founding of the CFTC in 1919 and the split within its ranks in 1964 with the creation of the CFDT. Also there were the teaching unions within the FEN (Fédération de l'éducation nationale), autonomous since 1948, which has also undergone a split with the creation of the FSU (Fédération syndicale unitaire) in 1992.

The strikes in 1936, which occurred three months after union re-unification, achieved what was a unique conjunction in French trade union history: a union victory (obtaining the 40-hour week, collective bargaining and paid holidays) in the aftermath of a political victory of the Left in the parliamentary elections. These strikes account for the soaring membership figures of the CGT, which rose from 750,000 to 4 million within a year. Like the December Movement of 1995, the 1936 strikes were a sudden reaction, a demonstration of workers' self-esteem as well as a response to the economic crisis of the 1930s which had not yet abated. December 1995 was also a demonstration of workers' self-esteem; there were scarcely any wage claims but the widespread fear of unemployment among increasing numbers of professional categories certainly worked in the strikers' favour – to such an extent that there was talk of strike by proxy; while public-sector employees still have the possibility of going on strike (because of job security), this is no longer the case for workers in the private sector. However, although unemployment had increased from 1931 to 1936, it rose much more dramatically at the end of the *trente glorieuses* (1945–75): 100,000 unemployed in 1953, 400,000 in 1968, one million in 1975, over three million today, not including part-time temporary jobs which have increased in even higher proportions with seven to eight million people affected. It must be said this phenomenon is not limited to France; it has affected most European countries to a greater or lesser extent (*Le Monde*, 30 March 1996).

As in 1917–20, the origin of the strikes of 1947–48 was profound social discontent caused by hardships endured during the war. These were further exacerbated by a new union split, the creation of Force Ouvrière, with the onset of the Cold War. The very violent strikes which the communists of the CGT did their utmost to step up ended in defeat, severe repression and a widespread loss of militant members. These strikes found no political outlet, nor did the December 1995 movement. In fact, the left-wing parties, the PCF and even more the PS, were embarrassed by the 1995 strikes and the attitude to adopt in opposition to Juppé's plan. The silence of the Communist Party can be explained by its desire not to prevent the CGT from acting alone, not to politicize the movement. It must also be recalled that the influence of the Communist Party has been in decline over the past 15 years in France. The uproar within the Socialist Party that followed the announcement of Juppé's plan was such that its leader Lionel Jospin had to call it to order. Subsequently the Socialist Party proved to be incapable of putting forward any alternative proposals or finding a way to resolve the crisis. December 1995 and the strikes of 1947–48 are different in the way politics intervened; whereas the strikes in 1947–48 were politicized in the extreme, even if there was no political resolution of the crisis, by contrast the strikes of December 1995 seemed to be a search for the greatest possible trade union autonomy from political parties.

Finally May 1968, the greatest strike in French history, did result in a trade union victory but only relatively speaking; wage increases were quickly eroded by inflation. It is not at this level that they should be compared to the December Movement. There is a more useful comparison to be made; in 1968, as in 1995, defence of the welfare system was a key factor. The CGT had been fighting the Jeanneney edicts since the summer of 1967, which under a supposed restructuring of the social security system had ousted the union from its management. Whatever the strength of the strike movement in 1968, the CGT did not succeed in making the government retract at all and the edicts remained, as did the main outlines of the Juppé plan in December 1995. In the history of the social security system 1967 and 1995 are turning-points; in the aftermath of the Liberation its management had been entrusted to trade union organizations. Through the Juppé plan the government is strengthening its control of the social security departments. Election of the administrators by employees has been abolished and from now on the board of directors of each department will have as many employer representatives as employees (*Le Monde*, 31 March–1 April 1996).

From one wave of strikes to another the number of strikers rose to a peak of seven million in 1968, whereas it must be stressed that numbers were much more restricted in 1995. Nevertheless, as the many demonstrations of December 1995 illustrate, particularly those in the provinces, these strikes were seen in a favourable light by large sections of the population.

To these six extensive strike movements could be added a seventh, in August 1953; it broke out against a government plan to cut 4000 posts in the public sector and to end certain pension rights, especially those of railway and post office workers. The movement spread rapidly and a few days later France came to a complete standstill. To the general astonishment of everyone there were nearly four million out on strike. By the end of August the government had to abandon its plans; here the similarity with the December 1995 movement is striking. As with most of the previous waves, the December 1995 strikes illustrated the failure on the part of the government to take union organizations into consideration. After drawing up his plan with no consultation whatsoever, the prime minister was forced to make far-reaching concessions. Once more it was proved that in France the government, and very often employers too, will not negotiate with unions unless forced to do so.

This latest industrial dispute has occurred in a France where unemployment and part-time jobs have been steadily increasing, whereas in 1953 there were 'only' 100,000 unemployed and in 1968 400,000. Furthermore, it happened against a background of denationalization and privatization: this development has weakened the public sector and the status of its employees. Widespread now in Europe, it began in France in 1986 and challenged everything that had been secured in the public sector from 1936 to 1981. The defence of the public sector was unequivocally stated by the strikers, while wage claims were of secondary importance.

The December 1995 movement also took place against the background of a serious union crisis. Over the past 15 years the CGT has lost two-thirds of its members; the CFDT and doubtless the FO have not fared any better even if the drop in numbers has been checked over the past three years. During its last national congress in Montpellier in March 1995, the CFDT claimed to have more members than the CGT (650,000 as opposed to 630,000). In fact membership of both unions is broadly similar. In the absence of any official figures from the FO it is estimated that its membership is around 300,000. The most recent professional elections in the SNCF in March 1996 saw the CFDT lose heavily while the CGT gained and a new trade union, SUD (Solidaires unitaires démocratiques), emerged, which had already made inroads among post office workers (*Le Monde*, 30 March, 1996).

Will the December movement regain lost ground for the trade unions? These disputes will possibly contribute to altering the relative strengths of the union movement. The past few years have seen a gradual shift, with more vociferous demands from the FO since Marc Blondel assumed its leadership in 1989, while the CFDT has been adopting a much more conciliatory position in an attempt to appear a 'responsible' union. The co-ordination committees which led the strikes of 1986–90 played no role in 1995, apart from those formed by students. Opposition to the Juppé plan revealed profound social unrest faced with rising unemployment and fear of the ending of pension rights and management of the social security system by the unions, a fundamental issue for the latter.

The international context

One final remark in this epilogue is that the five preceding waves of industrial action had all been affected to a greater or lesser degree by the international political situation (the Russian Revolution, unity of the Left against Fascism after 1934, the Cold War, the support of the

PCF for de Gaulle's line of independence in foreign policy). Contrary to previous divisions, the international situation played a very minor role in 1995. In different guises the Soviet Union had intervened in 1917–20, 1936, 1947–48 and certainly in 1968. This was no longer the case in 1995. For all that, the international context was not completely absent from the minds of many strikers, who expressed their reservations and worries about the implications for Europe of the liberalism of Maastricht. Equally, it should be noted how the movement was perceived in other European countries, where it was followed closely. Not enough attention has been given to the unqualified support given to the French government by Helmut Kohl at the height of the crisis; the German Chancellor congratulated the French government for its attempt to reduce the budget deficit. This interference by a government leader in the domestic politics of a foreign country went almost unnoticed; it was an expression none the less of the anxiety that similar strikes might spread to other European member countries.

In presenting his plan, Alain Juppé had undertaken to reduce the deficit of the social security system to 17 billion francs and to show a surplus of 11.8 billion francs in 1997. By the beginning of April 1996 it was obvious that this aim was unattainable, as the latest estimates forecast a deficit of 40 billion francs for 1996 alone (*Le Monde*, 4 April 1996). Since November 1995, there are another 50,000 unemployed in France. History does not repeat itself, but the latent causes of the November–December conflict remain. On the one hand, this strike could be the swansong for the history of social movement in France. With the decline of the industrial workforce it could be the end of a certain type of cycle of industrial conflict. On the other hand, however, it could be a renewal of industrial conflict in a Europe weakened by unemployment and an increased sense of job insecurity. No one, least of all an historian, such as the author of this chapter who was a close observer of these developments, is in a position to speculate on these possibilities, which nevertheless are worth raising.

Notes

1. The most heavily penalized will be the unemployed who will now be liable for contributions to refund the social debt, families with modest incomes or large families, whose benefits will be frozen in 1996, and those receiving small pensions whose sickness insurance contributions are subject to two successive increases of 1.2 per cent each in 1996 and 1997.

References

Beuve-Méry, A. (1995) L. Viannet rencontre des difficultés pour mettre en oeuvre les orientations du congrès de la CGT, *Le Monde*, 6 April.

Bezat, J.M. (1995) Le Plan Juppé envisage de modifier profondément le système de santé, *Le Monde*, Dossier 'Du Plan Juppé au sommet social', 21 December.

Bonn soutient la politique de rigueur de Paris, *Le Monde*, 9 December 1995.

Deux gauches face au mouvement social, *Libération*, 7 December 1995.

Le déficit de la Sécurité sociale devrait dépasser 40 milliards de francs en 1996, *Le Monde*, 4 April 1996.

Le gouvernement renforce son contrôle sur les caisses de la Sécurité sociale, *Le Monde*, 31 March–1 April 1996.

L'Europe en bataille pour l'emploi, *Le Monde*, 30 March 1996.

Près d'un million de personnes ont manifesté le 7 décembre, *Le Monde*, 9 December 1995.

Index